# Professional Development for Cooperative Learning

# PROFESSIONAL DEVELOPMENT FOR COOPERATIVE LEARNING

## ISSUES AND APPROACHES

ॐ

EDITED BY
CELESTE M. BRODY
AND NEIL DAVIDSON

STATE UNIVERSITY OF NEW YORK PRESS

Published by
State University of New York Press, Albany

© 1998 State University of New York

For information, address State University of New York Press,
State University Plaza, Albany, N.Y. 12246

Production by M. R. Mulholland
Marketing by Patrick Durocher

Library of Congress Cataloging-in-Publication Data

Professional development for cooperative learning : issues and
    approaches / Celeste M. Brody and Neil Davidson [ editors].
        p.   cm.
    Includes bibliographical references and index.
    ISBN 0-7914-3849-X (hardcover : alk. paper). -- ISBN 0-7914-3850-3
(pbk. : alk. paper)
        1. Group work in education.   2. Constructivism (Education)
3. Teachers--In-service training.   4. Teachers--Training of.
I. Brody, Celeste M.   II. Davidson, Neil.
LB1032.P76   1998
371.39'5--dc21                                          97-37732
                                                          CIP

10 9 8 7 6 5 4 3 2 1

# CONTENTS

# Part I

# Begin with the Teacher: Focusing Professional Development for Cooperative Learning

❦

# Introduction: Professional Development and Cooperative Learning

## Celeste Brody and Neil Davidson

"Cooperative learning." These two simple words have spawned many interpretations and models, and much debate about philosophy, research, and use over the last three decades. This volume describes different approaches to professional development for cooperative learning and how the use of cooperative learning for teacher learning is leading to new insights into professional growth in schools. The book has two main purposes: (1) to enable educators to make informed decisions and choices about selecting, implementing, and evaluating cooperative learning approaches with respect for the differences and diversity of goals among professionals, and the variations within school contexts, and (2) to consider the goals of teachers' professional development in the context of organizational reforms that foster systemic school change, such as the development of learning communities.

### Connecting Professional Development with Cooperative Learning

Professional development conveys a commitment to high-quality learning experiences for all the adults who work with students on a regular basis, including administrators and other non-teaching staff. It reflects an important theme of the book: cooperative groupwork practices can inform educators not only about the goals of professional development, but how to actually organize and craft professional development experiences for adults.

Many of the contributors use the term "staff development" because it conveys specific developmental activities within a school organization. It is important, however, to cultivate long-term, sustained support between colleagues who act differently in relation to one another than in traditional staff development efforts. Much staff development has taken the form of inservice training for teachers and administrators, and its aim is to equip teachers with new classroom strategies and experiences to assist the achievement of students. The experiences of the contributors (see also, Battistich & Solomon, 1995; Battistich, Solomon & Deluchi, 1993; Brody, 1992; Cohen, 1991/2; Dasho & Kendzior, 1995; Schmuck, 1991/2; and Watson, 1995), and others interested in teachers' professional development (Auer, 1994; Little, 1993; Richardson, 1994, 1996), however, suggest that simply providing information and experience results in only a minority of teachers who are still implementing the ideas and practices several months later.[1] Contributors will refer to "trainers" and "trainings," and we accept that language because it is still a reality; it communicates a particular kind of inservice education for teachers and administrators.

There is much that can be learned about good practices in the professional development of teachers and administrators from the consultants, teacher educators, and staff developers who for many years have been teaching classroom teachers and school administrators about one of the more complex instructional practices, namely, cooperative learning. The greater portion of this book, therefore, is devoted to approaches to cooperative learning and the authors' reflections about implementing good cooperative groupwork practices.

The book couples the ideas of professional development and cooperative learning because it is the relationship of the two that sustains not only good cooperative learning practices in schools and classrooms, but the larger goal of creating schools that are learning communities. Many of the contributors in this volume have evolved from focusing primarily on how to change teachers' classroom practices in order to improve student achievement, to considering factors that affect teachers' abilities to sustain new, more socially complex practices. This evolution reflects a trend in both the research and practitioner communities from positivist, out-side in, rule-based dissemination approaches which are acontextual, to approaches that account for context, and encourage teachers to situate their experiences and construct their own knowledge (Jacobs, 1997). Authors discuss aspects of the organization of schooling that are potential inhibitors and facilitators, or functions that affect teacher learning—the teachers' histories, their subject areas, grade levels, the culture of the school, the support of the principal, the district's commitment to professional development over time, and so on. The effect of sustaining this theme throughout the book is to communicate to all levels of educators the need for a shift in thinking about the questions:

*Who* is responsible for the continuing development of teachers? *What* is responsible practice for insuring continuous improvement in schools?

## Importance of Learning Communities

There is also the recurring theme in this book regarding how and why teachers, students, administrators, and staff developers should collaborate, and that is to develop a sense of collegiality in the interest of restructuring schools as learning communities (Cooper & Boyd, 1994; see also Forest, chapter 15 this volume). In learning communities there is the expressed value and goal that every child and adult learns; members have access to information, research, and training so they can learn continuously. Parties from the larger community engage in discussions to determine what kind of schooling they want for their community. If school people are to generate systemic reforms toward becoming learning communities, the learning of teachers must be central to any discussion. Creating collaborative learning communities requires a different epistemology and even a reconceptualization of the very concept of teacher.

## Teachers as the Focus for Developing Learning Communities

Teachers are the focus of this volume because we are interested in how classroom teachers construct knowledge and how this knowledge transforms their teaching and their sense of themselves as professionals. What is important about the selections in this volume is that they focus the discussions about cooperative learning on teachers and administrators and their professional growth and development. A highly effective way to create sustained implementation of cooperative learning, or any new approach for learning and teaching, is to focus on the teacher. The major work in transforming schools begins and ends with teachers because they stay the longest, have the most contact with students, and potentially have the power to change the social relationships of the school and classroom. Teachers' experiences in classroom life have been under-represented and ignored in the research literature, even through their experiences are very different from their students (Hargreaves, 1996). Educators have been increasingly interested in how teachers learn a new practice and how they adapt innovations through their own beliefs, conditions for teaching, and personal biographies (Connelly & Clandinin, 1990; Miller, 1990; Palmeri, 1996; Witherell &

Noddings, 1991). By inviting trainers, consultants and teachers who have worked systematically and carefully over the last three decades to tell us how they assist in teacher development for using cooperative groupwork effectively, we hoped to find more about teachers' experiences in adapting cooperative learning to their particular situations.

Cooperation as a Value

Another theme of this volume is that cooperation is a legitimate value to be examined in schools and classrooms (see Schniedewind and Sapon-Shevin, chapter 10, and Forest, chapter 15). Cooperation is one of the oldest concepts we associate with human and systemic survival. It is much more than a simple set of strategies and procedures for reconfiguring students or adults in schools. Cooperation can be viewed as a deeply rooted set of values and principles that align overt practices with more covert attitudes and beliefs. To embrace cooperation as a value worthy of guiding student social, moral, and intellectual development in schools may require not only a shift in the way educators do things, but also significant changes in the way we think, feel, speak, and view others.

Cooperation is grounded in the human moral and social capacity to take the position of the other through numerous forms of reciprocity, mutuality, and give and take. From this point of view, we are equally concerned about the developmental aspects of authentic cooperation in children, adolescents, and adults, as well as the complexity of using mutuality and reciprocity as processes for academic ends. Cooperation is an outcome as well as an approach to planning, delivering, and sustaining our educational institutions.

*Definitions of Cooperative and Collaborative Group Learning.* There has not been a time in western education when interest in cooperative group work has been greater, certainly not since the progressive era, when the philosopher John Dewey encouraged educators to build learning communities based on democratic principles and productive work, grounded in respect for others and the value of cooperation (1916, 1938). The national curricular reform programs of the 1960s in science, math, and the humanities anticipated the need for a more sophisticated understanding of why and how learners achieve while engaged in small group problem solving.[2] Many of those programs failed to take root because teachers were not equipped to manage the complexities of ill-structured but highly engaging tasks with student-directed group learning.

By the early 1970s educators were building classroom models based on studies of human social interaction and group learning. These pioneers of effective groupwork practices, for example, Ron Edmonds (1979), David and Roger Johnson (1970), Shlomo Sharan and Yael Sharan (1976), Robert Slavin (1983), Elizabeth Cohen (1994), and Patricia and Richard Schmuck (1968; 1997), stood on the shoulders of the research and theory of educators, sociologists, and psychologists such as Kurt Lewin (1948; 1951), Jacob Moreno (1953), John Dewey (1916; 1938), Ron Lippitt (1940; 1962), Morton Deutsch (1949), and Alice Miel (1952).[3] This strand of work eventually led to the development of many of the approaches to cooperative group learning discussed in this volume.

During this same period other educators were defining another framework for groupwork practices derived from theories about the social nature of human knowledge. The different roots of constructivism from Lev Vygotsky (1978), Jean Piaget (1978), George Herbert Meade (1978), Thomas Kuhn (1970), George Kelly (1955), and Richard Rorty (1979) created a context for different claims and practices in collaborative groupwork and classroom instruction. For example, in the area of whole language, a literacy approach that enacts the theory that knowledge is based on socially-constructed agreements, the role of groupwork is to promote rich contexts for purposeful talk (Britton, 1970; Bruffee, 1993). Teachers consider questions about classroom management and motivation in a context that places the student at the center of control over the content and the process. When one compares the constructivist orientation of, for example, the Child Development Center Project (see chapter 7 this volume), with other approaches to cooperative learning (see Kagan & Kagan, chapter 5, for one example) the differences become apparent. Table I.1 demonstrates some of the epistomological differences in how each tradition could guide the framing of questions for teaching and learning in the classroom (Brubacher, 1991).

Each of the different frameworks for cooperative and collaborative learning generated different methods and research, and lived alongside one another without much connection or conflict until the 1980s, when educators began to understand the implications of different practices for the classroom. These terms draw from different traditions, speak to different subject fields, and yet overlap in terms of means and ends. Cooperative and collaborative learning now embrace wide variations in formats and applications, as well as differences in underlying philosophies and theories of learning (Brody,1992; Matthews, et.al, 1995).

There are currently over 20 different cooperative groupwork models and methods that an educator can learn—tied together by the idea that all students can succeed in school, and by a loosely defined commitment to develop positive values and skills that promote democracy, equity, and productive interdependence through active involvement in small peer

TABLE I.1

Questions for Teaching and Learning in the Classroom

I. *Questions Teachers Ask From the Cooperative Learning Perspective*
   1. How do we teach social skills?
   2. How can we develop self-esteem, responsibility, and respect for others?
   3. How does social status affect learning in small groups?
   4. How do you promote problem solving and manage conflict?
   5. Are extrinsic or intrinsic rewards most effective?
   6. How can we prove that cooperative learning increases academic achievement?
   7. How do we teach children to take on various roles?
   8. How do you structure cooperative activities?
II. *Questions Teachers Ask from the Collaborative Learning Perspective*
   1. What is the purpose of this activity?
   2. What is the importance of talk in learning?
   3. To what extent is getting off topic a valuable learning experience?
   4. How can we empower children to become autonomous learners?
   5. What is the difference between using language to learn and learning to use language?
   6. How can we negotiate relevant learning experiences with children?
   7. How do we interact with students in such a way that we ask only real questions rather than those for which we already know the answer?
   8. How can we use our awareness of the social nature of learning to create effective small group learning environments?

Adapted from Mark Brubacher (1991).

group activities. From a macro-view, cooperative/collaborative learning is a system of organizing learning that changes student-to-student relationships, teacher-student relationships, the relationship of teacher and students to the school, the nature of knowlege and knowing, and students and teachers relationship to knowledge construction, as well as the locus of control, power, and authority in the classroom and school. On the micro level, cooperative/collaborative learning affects dimensions in the classroom depending on the level of use and complexity of the learning task, the physical organization of the classroom, teacher's instructional and communicative behavior, and student's social and academic behavior (Hertz-Lazarowitz, 1993). Cooperative learning most commonly refers to a method of instruction that organizes students to work in groups toward a common goal or outcome, or share a common problem or task in such a way that they can only succeed in completing the work through behavior that demonstrates interdependence while holding individual contributions and efforts accountable.

TABLE I.2

Common and Varying Attributes Among Major Cooperative and
Collaborative Learning Approaches

---

*Attributes Common to all Approaches*
1. A common task or learning activity suitable for groupwork.
2. Small-group student interaction focused on the learning activity.
3. Cooperative, mutually helpful behavior among students.
4. Interdependence in working together.
5. Individual accountability and responsibility for groupwork outcomes.

*Attributes that Vary Between Approaches*
6. Procedures by which students are organized into groups, (e.g., heterogeneous, random, student selected, common interest).
7. The value of and ways for structuring positive interdependence (e.g., goals, task, resources, roles, division of labor, or rewards).
8. The value of explicitly teaching groupwork skills: e.g., communication, relational (social), group maintenance, and task skills.
9. The use of reflection, processing, or debriefing among students and/or between teacher and students on communication skills, academic skills, or group dynamics.
10. The value of classroom climate-setting through class-building, team-building, community building, or setting cooperative norms.
11. Attention to student status by the teacher (identifying competencies of low-status students and focusing peers' attention on those competencies).
12. The use of group structures for organizing the communication pattern within the group.
13. The question of group leadership: whether responsibilities are rotated among students, shared by structures or roles, or not designated.
14. The teacher's role in different phases of the lesson, unit, or process.
15. Emphasis on the value of demonstrating equal participation by all students.
16. The importance of simultaneous interaction among students in pairs or small groups.

---

Adapted from Neil Davidson (1994). Cooperative and collaborative learning: An integrative perspective. In Thousand, Jacqueline; Villa, Richard; and Nevin, Ann. *Creativity and collaborative learning: A practical guide to empowering students and teachers.* Baltimore, MD. Paul H. Brookes, Co.


Table I.2 explains the common and varying attributes among major cooperative and collaborative learning approaches. The collaborative approach is prominently represented in perspectives from the United Kingdom. The editors have made a conscious decision to use the term "cooperative learning" as the generic concept to facilitate reader understanding. Where it is appropriate, both terms will be used to convey the conceptual breadth of this idea.

Widely-Known Approaches to Cooperative
and Collaborative Learning

There are many approaches to cooperative and collaborative learning. The most widely-known include Student Team Learning (Slavin, 1983; 1989), Learning Together (D.W Johnson & R. Johnson, 1987, 1989), Group Investigation (Sharan & Hertz-Lazarowitz, 1980, 1982, Sharan & Sharan, 1992), the Structural Approach (Kagan, 1993), Complex Instruction (Cohen, 1994), The Child Development Project (Watson, 1995), and the Collaborative approaches (Britton,1990, Bruffee, 1993). Four of these main approaches are included in Part II and III of this book: Learning Together (Johnson & Johnson, chapter 11, and Linda Munger Chapter 14), The Structural Approach (Kagan & Kagan, chapter 5), Complex Instruction (Lotan, Cohen & Morphew, chapter 6), and The Child Development Project (Watson, et.al, chapter 7).[4]

There are other approaches that are adaptations of these main-line approaches for different audiences for specific outcomes.[5] In this volume James Bellanca & Robin Fogarty (chapter 9) present an example of an adaptative approach in their cognitive model. Bellanca & Fogarty work extensively with middle and secondary teachers, representing the influence of cognitive psychology on organizing teacher learning (see also Davidson & Worsham, 1992). Other staff developers, such as Rolheiser & Stevahn (Bennett, Rolheiser & Stevahn, 1991; see also chapter 3) and Cooper & Boyd, (chapter 2) draw from several different approaches as the training situation determines. They represent new directions by staff developers and teachers who have learned the importance of situating knowledge for educators in demanding environments.

While all of the authors have evolved their approaches to cooperative learning training over many years, some consultants, teachers, and staff developers realized the effect of different requirements of grade level, subject-areas, and theoretical developments for their own work with teachers. Schmuck (chapter 12) built his work on the field of organization development. The considerations of subject matter pose adaptation questions for middle and secondary teachers in particular. The demands of mathematics teaching and the middle grades are thoughtfully represented in the work of Sydney Farivar and Noreen Webb (chapter 8) who developed their approach through systematic study of cooperative learning for mathematics (see also Davidson, 1990).

Two approaches may be more allied with the collaborative tradition: the constructivist developmental approach of the Child Development Project (Watson, et.al, chapter 7), and Socially-Conscious Cooperative Learning (Schniedewind & Sapon-Shevin, chapter 10). The Child Development Project demonstrates the influence of a pro-social values stance coupled with the constructivist developments in child psychology. The work of Nancy Schniedewind and Mara Sapon-Shevin represents approaches that systematically question the nature of curriculum itself in teaching cooperative or competitive values.

## A Framework for Understanding Conceptions of Cooperative/Collaborative Learning

Several authors in this volume refer to the variations in the epistemological orientations of different approaches to cooperative groupwork that affect both the selection of means as well as the aims of education. Brody (1992) adapted Miller and Seller's (1985) curriculum schema to assist in understanding general epistemological orientations and apply these to discern the value assumptions implicit in cooperative learning practices. In chapter 1 she defines these three orientations as transmissional, transactional, or transformational. Authors such as Cooper and Boyd (chapter 2), and Rolheiser and Stevahn (chapter 3) are examples of how experienced staff developers and consultants adapt and adjust their approaches to make sense to teachers who must be able to do the same with their own students.

It is important to resist the tendency to generalize and categorize approaches to cooperative learning because responsible disseminators learn from the teaching and training they do with teachers, and evolve programs and approaches over time. There is still, however, a distinction between approaches developed during the 1950s through the early 1980s when there was a need to create legitimacy for cooperative learning in the research community, and those that grew from the more recent developments based on social constructivist theory.

Approaches that grew out of the psychometric or social psychology tradition were deeply influenced by the need to create fidelity in the model in order to replicate results in the research related to student achievement (see Johnson & Johnson, 1987; Sharan, 1980; and Slavin, 1983, as examples of the research base). In order to conduct systematic research on the effects of cooperative learning on student achievement and disseminate widely to great numbers of educators, it made sense at the time to adopt carefully prescribed approaches to cooperative learning and staff development. The recent influence of constructivist theory in regard to student learning, however, provided a context for questioning large-scale dissemination models of any innovation, including cooperative learning (Jacobs, in press). Recent research about the effects of large-scale, generic implementation of any innovation indicates that generic approaches produce only a modicum of school improvement (Clandinin, 1996; Elmore, 1995, Richardson, 1994, 1996).

Consequently, there has been a shift in professional development for cooperative learning in four directions:

1.  Drawings from multiple approaches to cooperative learning and other related programs[6] for responsible work with the particular requirements and differences in learning environments.
2.  The evolution by those who have created "models" of cooperative learning, to shift their work with schools to longterm commitments over the course of many years (see Kagan & Kagan, chapter 5 and Johnson & Johnson, chapter 11; Bellanca & Fogarty, chapter 9; Munger, chapter 14; and Lotan, Cohen & Morphew, chapter 6 for examples of this approach to staff development).
3.  The recognition that the whole school must be treated if there is going to be any successful change in student learning (see Part III and IV).
4.  The understanding of and documentation through research of constructivist theories of learning for approaches that begin with how the learner—teacher or student—makes sense of an innovation or approach and learns through situation (Brody, chapter 1, Watson, et.al, chapter 7).

### The Organization of This Book

This book can assist all levels of educators—teacher educators, university researchers, independent consultants, staff development personnel, curriculum specialists, school and district administrators, or fellow teachers—who hold responsibility for the continuing development of teachers, aides, and administrators. One of our goals is to continue the dialogue about the nature of professional development that supports systemic change and the creation of learning communities. Reflections on the larger aims of a learning community are combined with selected approaches to cooperative learning and what the authors have learned about effective professional development. This includes ways to enable teachers to direct their own development through collegial collaboration, as well as organizational factors that influence the outcomes of professional development efforts.

Our contributors consider ways to promote comprehensive, learner-centered professional development for teachers. They raise concerns about how to best support instructional change, the relationship of adult learning and organization change to teacher beliefs, the research on teachers' adaptation of innovations, and the effects of differing cooperative learning philosophies and theories of learning on decisions about implementation. Each writer has made significant contributions in the fields of cooperative learning and professional development through research, writing, and consultation. The authors draw on their experiences to provide the texture and color for understanding the complexity of cooperative learning implementation. Their narratives help us to identify where there are gaps in our knowledge, and consequently, in well-grounded practices.

Part I:  Begin With the Teacher:  Focusing Professional Development
for Cooperative Learning

We begin by directing our lens toward the teacher. This section focuses on reflective practices—by teachers engaged in cooperative learning and other professional development practices, and by staff developers who make decisions about how best to serve and support teachers. This section also considers professional collaborative relationships. By engaging in different types of collaborative activities, teachers can help one another function as career-long students of their practices.

Professional collaboration is somewhat different than cooperation. While cooperation is helpful for effective group work, it is only a "prerequisite to collaboration between professionals" (Henderson, 1992, p.8). Professional collaboration is a facilitative relationship between two people who are willing to support another's professional autonomy and celebrate their diversity in the context of shared consideration and critical examination (Henderson, 1996, p. 187). In this section the authors consider the importance of collaboration for successful professional development efforts. They also focus on reflection as central to effective collaboration.

Anning (1988) and Schon (1987) point out that experience is educative only with reflection. Reflective practices allow a teacher to clarify and recast situations, rethink the assumptions on which the initial understandings of a problematic issue were based, and reconsider the range of possible responses he/she might use. The authors describe the changes this process can bring about in teachers, namely the ability to identify specific ways in which their practice may become more consistent with their beliefs and values about what is educationally sound.

In chapter 1, *The Significance of Teacher Beliefs in Professional Development*, Celeste Brody discusses how teachers' beliefs interact with instructional innovations such as cooperative learning, and how teachers reconstruct their assumptions and practices though reflective and critical approaches to professional development. Brody describes a schema that helps teachers understand where there are tensions and contradictions between their general epistemological orientations as teachers and those of the new practices that they are learning. Brody suggests a stance on the part of teachers, consultants and trainers who work in schools: by listening carefully to teachers and administrators we can begin to work "where teachers are" and validate what is important to them. In this way we will build our understanding of situated knowledge and adapt different cooperative/collaborative learning approaches to particular classroom contexts.

In chapter 2, *Creating Sustained Professional Growth through Collaborative Reflection*, Carole Cooper and Julie Boyd consider a rationale for inservice teacher professional development programs that cultivate collegial forms of learning implemented with and by teachers themselves. The authors discuss several different models that promote reflection through collaboration including partnering, small groups, and large group reflective practices. They describe the conditions that are essential for collaborative reflective practices that promote teacher growth and change.

In chapter 3, The *Role of Staff Developers in Promoting Effective Teacher Decision-Making*, Carol Rolheiser and Laurie Stevahn invite us to consider how to support teachers' decision-making capacity while they are in the process of learning and adapting cooperative learning in the classroom. They outline four general guidelines that should direct leaders' decisions and the conduct of training programs for cooperative learning. These will be echoed in greater detail by the contributors in Part II. Based on the premise that effective use of cooperative learning is effective decision-making, Rolheiser and Stevahn emphasize the role of the program leader in creating training conditions that foster teacher reflection. The goal of training is to assist teachers in making purposeful choices for context-specific implementation of cooperative learning.

Chapter 4, *Staff Development That Makes a Difference* by Pat Roy, invites the reader to consider the major research findings about effective staff development components and relates these to cooperative learning. Roy, who is a former president of the National Staff Development Council, discusses six approaches to staff development and describes how cooperative learning training would be handled within these approaches. She concludes with suggestions for selecting cooperative learning as a focus for teachers' professional development. In so doing, she provides an effective transition to the next section of the book.

Part II: Lessons From the Field: Approaches to Cooperative Learning
and Implications for Professional Development

The contributors in this volume were invited to reflect on the following questions:

1.  How does the research on best staff development practices inform your selection and implementation of cooperative and collaborative learning?
2.  What have you learned about professional development by working in the field of cooperative learning education?
3.  What have you learned from working with teachers about cooperative learning that can provide better portraits of teachers' learning, and schools undergoing reform?

Contributors share their experiences and/or research on teacher implementation of cooperative learning, and the lessons they have developed through years of practical refinement that further informs their models. Contributors fall into two categories: they are either educators who conduct research on their approaches while they disseminate (Lotan, Cohen, & Morphew, chapter 6; Watson, et.al., chapter 7; Farivar & Webb, chapter 8; Johnson & Johnson, chapter 11 and Schmuck, chapter 12), or they are university-based or independent consultants who are primarily concerned with teaching and learning.

Three of the approaches in this section speak directly to the content of the curriculum: Lotan, Cohen & Morphew focus on the nature of the groupwork task and the challenges to teacher learning of creating rich, complex curricula. Schniedewind & Sapon-Shevin emphasize the importance of integrating the subjects of competition and cooperation into everyday curriculum. The approach presented by Sydney Farivar & Noreen Webb is an example of thoughtful adaptations to specific needs, audiences, and questions for inquiry in mathematics.

Spencer Kagan has developed what is often referred to as the structural approach to cooperative learning. In chapter 5, *Staff Development and the Structural Approach to Cooperative Learning*, Spencer Kagan and Miguel Kagan describe the basic principles of the structural approach, dubbed PIES, and how it is actually a curriculum in itself for teachers. It defines the content for staff development. The Kagans conclude with a review of four different models of training that vary from emphasis on individual training to district wide implementation programs.

In chapter 6, *Beyond the Workshop; Evidence from Complex Instruction*, Rachel Lotan, Elizabeth Cohen, and Christopher Morphew explain how their program for complex instruction employs cooperative learning as a key part of its instructional strategies for teaching in heterogeneous classrooms. The staff of the Program for Complex Instruction has carried out systematic sociological research on the effects of staff development and support from principals and other teachers on the implementation of this approach in the classroom. Using sociological theory they have also found some key differences between the elementary and middle school levels. They focus on those findings that can be generalized to other demanding strategies of cooperative learning.

The social constructivist approach to staff development and cooperative learning is exemplified in chapter 7, *A Social Constructivist Approach to Cooperative Learning and Staff Development: Ideas from the Child Development Project*. This is a carefully evaluated project, particularly in terms of students pro-social and moral development. Marilyn Watson, Sylvia Kendzior, Stefan Dasho, Stanley Rutherford, and Daniel Solomon are on the staff of the CDP. They have developed an effective approach to staff development and conducted research based on the principles of social constructivism with adult learners. The overall goal of the CDP is to help schools to become "caring communities of learners." The sense of the school as a community is the critical mediating variable in their model of program effects.

Sydney Farivar and Noreen Webb focus on a cooperative learning program that builds students' small-group communication and helping skills, and how four middle school teachers were prepared to implement the program in their mathematics classroom. In chapter 8, *Preparing Teachers and Students for Cooperative Work: Building Communication and Helping Skills,* they describe the theoretical and empirical basis for the cooperative learning program, how teachers are prepared to implement the program, the dilemmas they faced during the course of preparing teachers, and their reflections about preparing teachers for such a program in the future. This chapter contributes to the discussion about the particular instructional demands of and differences between the content areas, for example, mathematics and language arts. Middle and secondary level teachers need to see how cooperative learning approaches fit their understanding of their academic disciplines and the particular discourse structures of those disciplines.

James Bellanca & Robin Fogarty add a unique dimension to this volume. In chapter 9, *The Cognitive Approach to Cooperative Learning: Mediating the Challenge to Change,* they discuss how they evolved the cognitive approach from several theoretical bases. They then worked to institutionalize it through a university-based master's program and a professional network. Both of these strategies hold useful lessons for local professional development efforts.

Nancy Schniedewind and Mara Sapon-Shevin, in chapter 10, *Professional Development for Socially-Conscious Cooperative Learning*, detail an approach to cooperative learning and professional development that creates links between cooperative learning in the classroom and broader, societal issues. Within this approach, called Socially-Conscious Cooperative Learning, cooperative learning is both pedagogy and content, and the strategies used are compatible with the broader goals of social justice and equity within a democratic society. The authors discuss the rationale, ways of working with teachers to enhance their full understanding of the potential of cooperative learning and critical pedagogy, examples of ways in which teachers have implemented such a model, and samples of materials for use in such training. They consider the complexities involved in helping teachers to embrace a more holistic, inclusive vision of cooperative learning and cooperative classrooms, and strategies for overcoming resistance and limited implementation.

### Part III: The Learning Community: Cooperative Learning and Organizational Change

In the third section contributors consider the effect of the whole on its parts: how does an organization support cooperative learning at each level—faculty to faculty, faculty to administration, and administration to staff? The questions arise from the structural problem of how to fit opportunities for professional development to a principled redesign of schooling, not simply how to organize training and support to implement a program or set of transferable practices (Little, 1993, p. 132).

Section three begins with David and Roger Johnson's chapter, *Effective Staff Development in Cooperative Learning: Training, Transfer, and Longterm Use*. In chapter 11 the Johnsons outline the requirements of professional development sessions to promote effective longterm use of cooperative learning. They review those studies that involve cooperative learning implementation and discuss these in the context of their 30 years of training teachers and trainers. They may be best known for their cooperative learning model, Learning Together, but they also function as the major disseminators who have implemented organizational change programs to support longterm use of cooperative learning in the schools. The Johnsons relate closely to the literature on innovation in education.

In chapter 12, *Mutually-Sustaining Relationships Between Organization Development and Cooperative Learning*, Richard Schmuck positions professional development and cooperative learning in context with organization development. Schmuck considers empirical relationships between organization development for the school staffs and use of cooperative learning in the classroom. He offers data from case studies on how OD interventions increase readiness for teachers to risk trying co-operative learning strategies in their classrooms. Conversely, schools in which a critical mass of teachers are already trying cooperative learn-ing, are ripe environments for organization development endeavors with the adult staff.

Chapter 13, *Faculty Development Using Cooperative Learning* by Su-san Ellis, describes a systematic program to teach cooperative learning structures to a school faculty to enable them to address and resolve school issues. The faculty experience a variety of cooperative activities to promote team-building and solve problems that they have identified, and they reflect on ways they can use these procedures with their stu-dents to address both social and academic issues in the classroom. Ellis reviews specific strategies for instructing adult groups in how to use co-operative structures to solve problems.

Linda Munger offers a case example in chapter 14, *Developing a Collaborative Environment through Job-Embedded Staff Development: One District's Journey.* Through this narrative Munger details how to make significant changes in many schools and classrooms when there is a dis-trict-wide commitment to professional development and cooperative learning. Munger's work adds another piece to the cases about struc-turing initiatives that make significant learning demands on teachers, and she adapts several approaches to cooperative learning as she evolves with her staff.

### Part IV: Return to the Vision of Community

Liana Forest's chapter 15, *Cooperative Learning Communities: Ex-panding from Classroom Cocoon to Global Connections* is positioned care-fully to re-focus the reader on the larger vision of this book: imagining the future and the place that learning communities have in creating con-texts for teachers and students to be learners together. Forest tells the story of her evolution from anthropologist to teacher who tries contin-ually to see the world through the lessons of her early field work in a communal society. This chapter typifies the evolution of many consul-tants, teachers, and trainers who began working with teachers in class-rooms but soon confronted the problems of and obstacles to longterm implementation—the lack of a coherent organizational context to sup-port the classroom community and the need to address the effects of the larger society on the school as a learning community.

In the *Afterword: Promising Practices and Responsible Directions*, the editors return to the goals of this book, reflect on how the central questions were addressed, and identify areas that have not been discussed by the contributors. They point to promising lines of inquiry and suggest how teachers' classroom research could be better supported for finding situational answers to some of these questions. They reflect on the challenges in professional development for teachers, administrators, and staff developers who are working to restructure schools toward becoming learning communities.

We hope our readers will find this book intellectually rich and practically oriented so that they can participate knowledgeably in the dialogue about how best to reform education.

## Notes

1. For more discussion of this topic, see the *Cooperative Learning Magazine,* particularly, Staff Development: Building Communities of Learners, 12 (2), 1991/2.

2. The Curriculum Project, *Man a Course of Study,* developed at Harvard University under the leadership of Jerome Bruner was an example of this difficulty. While this curriculum came under attack for numerous reasons, among them the nature of the content itself, the inquiry approach required a new set of strategies for teachers, and the support for learning these was not often available.

3. See Schmuck & Schmuck, 1997, for a complete discussion of these influences.

4. More than 25 developers of approaches to cooperative/collaborative learning were invited to contribute to this volume. Many declined to write because of time constraints. No one was omitted due to philosophical differences with the editors.

5. There are many approaches that have been important to the development and dissemination of cooperative learning not included in this volume. For example, see Aronson, et.al., 1978, Clarke, Wideman, & Eadie, 1990; Dalton, 1985; Gibbs, 1987; and McCabe & Rhoades, 1990.

6. See also Albert, 1989, and Freiberg, in press, as an example of a program in classroom management that addresses the trend toward approaching discipline as school-wide, and requiring the adoption of care and cooperation as central values.

## References

Albert, L. (1989). *A teacher's guide to cooperative discipline: How to manage your classroom and promote self-esteem.* Circle Pines, MN: American Guidance Service.

Anning. A. (1988). Teachers' theories about children's learning. In J. Calderhead (Ed.), *Teachers' professional learning* (pp. 128–141). NY: Longman.

Aronson, E. Blaney, M., Stephan, C, Sikes, J. & Snapp, M. (1978). *The jigsaw classroom*. Beverly Hills, CA: Sage Publications.

Auer, M. (1994). The need to "no:" Resistance to cooperative learning. Paper presented at the international meeting of the International Association for the Study of Cooperation in Education, Portland, OR.

Battistich, V. & Solomon, D. (1995). Linking teacher change to student change. Paper presented in symposium at the annual meeting of the American Educational Research Association, San Francisco, CA.

Battistich, V., Solomon, D., & Delucchi, K. (1993). Interaction processes and student outcomes in cooperative learning groups. *The Elementary School Journal, 94,* 19–32.

Bennett, B., Rolheiser, C., & Stevahn, L. (1991). *Cooperative learning: Where heart meets mind.* Toronto, ON: Educational Connections.

Britton, J. (1990). Research currents: Second thoughts on learning. In M. Brubacher, R. Payne & K. Rickett (Eds.), *Perspectives on small group learning.* Canada: Rubicon Publishing, Inc.

———. (1970). *Language and learning.* Portsmouth, NH: Boynton/Cook

Brody, C. (1994). Using co-teaching to promote reflective practice. *Journal of Staff Development.* 15 (3). 32–37.

———. (1993). Co-teaching, teacher beliefs and change: A case study. Paper presented at the annual meeting of the American Educational Research Association, Atlanta, GA.

———. (1992). Cooperative learning and teacher beliefs: A constructivist view. Paper presented at the meeting of the International Association for the Study of Cooperation in Education. Utrecht, Netherlands.

Brubacher, M. (1991). But that's not why I'm doing it. *Cooperative learning magazine* 11(4), 2–3.

Bruffee, K. (1993). *Collaborative learning: Higher education, interdependence, and the authority of knowledge.* Baltimore, MD: Johns Hopkins University Press.

Clandinin, D. J. & Connelly, F. M. (1996). Teachers' professional knowledge landscapes: Teachers stories—stories of teachers—school stories—stories of schools. Educational Researcher 24(3). 24–30.

Clarke, J., Wideman, R. & Eadie, S. (1990. *Together we learn.* Englewood Cliffs, NJ: Prentice Hall.

Cohen, E. (1994, 2nd edition). *Designing groupwork.* NY: Teachers College Press.

————. (1991/2). Staff development for cooperative learning: What does the research say? *Cooperative Learning Magazine*. 12(2), 18–21.

Connelly, F. M. & Clandinin D. J. (1990). Stories of experience and narrative inquiry. *Educational Researcher*, 19(5), 2–14.

Cooper, C. and Boyd, J. (1994). *Collaborative approaches to professional learning and reflection*. Tasmania, Australia: Global Learning Communities.

Dasho, Stefan, & Kendzior, S. (1995). Toward a caring community of learning for teachers: Staff development to support the child development project. Paper presented in symposium at the annual meeting of the American Educational Research Association, San Francisco.

Davidson, N. (Ed.) 1990. *Cooperative learning in mathematics: A handbook for teachers*. Reading, MA: Addison-Wesley.

Davidson, N. & Worsham, T. (Eds.). (1992). Enhancing thinking through cooperative learning. NY: Teachers College Press.

Deutsch, M. (1949). A theory of cooperation and competition. *Human Relations* 2, 129–152.

Dewey, J. (1938/1963). *Experience and education*. NY: Collier Press.

————. (1916/1994). *Democracy and education*. NY: Macmillan, reprinted by Shelburn, VT: Resource Center for Redesigning Education.

Edmonds, R. (1979). Effective schools for the urban poor. *Educational Leadership*. 37(1), 15–24.

Elmore, R. (1995). Structural reform and educational practice. *Educational Researcher*, 24(9), 23–26.

Freiberg, J. (in press). *Consistency management & cooperative discipline: From tourist to citizen*. Ohio: Merrill.

Freiberg, H. J. & Huang, S., (1994). *Study 2.4: Longitudinal study of the life-cycle of improving schools: Final report*. Philadelphia, PA: National Center on Education in the Inner Cities

Gibbs, J. (1987). *Tribes: A process for social development and cooperative learning*. Santa Rosa, CA: Center Source Publications.

Hargreaves. A. (1996). Revisiting voice. *Educational Researcher*. 25(1), 12–19.

Henderson, J. G. (1996, second edition). *Reflective teaching*. Englewood Cliffs, NJ: Merrill Press.

————. (1992). *Reflective teaching: Becoming an inquiring educator*. NY: Macmillan.

Hertz-Lazarowitz, R. (1993). On becoming a cooperative learning teacher: Using the six mirrors of the classroom to document transition of two teachers. *Texas Researcher*, 4 97–110.

Jacob, E. (in press). *Cooperative learning in context.* Albany, NY: SUNY Press.

———. (1997). Context and cognition: Implications for educational innovators and anthropologists. *Anthropology and Education Quarterly.* 28(1), 3–21.

Johnson, D. W., Johnson, R. T. & Holubec, E. (1987). *Circles of learning.* Edina, MN: Interaction Book Company. Johnson,

Johnson, D., W. (1970). *The social psychology of education.* NY: Holt, Rinehart & Winston.

Joyce, B. (1991/2). Cooperative learning and staff development. *Cooperative Learning Magazine.* 12(2). 10–13.

Kagan, (1993). *Cooperative learning: Resources for teachers.* San Juan Capistrano, CA: Kagan Cooperative Learning.

Kelly, G. (1955). *A theory of personality.* NY: Norton & Company.

Kuhn, T. (1970). *The structure of scientific revolutions.* 2nd edition. Chicago: University of Chicago Press.

Lewin, K. (1948). *Resolving social conflicts.* NY: Harpers.

———. (1951). *Field theory in social psychology.* NY: Harpers.

Lippitt, R. (1940). An experimental study of the effect of democratic and authoritarian group atmosphere. *University of Iowa Studies in Child Welfare* 16, 43–165.

———. (1962). Unplanned maintenance and planned change in the group work process. In *Social Work Practice.* NY: Columbia University Press.

Little, J. W. (1993). Teachers' professional devleopment in a climate of educational reform. *Educational Reform & Policy Analysis.* 15(2), 129–151.

Matthews, R. S., Cooper, J. L., Davidson, N. & Hawkes, P. (1995). Building bridges between cooperative and collaborative learning. *Change.* 35–40.

McCabe, M. & Rhoades, J. (1990). *The nurturing classroom.* Sacramento, CA: ITA Publications.

Meade, G. H. (1934). *Mind and society.* Chicago: University of Chicago Press.

Miel, A., et.al., (1952) *Cooperative procecures in learning.* NY: Teachers College Press.

Miller, J. (1990) *Creating spaces and finding voices.* Albany, NY: SUNY Press.

Miller, J. P. & Seller, W. (1985). *Curriculum perspectives and practice.* NY: Longman.

Moreno, J. L. (1934/1953). *Who shall survive?* Washington, D.C.: Nervous and Mental Diseases Publishing Co., Reprinted NY: Beacon House.

Osberg, A. (1986). Staff development through individual reflection on practice. Paper presented at the annual meeting of the American Educational Research Association, San Francisco, CA.

Palmeri, A. B. (1996). The role of teachers' beliefs on the planning and implementation of second-grade science curricula. Paper presented at the annual meeting of the American Educational Research Association, New York City.

Piaget, J. (1978). *Success and understanding.* Cambridge, MA. Harvard University Press.

Richardson, V. (Ed.) (1996). Teacher change and the staff development process: A case in reading instruction. NY: Teachers College Press.

Richardson, V. (1994). Conducting research on practice. *Educational Researcher,* 23(5), 5–10.

Rorty. R. (1979). *Philosophy and the mirror of nature.* Princeton: Princeton University Press.

Sapon-Shevin, M. & Schniedewind, N. (1992). If cooperative learning is the answer, what are the questions? *Journal of Education,* 174(2), 11–37.

Schon, D. (1987). *Educating the reflective practitioner.* San Francisco: Jossey Bass.

Schmuck, R. A. (1991/2). Richard Schmuck: Organization development: Building a community of learners. Interviewed by Judy Clarke. *Cooperative Learning Magazine.* 12 (2), 14–17.

Schmuck, R. A. (1968). Helping teachers improve classroom group processes. *Journal of Applied Behavioral Science* 4, 401–435.

Schmuck, R. A. and Schmuck, P. (1997, 7th edition). *Group processes in the classroom.* Dubuque, IA: Brown and Benchmark Publishers.

Sharan, S. (1980). Cooperative learning in small groups: Recent methods and effects on achievement, attitudes, and ethnic relations. *Review of Educational Research,* 50, 241–271.

———. (1990). The group investigation approach to cooperative learning: Theoretical foundations. In M. Brubacher, R. Payne & K. Rickett (Eds.), *Perspectives on small group learning.* Canada: Ribicon Publishing, Inc.

Sharan. S. & Hertz-Lazarowitz, R. (1980). A group investigation method of cooperative learning in the classoom. In S. Sharan, P. Hare, C. Webb & R. Hertz-Lazarowitz (Eds.) *Cooperation in education* (pp. 14–46). Provo, UT: Brigham Young University Press.

———. (1982). Effects of an instructional change program on teachers behavior, attitudes and perceptions. *Journal of Applied Behavioral Science,* 18, 185–201.

Sharan. S. & Sharan, Y. (1992). *Group investigation.* NY: Teachers College Press.

————. (1976). *Small group teaching.* Englewood Cliffs, NJ: Educational Technology Publications.

Slavin, R. (1983). *Cooperative learning.* NY: Longman.

————. (1989/90). *Research on cooperative learning: Consensus and controversy.* Educational Leadership, 47(4), 52–55.

Watson, M. (1995). Giving content to restructuring: A social, ethical and intellectual agenda for elementary education. Paper presented in symposium at the annual meeting of the American Educational Research Association, San Francisco, CA.

Witherell, C. & Noddings, N. (1991). *Stories lives tell: Narrative & dialogue in education.* NY: Teachers College Press.

Vygotsky. L. S. (1978). *Mind in society: the development of higher psychological processes.* In Michael Cole, Vera John-steiner, Sylvia Scribner & Ellen Souberman, (Eds.), Cambridge: Harvard University Press.

# 1

## The Significance of Teacher Beliefs for Professional Development and Cooperative Learning

### *Celeste Brody*

Teachers' beliefs may have the greatest impact on what teachers do in the classroom, the ways they conceptualize their instruction, and learn from experience. Until recently educators knew relatively little, however, about how teachers change their beliefs, how they interact with instructional innovations, and how teachers reconstruct their assumptions and their practices once they complete a professional development experience (Clark & Peterson, 1986; Cuban, 1988; Nespor, 1987; Richardson, et.al, 1991; Richardson, 1990, and Tobin, 1987). Many development practices simply disregard the connections between the belief orientations implicit in the innovation itself and those of the teacher engaged in the adoption of the practice. The focus on being able to adopt the innovation can distract from a teacher's practical and situational response to it which is unique and a result of complex variables: personal and professional histories, age, and the grade level and subject matter they teach.

This chapter presents a framework for understanding basic aspects of teachers' beliefs regarding: locus of control and authority in teaching, the nature of knowledge and knowing, and conceptions of the teacher's role in decision-making, for those who work with teachers on any instructional innovation. I draw on several studies and then present one case to demonstrate the importance of paying close attention to teachers' meanings for selecting and tailoring approaches for teachers who are learning cooperative learning.

### The Importance of Teacher Beliefs for Practice

Beliefs are "conceptual representations that signify to its holder a reality or given state of affairs of sufficient validity, truth, and/or trustworthiness to warrant reliance upon it as a guide to personal thought and action." (Deford in Richardson, et.al, 1991, p. 562). Beliefs have a certain functionality for teachers. Because the contexts in which teachers work are often ill-defined and multi-faceted, beliefs allow teachers to make sense of ambiguity and role diffuseness. Belief systems can be understood as deeply-etched patterns reflecting orientations that guide the task of teaching (Von Glasersfeld, 1984; Kelly, 1955). They create a set of personal constructions that guide a teacher in interacting with new ideas and practices. When beliefs change it is more likely a matter of a gestalt shift than the result of argumentation or marshalling of evidence (Nespor, 1987).

When staff developers and teacher educators fail to make explicit their own value and belief orientations and that of the innovation they are introducing to teachers, they complicate a situation that is already complex. This may pose additional discrepancies or contradictions for teachers.

Cooperative learning is a case in point. Some refer to it as a generic tool for teaching, adaptable to any teaching/learning situation. Others consider it a philosophy in itself (see Schniedewind & Sapon-Shevin, chapter 10; and Forest chapter 15 this volume). Some even argue that changing to a cooperative, or a collaborative perspective, requires a shift in sensibility, a shift in fundamental assumptions and beliefs about learning, knowing, and authority (Britton, 1990). There is truth in each view, but how teachers implement cooperative learning depends partly on the particular beliefs about education they hold, as well as the match between the models they are implementing or learning, and their beliefs. While many cooperative learning training programs are well-grounded in research and theory, we need to provide more opportunities for teachers to reflect on the range of implicit assumptions in the innovation in relation to their own beliefs and personal constructions.

An example may be useful here. Several years ago during a year-long cooperative learning professional development program, I arranged for the participating teachers and administrators to experience three well-known cooperative learning approaches. The participants also read research from the collaborative learning tradition, teacher change, and reflective practice. We held monthly meetings to talk about our progress of learning more about cooperative learning. We analyzed emerging classroom practices in light of each of the cooperative learning models as they were introduced and considered. In the spring a representative of one approach came and demonstrated strategies from several of their programs. The responses of the teachers and administrators to the approaches were so negative, however, that they outright rejected it—despite the powerful research base for this model! The teachers described a negative sense of self while participating in the activities. They criticized the conceptions of knowledge that formed the basis of the math and language arts programs. They argued that there was little evidence of problem-solving, opportunities for students to invent, create, critically think, and construct their own meanings. They were disturbed by the standardized curriculum of the program, the lack of emphasis upon social values, and the use of competition to achieve academic ends. Interestingly as well, three teachers who had been introduced to this same approach through their district before this program began, had been initially reticent to participate in this year long program because they did not think that cooperative learning, as they assumed this particular approach represented in totality, matched their notions of authority, control, and curricular structures. A first grade teacher described her initial reaction to the approach:

> It was kind of subject oriented, almost a programmed kind of thing. I visualized it as a good way to meet the needs of learners who were behind the norm, but it was very subject-oriented, and rather rigid. If I ever had just that model, having to do that real structured stuff, you know, count up the points, that would not fit for me. I would pack it in. That doesn't interest me.

One might argue that these educators did not understand thoroughly the approaches and programs or they would not have rejected them so quickly. Possibly, but given the high sense of efficacy of this group, the approaches in this particular workshop simply contradicted their beliefs. What was also interesting about the discussions was that the teachers did, in fact, appreciate the research base of the approaches. They relied on many of the findings regarding student achievement to craft their rationales for using cooperative learning in their classrooms. But the implication of their response to the programs was clear: any school-level decision to import these particular approaches of cooperative learning for this faculty to learn and implement without accounting for the faculty's practical knowledge and beliefs would be asking for problems and resistance right from the start.

## Conceptions of Cooperative Learning

When working with staff or a group of teachers, I use a framework that can assist them to understand general epistemological assumptions implicit in most practices, including cooperative learning. I (Brody,

1992) adapted Miller and Seller's (1985) curriculum schema to assist in understanding general epistemological orientations and apply these to discern the assumptions implicit in cooperative learning practices. These three orientations summarize curriculum and instructional approaches as transmissional, transactional, or transformational in regard to the aims of education and learning, the nature of knowledge and knowing, the locus of control and authority in relationship to goals, objectives and the learning process, the teacher's conceptions of his or her role, and the teacher's orientation to decision-making regarding the curriculum and instruction[1] (see Table 1.1). When this framework is used in conjunction with a collaborative interview, for example, (see Table 1.2), it can assist teachers in breaking down stereotypes and assumptions about colleagues, and facilitating reflective professional development practices. Collaborative reflective processes can enhance teachers' examination of their assumptions and beliefs by encouraging awareness of their own and others' perspectives on their inclinations and actions. (See Cooper & Boyd, chapter 2, for more discussion on reflective practices.)

The Transmission Approach

A transmission orientation, as the name suggests, promotes the aim of education as the transmission of knowledge to students in the form of facts, skills, concepts, and values; it is sometimes referred to as a "technical" orientation (Gitlin, 1990; Taylor, 1990). Students respond to a structured learning situation, usually initiated by the teacher, who plans and sequences materials so that the students can proceed through the units. Teachers play a strong, directive role in students' learning and in determining how students spend their time. Knowledge is construed as "an objective body of information whose existence is unrelated to human subjectivity, and schools must transmit this knowledge intact, i.e., free of error, to the learner" (Sharan, 1990 p. 35). Content is, therefore, relatively fixed, and the focus is on public knowledge, usually gathered from texts or standard sources. There is an emphasis on external rewards and external reinforcers, usually with little room for individual differences; students are considered competent or successful when they have mastered the curriculum.

A staff developer holding this view might convey that cooperative learning can be mastered through applying discrete strategies to solve any number of educational and pedagogical problems. Cooperative learning would be used consistently to achieve narrow academic ends—the teaching of a standard, or pre-packaged curriculum with a largely teacher-directed approach. The transmission view could refer,

TABLE 1.1

Teachers' Beliefs about Cooperative Learning and Pedagogy

| Transmission | Transaction | Transformation |
|---|---|---|
| *Conceptions of Cooperative Learning* | | |
| Cooperative learning is a technique to be mastered primarily to extend one 's tools for managing groupwork. It improves achievement test scores and is used most often for mastery learning, review. | Cooperative learning fosters problem-solving, higher levels of thinking and pro-social behaviors. | Cooperative learning is a philosophy whereby a set of values are explicit regarding relationships and learning, i.e.,creating a community of learners who can engage in critical dialogue and inquiry. |
| *Locus of Control and Sense of Authority* | | |
| Teacher-Centered Authority for knowledge rests primarily with the teacher who is responsible for all aspects of learning and the learning conditions. | Learner-Centered Authority for knowledge is shared with students. The teacher is authoritative, not authoritarian. The goal is to assist the learning to become more intrinsically motivating. | Constructed Communities Authority is derived from the community. Teacher is primarily concerned with the effect of community—creating new knowledge. Students are capable of defining the conditions of learning. |
| *The Teacher's Role* | | |
| Teacher is performer, director, manager. | Teacher is facilitator, encourager, orchestrator | Teacher is co-learner and an integral part of the community. |
| *Conceptions of Decision-making in Teaching* | | |
| There are prescribed processes for most situations. Effective practice can be tied to discrete teacher behaviors. | Teaching is a complex, relational craft and decisions are best made through reflection and consultation, consciously and tentatively. | Teaching is a complex, relational craft and decisions are best made through reflection and consultation, consciously and tentatively. Teacher considers a full range of pertinent, contextual and pedagogical factors, but dialogue focues on issues of power and social justice. |

TABLE 1.1  *Continued*

| Transmission | Transaction | Transformation |
|---|---|---|
| *The Nature of Knowledge and Knowing* | | |
| Knowledge is an objective body of information transmitted from teacher/texts to students. "Knowing" emphasizes logical, linear paradigms. Covering curriculum dominates decision-making. | Knowledge is dynamic and changing. Knowing is in relation to the knower, a process related to various modes of inquiry. Depth is valued over breadth in curriculum. | Knowledge is dynamic, changing, and constructed. Knowing is multi-dimensional and contextual or situational. Dialogue is central to creating a community. Students and teachers are co-authors, co-learners. The goal of knowledge is transforming society through community action. |

however, to any construction of cooperative learning whose aims are to leave fundamental assumptions unchallenged, particularly in relation to the nature of knowledge, authority and human interactions.

The Transactional Approach

A transactional orientation represents education as a dialogue between the student and the curriculum, and the student as a problem-solver. The aim is to develop intelligence in general, and complex problem-solving skills in particular. Learning can occur within any number of frameworks of an academic discipline, through an interdisciplinary approach, or within a social context. The teacher views herself as a facilitator who provides appropriate resources and questions for inquiry. In the transactional orientation social skills for a democratic society are as important as acquisition of complex intellectual frameworks. Students share control of the learning because students need opportunities to experiment and try out different solutions to a problem. Knowledge is in relation to the knower; it is a process related to the various modes of inquiry of the disciplines and, as such, is an integral aspect of content. Motivation is intrinsic, that is, the individual needs to resolve problems, but the environment needs to support problem-solving. Each student's level of development is considered in relation to the learning activities.

What also distinguishes transactional approaches to cooperative learning is the degree of structure associated with the teaching of cooperative skills, the importance of the nature of the dialogue and discourse, and the view of motivation and control in learning. Academic achievement is not in contradiction with social goals and values; in fact, learning social goals and values enhances the classroom environment and, hence, the context for achievement. Teachers consider the impact of cooperative learning on the scope and sequence, depth and breadth of learning. The teaching of social skills and the commitment to expressing prosocial values is equally important; the teacher is a facilitator of the learning environment. In this volume most of the approaches fit this orientation: David and Roger Johnson's Learning Together Approach (chapter 11), Complex Instruction by Elizabeth Cohen and Rachel Lotan (chapter 6), Sydney Farivar and Noreen Webb's communication and helping skills in mathematics (chapter 8), the cognitive approach of Jim Bellanca and Robin Fogarty (chapter 9), Spencer and Miguel Kagan's structural approach (chapter 5) and Laurie Stevahn and Carol Rolheiser's work (chapter 3).

Transformational Approach

In the transformational approach, the aims of education are social change and personal actualization. Learning focuses on the integration of the physical, cognitive, affective, and spiritual/moral dimensions, and the teacher's role is to link skills with these aspects of life. Students have as much control as possible over their own learning so that they can become self-motivated, self-directed problem solvers. Because knowledge is not separate from the individual, it is rooted in personal meaning systems. New knowledge is the effect of community where texts or curricula emerge from the collective experiences of the learners (Britton, 1990). Multiple perspectives are cultivated and promoted, and are subject to further exploration through collaboration and dialogue.

Cooperative and collaborative learning from the transformational approach emphasizes the aims of learning; for example, it may be a developmental stage towards a major philosophical change in the way teachers and students structure their classes, and ultimately, how schooling is structured (Kohn, 1986). Proponents who share this orientation often advocate cooperative learning as providing an ideal entree into the exploration of the possible in education and opportunity for considering the moral ramifications of education (Sapon-Shevin, 1991). Cooperative learning can provide a framework for thinking about how power is allocated, how decisions are made, and how multiple perspectives can be heard and validated. It can allow the creation of par-

TABLE 1.2

Collaborative Interviewing: Supporting Collegial Respect for Beliefs

*Interview I* focuses on histories, goals, and beliefs about one's teaching. Teachers reflect aloud on a critical incident or particular memory of teaching or learning. *Interview II* explores teachers' professional goals and teaching styles and lays the groundwork to discuss progress toward these goals. These interviews set the stage for discussing similarities and differences in motivation and intention.

Interview I: Histories, Goals, and Beliefs about Teaching

*Taking Turns, Ask Your Colleague:*

1. Describe a memorable event or critical incident from your teaching or learning experience.
2. Interpret the meaning of this event: Why is this particular experience so memorable? How would your define the theme(s) of this event?
3. Explore the connection of this theme to your core beliefs: What is important to you as a teacher? If you were to accomplish nothing else with your students this year, what would it be? What are your beliefs about learning?
4. Acknowledging that we have lives outside of school, what matters most to you when you are not teaching?

*Together, Let's Reflect On:*

How are we similar, how are we different, in our histories, beliefs, and goals? What do we want that is the same/different, for our students? ourselves? our colleagues?

Interview II: Examining Professional Goals and Teaching Styles

*Take Turns, Ask:*

1. Describe your teaching style, i.e., the way you see yourself relating to students, the way you would describe your role in the clasroom, and how you manage the classroom.
2. How do you expect your ideal cooperative learning classroom to look? How do you describe your role in a cooperative classroom?
3. What do you consider as your strong points as a teacher in a cooperative classroom? Where do you feel you need help and want to grow?
4. What do you want to learn through this experience of . . . (e.g., working together, team teaching, and so on). How can I support you in your learning?

*Together, Let's Reflect On:*

How are we similar, how are we different in each of these areas? What do we want that is the same? What do we want that is different?

This first appeared in a different version, in the *Journal of Staff Development*, (Brody, 1994): Using co-teaching to promote reflective practice.

ticipatory communities, classroom models of democracy, spaces for discourse, and the critical examination of the ways in which certain voices are silenced by our current models of schooling and government. Social justice and social action through the coordination of members is a goal. It is exemplified in the work of the Sharans (1992) and in this volume, the approaches of Liana Forest (chapter 15), Nancy Schniedewind and Mara Sapon-Shevin (chapter 10), the Child Development Center Project (chapter 7), and Carole Cooper and Julie Boyd (chapter 2).

For many teachers there will be marked congruency with the practice as it is represented to them, or as they perceive it; for others such as the teachers in the earlier example, it will not "fit" at all, or they will modify the practice to fit their existing beliefs. Teachers will alter a viewpoint, however, even if it is an integral part of their beliefs, if they become aware of the personally meaningful implications of an alternative. With the proper support they will explore alternative views even though these may cause dilemmas or contradictions between their prevailing or dominant orientation and the new epistemologies within their own constructs. Teacher educators and staff developers need to understand how teachers adopt an innovation such as cooperative learning from the point of view of their system of beliefs (Pope & Scott, 1984).

## Teachers' Beliefs and Cooperative Learning

This section considers the importance of listening closely to teachers as they move through their learning process in regard to cooperative learning. How teacher educators and staff developers pose questions and invite dialogue is critical to a learner-centered professional development environment, especially when the learners are teachers. We need to remain open to teachers' views of their role, their notions of the nature of knowing and knowledge, their understandings of cooperative learning, and their resolutions of the dilemmas of practice. We begin by asking teachers to discuss what they understand cooperative learning to be and what significance they attach to it (See Table 1.2). We read teachers' journals to understand how they construct their concerns about adopting cooperative learning. The content is unique to each teacher and it is important for the staff developer and teacher to know and understand it in order to assist them to consider new directions.

### Persistent Themes in Teachers' Constructions
of Teaching and Learning

There are four areas that are persistent themes for teachers when they talk about their work. These are: (1) the locus of control and sense of authority, (2) teacher's role, (3) how decision-making is viewed, (4) the nature of knowledge and knowing (Berlak & Berlak, 1981). I have added a fifth, conceptions of cooperative learning, because it is directly related to professional development and levels of use. That is, teachers in their first or second year of adoption of cooperative learning talk most frequently about issues of control and their role as teacher: "What do I do when it gets too noisy and takes so much time to set up?" "Now that they are working in groups, what is my role? I'm not needed in the same way anymore." Those with more than two years of experience using cooperative learning talk more often about epistemological dilemmas (Brody, 1992): "How do I balance a district-driven curriculum with what I see students needing to do within their cooperative groups?"[2]

In interviews (Brody, 1992) we[3] conducted with educators six months after a year-long program in cooperative learning, we explored and described the participants' changes in beliefs about cooperative learning. The teachers, called Sharon and Betty, represent the variation in motives for adopting cooperative learning, and the constraints on and possibilities for how each teacher will use it.

*Sharon.* Sharon,[4] a 15 year veteran, made many of her instructional decisions based upon a view that students and teachers are co-learners, and that students construct the knowledge for themselves. She described herself as a teacher "in transition" who only made a serious "choice" about teaching within the last five years. Through cooperative learning training she realized that she needed to reaffirm her life's work; and only recently had she made a conscious commitment to work for change in education. She had fallen into teaching for lack of anything else to do when she returned from the Peace Corps years before. For Sharon, cooperative learning training contributed to developing constructivist ideas about learning often associated with transformational orientations.

> Cooperative learning is about how kids construct knowledge. . . .
> I am attempting to create situations in which kids will pose their own questions and present their own conflicts, and go off in other directions. Before, I might have looked at some tangent that some kid would take, and say, "Why?" I am now looking at that and saying, "What is the potential for this? How can I take advantage of this opportunity to help create a situation that will provide some learning for these kids?"

For Sharon, decision-making depends on the context she is in, and is a negotiated process which accounts for the teacher's reasons for why she is doing what she is doing. All decisions must be considered within a standard of fairness and respect for students:

> Regarding positive interdependence (as other teachers use it), I think it's easy to threaten kids instead of encouraging them. Some of the ways that are suggested (in cooperative learning trainings) for creating positive interdependence, averaging the test scores for kids in your group, I think that's a valid thing to do if you know your kids well enough, and you know where they are with regard to cooperation; and you know they'll see that as a fair thing to do. But if they haven't had some experience, enough experience to get them to a point where they view it as a fair thing, then you can have some real trouble, and create a lot of anger and hostility.

Sharon considers cooperative learning, quite literally, as involving "disagreement and conflict:"

> For me that's been the scariest part of cooperative learning, and the most threatening part. It's inevitable, when kids sit down to work together that there's a lot of conflict. I have trouble dealing with conflict myself. So it's a real challenge to me to help kids deal with their conflict. The thing I'm trying to learn is that conflict is really good, and it's valuable. And trying to help kids see that is a big challenge.

*Betty.* Betty is an elementary teacher in her second year of using cooperative learning. Like Sharon she has been teaching for over 20 years. She came from a large, ethnically diverse city years before, and she described that influence on her purpose for teaching: fostering racial and ethnic harmony and understanding.

> I was drawn to cooperative learning from observing kids over a period of time and watching kids from different cultures. I taught Mexican kids, and they are totally different. You look at those kids who are from Mexico, and they have extremely good manners. They always want to help. They are attentive. It's all of us working together. So I saw cooperative learning as the way to give kids an experience that will have them relate to each other differently.

In structuring her classroom for cooperative groupwork, Betty puts her students in a single group for the entire year because she wants them to learn to "love one another. And they do learn to do that." Managing the groups so that there was as little disruption as possible with the greatest amount of harmony is an often repeated concern for her. She does not approve of the generally recognized practice in cooperative group learning of giving students opportunities to move to other groups so they can learn to work with a variety of people. Furthermore, she is not certain about distinguishing individual activity from group activity:

> Cooperative learning is helping each other, and knowing you're responsible for helping somebody else. The kids do really help each other a whole lot; as a matter of fact, it gets so bad they help each other too much. They never stop. The few times I want them to do their own stuff, they're very helpful.

Her view on knowledge is that the curriculum is determined by the texts, or set by her fourth grade team, and her job is to dispense it and make it as interesting as possible:

> You can't use (cooperative learning) 100% of the time, but I try to use it as much as I can. The daily oral language that they have to do, the way it's written up in the book, is for you to pick a child to come up and find one thing wrong in the sentence. These happen to be pretty easy sentences and the kids didn't have too much trouble with them, so I'll pick two kids from the same team to come up and work at it. If they get stuck, like if I told them there is one more thing, they go back and consult with other members of their team, "Did you get all of them?" Then they earn points for all of their team up there.

Because "the curriculum is repeated so often through grade school and the middle years, that whatever they don't get, or have forgotten one way or the other, they'll get again," she describes her role as an orchestrator of learning activities: "I provide materials for you (the student), but whatever you learn is what you get out of it yourself." Betty does not give students multiple informal group experiences at the first part of the year to observe and learn how her students interact—a common recommendation in cooperative learning trainings as a good way to begin the year—because she wants "to avoid conflict" between students. At holiday time, she often puts the children back in rows, because "that's when they all get a little bit crazy and that's the time when you want everybody doing their own thing, in little rows, and quiet things down because they get so excited this time of year." Decision-making for this teacher, in contrast to Sharon, centers on how to create harmony, how to foster love between students, and how to invite students to partake of the standard curriculum that is offered.

*Generalizing From Patterns.* We should resist judging teachers' beliefs, but it is helpful to generalize patterns in order to understand teachers' contradictions and dilemmas. Table 1.1 summarizes a framework for discussing these. Teachers do reveal their implicit beliefs in a non-judgmental context such as an interview setting among peers. My interviews with teachers who made the transition from novice to more expert in using cooperative learning suggest these teachers have more-elaborated, more-organized schema in regard to the pedagogical themes; teachers revealed the complexity and contextual nature of their knowledge, and their narratives referred to constructs that guided their actions.

Teachers may talk about practices that might be characterized as traditional and, in the same breath, draw upon the theories also fundamental to transformative approaches to explain their goals. The categories in Table 1.1 represent generalized themes; they are not necessarily exclusive nor separated in teachers' thinking. Teachers talk more often about issues of control and authority than about epistemological questions; however, the more experienced the teachers are with cooperative learning, the more likely they are to address dilemmas about the nature of knowledge and knowing. These orientations are representational positions along a continuum, with views shifting, depending upon contexts, histories, and experiences. This is not a static framework and is meant only to paint a broad picture.

I often introduce this framework early in a cooperative learning program and invite teachers to reflect on their own practices in several ways—through journal writing, small group discussion, and dialogue. Teachers realize that conflicts with colleagues are not necessarily based on personality; they may be epistemological. Recognizing similarities and differences is the first step toward accepting differences and respecting their colleagues' practical knowledge. Differences are particularly important because they create opportunities for colleagues to help one another across gaps of understanding and to push the boundaries of practice (Brody, 1994).

## The Locus of Control and Sense of Authority

Issues of control pose the most dilemmas for teachers adopting cooperative learning because cooperative learning requires them to reconstruct not only their practices but their notions of control and authority. Teachers will often compare their initiation period into cooperative learning to their first years of teaching when they clarified their classroom management. As they consider what a "learner-centered" environment means, they may redefine teacher control as a function of structure over the conditions for learning.

> Anne: When the teacher loses the authoritarian role, the control comes from the written lesson plans, and how well that teacher has organized the cooperative learning lesson. If it's not organized well, then the kids will be out of control. So you need to organize your lesson, and that's where your control is. Then kids will have the control within that lesson structure.

For many teachers the goal of their structuring is to promote more student-directed learning and inquiry. This teacher reveals a complex understanding about the issues of control and authority.

> Sharon: Teachers can be in control (with cooperative learning). It depends on what you want to be in control of. Setting up cooperative groups doesn't mean a teacher totally abdicates control in the classroom. In some ways, the teacher has to be more in control, in terms of structuring the groups, and setting some parameters, and some guidelines, and some clear expectations, but you can't control the outcome. You can't control the learning. If I haven't learned anything else this year, I'm learning that it's the kids who create learning from themselves. It's internal; and there is no way I can make a kid learn. There's a lot I can do to set up a more ideal situation, or situation that is favorable to a kid's constructing some meaningful learning.

Other narratives demonstrate elements of both transmissional and transactional beliefs:

> Marion: I'd probably say I'm authoritative, but not authoritarian. For the teachers who don't feel the need to be "in charge," be in control, cooperative learning is a comfortable way to teach. But if I felt it would reflect on me if students were out of their desks— because with cooperative learning they probably would be—if having a quiet classroom is important, it could feel out of control. I was observed last year, and I had a big class. In my evaluation she put, "Ms. K's classroom is not quiet, but it is controlled."

Experienced teachers notice a shift in their notions of control and authority once they begin using cooperative learning. The shift may be subtle, because there may already be a high degree of congruence with their conceptions of the goals of cooperative learning and their notions about control and authority. Sharon explained:

> I get very excited when I see kids taking charge. At the same time, it does create a little discomfort for me, because I know that I've been used to being in control. One of the things about putting kids into groups, is that you never know what's going to happen and you have much less control. You are setting up more potentially volatile situations, not just in the sense that they may get into an argument, but volatile in that their direction of their learning can just go anywhere.

Many teachers have not considered the notion of a teacher-centered versus learner-centered classroom before cooperative learning training unless they have already developed a highly-articulated philosophy that centers on these values, such as a whole language or a child-centered classroom. Having a mental image of a learner-centered environment as opposed to a teacher-centered classroom clarifies these goals and provides teachers with language to assess their practices more clearly.

## Teachers' Conceptions About Their Roles

Intimately connected to beliefs about control and authority are teachers' conceptions of their roles. Teachers have metaphors to describe how they see their role as a teacher in cooperative learning: whether they see themselves as a performer in a teacher-centered environment, or a facilitator in a student-centered environment. Teachers who self-select into a cooperative learning training program usually hold a facilitator view of their role before they begin. Cooperative learning greatly appeals to teachers if they see their role as one of "facilitator," or "encourager" of learning. This teacher defines her facilitator role in terms of control:

> The teacher's role is a facilitator. She'll be around to the tables helping with her control paper (directions). She can give that up, and work with the group then. A lot of teachers that do really well (with cooperative learning) just say, "If you have a question, make sure no one in your group can answer it before you ask me."

Jane defines her role consistent with a transformative approach, revealing a definite child-centered view:

> Through that observation, you become informed about what that child is thinking, how he is putting the pieces together. You hear a little vignette here or there and you think, "Oh, that's what he's thinking," or "I see what he needs."

## Conceptions of Decision-Making

Cooperative learning requires teachers to make many more decisions than they had before, and they are more conscious of the discrepancies between their intent, what they want to see happen in the class, and what actually occurs. This is what makes cooperative learning so risky. For the teachers who have previously construed their role narrowly and technically, decision-making is often a matter of trying to "get the situation right." It is difficult to consider that what they relied on previously for their decisions is no longer adequate within a cooperative classroom. Teachers whose decision-making approach is consistent with principles of reflective practice, generally welcome the new decisions. They notice that cooperative learning makes them better observers and assessors of students and the learning process. They welcome more complex information about students and this actually gives them time for reflection-in-action.

> Debbie: I get people started in the lesson by giving them what they need to get going, and then I turn them loose. That's when I see the goal completely changing from what it had been in the past. I now become an observer, a facilitator, an intervener of what's going on—if there are problems that are occurring—either lack of content knowledge, or lack of direction on the part of the kids of what they're really supposed to be doing, or a lack of being able to work together with one another to solve whatever a situation requires.

The language associated with cooperative learning gives teachers an increased sense of power in regard to interpreting and understanding learning, enabling them to describe their previous tacit knowledge more intelligently and forcibly to themselves, students, colleagues, and parents.

> Andy: The class ran itself. The students ran the operation. I know more about individual kids now, primarily because I can go

around listening to kids. I can find out what's going wrong and what's going right in the groups. I'm getting more information than I had before. Before my cooperative learning training I don't think it mattered.

The greater the sense of self-efficacy the more likely the teacher will selectively use cooperative learning (Brody, 1992). If the administration is not supportive, or the size of the class not conducive, or the number of preparations too many with too little time, or if there are other job demands (e.g., team teaching or job sharing), experienced teachers judge about the conditions under which they could use cooperative learning.

Kim: What's changed for me are the details, the how to's, facilitating it, getting more kids doing more. I've always done groupwork, we've always talked over problems, I've always had expectations of how kids should be to each other in a classroom. This just makes it a lot easier. I don't hesitate to change strategies, but it's really important to me now not to put myself in extremely stressful situations by letting kids continue with something that is not working.

When teachers begin using cooperative learning decision-making centers initially on choosing when or when not to use cooperative learning, rather than on how complex the collaborative environment should become over time. (See Lotan, Cohen, Morphew, chapter six, for more discussion about complex, demanding tasks.)

The Nature of Knowledge and Knowing

Fundamental assumptions about the nature of knowledge and how people come to know what they know, are deeply held beliefs and often the most resistant to change. Teachers can hold transmissional ways for constructing knowledge while welcoming new forms to promote learning. They might consider themselves as co-learners and co-inquirers who look to students to teach them about themselves, but the questions for inquiry might be the typical ones accepted by the field, or directed by the text. Dick, a math teacher, explains his new conceptions of math after cooperative learning training:

In the early days . . . I was always the center, I was always the font of knowledge. I was the one that had everything, and I would have been in direct control. (Today) the amount of content that we cover

becomes less important than the richness of the experiences that
you give them . . . the breadth of experiences as opposed to the
accelerated kind of thing which you get when you have people
working pretty much by themselves, and you're the one in control.
(Working with cooperative learning) someone will take (an approach) to solve a problem or something that I never thought of in
my entire life, that just is so different with the way that I would approach the problem, and it's a real awakening for me and just really expands my horizon.

If the staff developer approaches cooperative learning training
from a consideration of the demands of creating student-centered tasks
and environments, teachers will eventually confront issues of "depth
over breadth" in the curriculum.

From my data, teachers who stay with cooperative learning more
than two years typically believe that the synergy of the cooperative
group produces complexity in both knowledge and knowing and potentially superior learning results (Brody 1992, 1993). Dilemmas of practice become obvious in light of their decisions to ignore curriculum
mandates to cover a certain amount of material. Teachers who are able
to implement cooperative learning comfortably often resolve these
dilemmas as a matter of achieving some kind of a truce or balance between external mandates, pressures from their colleagues, and their
own beliefs about how children best learn.

Teachers who value the social benefits of dialogue often point to
the importance of "verbal rehearsal" time in a group, but it takes several years of consistent support for teachers to understand the nature
of dialogue in creating a community of inquirers who construct a curriculum together. Theoretical understanding about how dialogue informs learning and a community of inquirers is a relatively new notion
to most teachers except for those who had, for example, a whole language background.

## Using Teacher Beliefs as a Way to Assist Teachers

Educators whose work is to support growth and learning in teachers understand the limits of formal training programs in assisting teachers to adapt approaches to the different demands of grade levels, subject
fields, departmental policies, and organizational cultures. Once teachers understand the general principles of cooperative learning (See introduction, Table 1.2 for a summary of these), for example, a staff
developer may need a great deal of expertise in various approaches to
assist teachers to go beyond simple task usage. The following case

demonstrates how complex the adaptation and professional development process is when one considers teachers' particular professional histories, core beliefs, and context demands.

## Marilyn: A Case Study

Marilyn and I met through an inservice training in cooperative learning I conducted at her urban middle school. She spoke about her frustration with going the "next steps" in using cooperative groupwork. In our initial interviews she stated that she believed that learning was the result of community and that community was the result of learning together. But she could not figure out how to implement this vision organizationally. She needed a system that would allow her to manage 30–35 sixth graders in a combined language arts/social studies "block" for 2 1/2 hours per day. Her overarching goals were for students to (1) develop self-respect regarding what they can do; (2) become responsible for themselves as learners; (3) regard themselves as growing in the process of knowing; and (4) develop concepts about organization in order to handle the many and varied demands of middle school. Building an environment of "safety—trust and care among the students—is my first and most important job."

In looking at the curriculum Marilyn developed, it was evident she understood inquiry processes and how to construct complex tasks for group investigation, but she became overwhelmed with managing these exercises with so many students. She could not free herself up to listen to student talk so she could understand their conceptions and misconceptions.

Marilyn provided valuable information in our interviews that focused my attention on certain features of her classroom organization in light of her values and goals for her students. The first thing I suggested was that Marilyn participate in a *Tribes* training for teachers (1994), a curriculum and process for social development and cooperative learning developed by Jeanne Gibbs. It affected Marilyn deeply. *Tribes* training allowed her to surface long-held beliefs established in her primary-grade teaching about the significance of class-building and community norms that went beyond simple routines and activities. These beliefs, which had drawn her into teaching, were not supported in her middle school. *Tribes* gave her the "community view" as distinguished from cooperative learning training which stressed curricular aspects and working as a team through an activity. The program supported the time it takes to build community, and the workshop experience even gave her a model for structuring our reflective processes together.

After *Tribes* training Marilyn began the class with a community circle and continued this structure through the entire year, using it daily to begin and end the time together; later she enlarged the idea of community circle to include classwork with writing, reading, old business, and new business. Most importantly, Marilyn was now creating the kind of environment she valued.

Establishing cooperative learning groups was next. Marilyn wanted an approach that would allow the students to manage the classroom—in keeping with her goal of establishing student responsibility for their own learning. Instead of focusing on curricular tasks, we initiated home groups, selected four roles that would rotate around the four students—materials handler, homework checker, spokesperson, and group recorder—to manage the period and the activities of the week. (This idea is in keeping with Cohen's (1994) suggestion that group roles focus on management aspects not intellectual abilities.) Once students understood these roles, they were managing the class in a few weeks, allowing Marilyn to use her time on more complex curricular tasks, and working with individual student needs. The accountability to the group remained high and students were then able to change their groupwork partners often throughout the period—moving into writers' groups, readers' grand conversation groups, and back to home groups.

By the end of the year, the students were, indeed, running their own classroom. Groups of students revised her independent reading unit called "Grand Conversations," by developing their own scoring guides and rewriting the directions for students. The sense of community was so high that students were willing to work with any student, but more importantly, they moved from task to task, making appropriate choices in whom to work with on what task.

As Marilyn's guide for the year, I learned how important it is to start where the teacher is, and provide consultation, training, observation, ideas, and in-class support for cooperative groupwork from the point that makes the most sense for the teacher. I realized how important management issues were to even experienced, highly competent teachers who were already knowledgeable and skilled at orchestrating demanding learning tasks, but that the organizational issues for a middle school "block" teacher were different than, for example, a high school math teacher. It is important that the staff developer understand different approaches to cooperative groupwork, so that she can draw in approaches that make sense to the teacher at her beginning point.

## Conclusions

The value and premises teachers hold toward their work, including their own stance toward knowledge, both within a discipline and toward the student as a knower, are important and potentially significant knowledge for staff developers and teacher educators. Educators do identify different epistemological positions, and individuals can hold various and shifting beliefs. These beliefs may change over time and, within a given epistemological perspective, approaches to knowing may vary. Certain models of cooperative learning may represent such great departures from teachers' beliefs that they are likely to be categorically rejected by these same teachers. Because cooperative learning requires so many new and different kinds of decisions, some teachers at first feel divested of a kind of ownership, prerogative, or control. The authority arrangements in the classroom are suddenly exposed. Cooperative learning challenges teachers' fundamental conceptions about human interaction and poses dilemmas because it departs from prevailing practice. It can separate teachers who move toward this approach from their colleagues who do not, and can strain professional relationships because the shared norms and expectations have changed; dialogue between colleagues with different views becomes difficult. One can expect resistance when contradictions are so many.

Teachers need support to continue evolving their conceptions of cooperative learning. Some teachers are more cognizant of developing their practices to become more congruent with their ideal vision of a cooperative classroom; others need a safe environment in which to explore what an ideal cooperative classroom would be for themselves (See Table 1.2 for an example of collaborative interviewing; also Cooper and Boyd, chapter 2, and Rolheiser & Stevahn's activities to accomplish this in chapter 3.) Some teachers, relying only on school-based support, have no other forum to resolve dilemmas associated with experiences that arise and frustrate them, and they have to rely upon their well-honed, intuitive sense of what works and does not work.

Professional development programs should encourage teachers to critically examine any innovation in light of their existing beliefs, assumptions, and dilemmas-of-knowing that the innovation poses for them. They need support in undergoing shifts in beliefs about teaching and learning that run counter to the existing status-quo and make dialogue between colleagues necessary but problematic and difficult.

Staff developers should consider issues of control relating to the innovation itself, the context of the change, teachers' histories and biographies, and the nature of the learning situation as "text" for the process of change. They need to recognize that the practice under consideration may be altered quite dramatically due to teachers' beliefs, but these beliefs can be subject to socially negotiated processes respectful of conceptual change. Innovations or practices that represent great

departures from teachers' educational beliefs may pose particular contradictions and dilemmas for teachers that may only be resolved
through a dialogical and supportive context, with opportunities for
making educational orientations explicit.

## Notes

1. John Myers, a secondary school curriculum consultant with the Board
of Education for the City of Toronto, Ontario, Canada, has adapted professional
development materials designed to explicate teachers' belief systems using
Miller and Seller's model. He discusses the application of this model to the various approaches to cooperative learning in the Great Lake Association for Cooperation in Education newsletter, Cooperative Classroom 3 (1988): 7–8.

2. This is consistent with the Concerns Based Adoption Model developed
by the Research and Development Center for Teacher Education, The University
of Texas at Austin. Within the six stages of concern that adults typically express
about the innovation, stage three addresses management and consequences, that
is, "How is my use affecting my students and my classroom?"

3. I acknowledge the assistance of Leslie Rennie-Hill in conducting these
interviews. Members of the Northwest Cooperative Learning Leadership
Network were also helpful in thinking through the design of our year-long
cooperative learning training and the subsequent stages of thinking regarding
cooperative learning and teacher beliefs.

4. These are not the real names of the teachers who participated in this
study.

## References

Aronson, E. (1978). *The jigsaw classroom.* Beverly Hills, Ca: Sage.

Bellanca, J. & Fogarty, R.(1991). *Blueprints for thinking in the cooperative classroom.*
    Palatine, Illinois: Skylight Publishing.

Berlak, A. and Berlak, H. (1981). *Dilemmas of schooling.* New York; Methuen.

Britton, J. (1990). Research currents: Second thoughts on learning. In M.
    Brubacher, R. Payne & K. Rickett (Eds.), *Perspectives on small group learning.*
    Canada: Rubicon Publishing, Inc.

Brody, C. (1994). Using co-teaching to promote reflective practice. *Journal of Staff
    Development* 15 (3) pp. 32–37.

———. (1993). Co-teaching, teacher beliefs, and change: A case study. Paper presented at the annual meeting of the American Educational Research Association, Atlanta, GA.

———. (1992). Cooperative learning and teacher beliefs: A constructivist view. Paper presented at the meeting of the International Association for the Study of Cooperation in Education, Utrecht, Netherlands.

Clark, C. M. & Peterson, P. L. (1986). Teachers' thought process. In M. C. Wittrock (Ed.), *Handbook of research on teaching* (3rd ed.) New York: Macmillan.

Cohen, E. (1994, second edition). *Designing groupwork*. New York: Teachers College Press.

Connelly, F. M. & Clandinin, D. J. (1988). *Teachers as curriculum planners: Narratives of experience*. New York: Teachers College Press.

Cuban, L. (1988). Constancy and change in schools (1880s to the present). In P. Jackson (Ed.), *Contributing to educational change: Perspectives on research and practice* (pp. 85–106). Berkley: McCutcheon.

Doyle, W., & Ponder, R. A. (1977). The practicality ethic in teacher decision-making. *Interchange*, 8, 1–12.

Glasersfeld, E. von. Learning as constructive activity. (1984). In E. von Glasersfeld (Ed.) *The construction of knowledge: Contributions to conceptual semantics* Salinas, CA: Intersystems Publications pp. 307–333.

Gibbs, J. (1994, second edition). *Tribes*. Santa Rose, CA: Center Course Publications.

Gitlin, A. (1990). Educative research, voice and school change. *Harvard Educational Review*. 60 (4), 443–466.

Henderson, J. G. (1996) *Reflective teaching*. Second edition. Englewood Cliffs, N.J: Merrill Press.

———. (1992). *Reflective teaching: Becoming an inquiring educator*. NY: Macmillan.

Johnson, D. W. , Johnson, R. T. & Holubec, Edythe J. (1986). *Circles of learning* Edina, MN: Interaction Book Company.

Kagan, S. (1993). *Cooperative learning* San Juan Capistrano, CA: Kagan Cooperative Learning.

Kelly, G. (1955). *A theory of personality*. NY: Norton & Company.

Miller, J. P. & Seller, W. (1985). *Curriculum perspectives and practice*. New York: Longman.

Myers, J. (1988). Great Lake Association for Cooperation in Education newsletter, *Cooperative Classroom* 3 :7–8.

Nespor, J. (1987). The role of beliefs in the practice of teaching. *Journal of Curriculum Studies.* 19 (4), 1–11.

Olson, J. (1980). Teacher constructs and curriculum change. *Journal of Curriculum Studies,* 12, 1–11.

Osberg, A. (1986, April). Staff development through individual reflection on practice. Paper presented at the annual meeting of the American Educational Research Association, San Francisco, CA.

Pope, M. L. & Scott, E. M. (1984). Teacher's epistemology and practice. In R. Halkes & J. Olson (Eds.). *Teacher thinking: A new perspective on persisting problems in education.* London, Swets & Zeitlinger pp. 112–122.

Richardson,V. (1990, Oct.). Significant and worthwhile change in teaching practice. *Educational Researcher* 19 (7) pp. 10–18.

Richardson, V., Anders, P, Tidwell, D. & Lloyd, C. (1991). The relationship between teachers' beliefs and practices in reading comprehension instruction. *American Educational Research Journal,* 28 (3), pp. 559–586.

Sharan, S. & Sharan, Y. (1992). *Group investigation.* New York: Teachers College Press.

Shephard, L. (1991). Psychometrician's beliefs about learning. In *Educational Researcher,* 20 (6), pp. 2–16.

Sparks-Langer, G. M. & Colton, A. B. (1991, March) Synthesis of research on teachers' reflective thinking. *Educational Leadership,* 48 (6) 37–44.

Taylor, P. C. S. (1990). The influence of teacher beliefs on constructivist teaching practices. Paper presented at the annual meeting of the American Educational Research Association, Boston, April 1990.

Tobin, K. (1987). Forces which shape the implemented curriculum in high school science and mathematics. *Teaching and Teacher Education,* 3, 287–298.

Webb, N. M. (1991). Task-related verbal interaction and mathematics learning in small groups. *Journal for Research in Mathematics Education,* 22(5), 366–389.

# 2

# CREATING SUSTAINED PROFESSIONAL GROWTH THROUGH COLLABORATIVE REFLECTION

## CAROLE COOPER AND JULIE BOYD

Several years ago, the highly respected Australian educator, Garth Boomer, said "putting money into professional development for teachers is tantamount to pouring it down a drain" (1986). Boomer was referring to the lack of sustained professional development opportunities that enable teachers to develop a principle-based approach to their own professional learning and teaching. Over the past decade there has been a slow but steady upsurge in the realization that professional growth involves teachers not only having access to new information and a broader world view, but most importantly, time and opportunities to practice, dialogue, reflect, support, and challenge each other. In-service education alone does not create sustained change, without some form of on-site peer support (Joyce and Showers, 1982). There are many forms that this peer support can take and it is essential that educators have a variety of learning strategies to apply and use for their own growth and development. These are described here as collaborative reflective practices.

In this chapter, we describe the conditions that are essential for collaborative reflective practice, as well as the rationale for using a variety of methods of reflection in facilitating educators' change and growth. The essential conditions for interactive reflection are:

1. Understand the variety of methods and approaches available;
2. Establish the conditions of collaboration; and
3. Establish ways to begin implementing these practices.

### Collaborative Reflective Practices

Collaborative reflective practices are methods for reviewing one's learning and development with a peer colleague. The purpose is for the teacher, administrator, or aide to become more aware of her attitudes, skills and knowledge, by gaining understanding and creating new meaning in one's craft. Engaging in on-going reflective practices affirms and reshapes our knowledge. Reflection helps us to analyze our actions, decisions, or products by focusing on what we did or are doing, so we can learn lessons that can be applied to new situations. Reflection involves a particular stance toward one's thinking and behavior, an awareness of what information we are perceiving and how we process that information. It can occur "on" our actions, "for" new action, and while doing our work "in" action.

Reflection-on-action occurs after the fact as we examine our actions and practices. Reflection-for-action is the generation or clarification of knowledge, skills, and attitudes that enable new action in our work. Reflection-in-action is the observation and mental processing of actions as they occur (Killian & Harrison, 1992). This involves a sensitivity and responsiveness to the thoughts and feelings we observe in ourselves. It includes jotting notes to ourselves and pausing to make conscious decisions as we are teaching or learning, and describing to group members what we are experiencing and thinking so they can see and relate to our processing and help us make meaning from it. There are several forms of reflective practice that involve all three types of reflection.

Not only does professional growth require conscious thinking and meta-cognition about our craft, it also requires taking the time to reflect and a structure for doing so. First, we will address the types of collaborative reflective approaches as outlined in Table 2.1.[1]

Partner and small group reflective practices need to be a part of a school/district's sustained professional development plan. Individual practices, listed in Table 2.1, are formats one could use in many of the more collaborative approaches. For example, in peer support groups individuals can share their portfolios or case study writing; action research projects could employ the checklists, rating scales, and surveys needed for self-contracting and self-monitoring.

Partner Reflective Practices

In partner relationships, there is reciprocity in learning. Each person commits to helping facilitate personal improvement and growth as well for the other person.

Learning Buddies are two people who are in similar positions in an organization. They share common concerns and agree to work together to discuss and plan ways to resolve those concerns. They may or may not actually observe the other in action. They may be teachers at the same grade level who plan lessons together and discuss how the lessons went

TABLE 2.1

Summary of Collaborative Reflective Practices

---

*Individual Reflective Practices*
- Self-Contracting and Monitoring
- Portfolios
- Journals
- Case Studies
- Professional Reading, Writing and Study

*Partner Reflective Practices*
- Learning Buddies
- Mentoring
- Peer Coaching
- Work Exchanges or Shadowing

*Small Group Reflective Practices*
- Action Research
- Study Groups
- Peer Support Groups
- Professional Dialogue Groups

*Large Group Reflective Practices*
- Assessment Centers
- Exhibitions and Panels
- Presentations
- Professional Development Schools
- Teacher Centers
- Teacher Institutes
- Partnerships

---

and what they are learning about their own teaching, students, or the curriculum. Learning Buddies may be two teachers who work at different grade levels or in different departments, who want to join their two classes together periodically for learning experiences, or two principals from two schools who agree to meet and focus regularly on specific topics in order to increase understanding and improve performance. Team teaching could be a structured learning buddy arrangement if the two parties actually plan and de-brief their learning together. It is not a learning buddy relationship if they devote little or no time to facilitating each other's learning and growth. A learning buddy relationship is a good way to begin staff collaboration. It helps teachers ease into reflective practice and it can improve their ability to plan, consider the needs of students and others, articulate results and reactions to the implementation of cooperative learning, and begin to self-assess their teaching.

Mentoring has recently enjoyed a resurgence in business, health, law, and finance professions. It is similar to Learning Buddies; however, there may not be the equality in roles. Mentors are trusted and experienced practitioners who have an interest in the development of less experienced individuals. Protégés are people who want to improve their professional knowledge, skills, and attitudes by entering into a relationship with a mentor. This is particularly effective for improving teachers' implementation of cooperative learning. People who have become experienced in cooperative learning often cite the importance of a role model at the beginning to help refine the complex subtleties of collaborative classroom work. Like the sages of the past, mentors can help set educators on their paths.

Peer Coaching involves an on-going relationship with a partner, but includes classroom observation and a frequent cycle of planning, observing, and de-briefing. The partner relationship is strong as in mentoring, yet more mutual and equal. Unlike the mentoring, however, there is no external evaluation in the peer coaching relationship. There are generic coaching programs, aimed at the self-directed concerns of the teacher, or content-specific coaching programs, aimed at a particular teaching strategy, such as cooperative learning. However, whether generic or specific, in each coaching cycle there is a declared area of improvement, content of the coaching, for each partner. [See Table 2.2, The Peer Coaching Cycle, and Table 2.3, What to Coach for Cooperative Learning.]

Coaching takes skill, commitment, and time; yet it is essential to the on-going refinement of teaching practice, especially cooperative learning, where the goal is for students to construct new ideas, attitudes, skills, and meaning.

Small Group Reflective Practices

These are reflective methods that typically involve more than two people. Action research, study groups, peer support groups, professional dialogue groups and electronic professional development networks provide opportunities for teachers to collaborate with others to refine their knowledge and improve their implementation of cooperative learning. Each works to remove the isolation of teachers and to improve the learned practice of professionals.

*Action Research.* In the past, teachers and administrators have been more consumers of research data than creators of it. As a result, studies do not always have the impact they could on teacher knowledge and practice. Some of the questions academic researchers ask are not

TABLE 2.2

The Peer Coaching Cycle

---

1. *Establish the Relationship*
*Build Trust:* getting to know each other, commitment to the coaching process and to each other, openness around the craft of teaching, and goals for effective teaching and learning;
*Discussions about Coaching:* what it is and is not, benefits, problems, and defining expectations.
2. *Conduct the Pre-Conference*
May involve planning lessons and visualizing each step of the way;
Always includes setting the date, time, place, role of coach, focus for observation, and data collection;
3. *Observe the Teaching*
Non-judgmental collection of data on focus area;
May be a narrative, or checklist of critical incidents
4. *Engage in Self-Reflection*
For the coach: review notes, mentally replay and formulate open-ended, probing questions;
For the teacher: review notes from observer, mentally re-play the events, draw conclusions;
5. *Conduct a Post-Conference and Debriefing*
May involve teacher sharing general impressions;
Always involves teacher focusing on an area and what it means for his or her teaching;
Does not involve evaluation by the coach;
6. *De-brief the Coaching Session*
Coach solicits feedback on her assistance and on the coaching process.

---

pertinent to teachers, and conversely, some of the questions most relevant to classroom teachers are not studied. Action research, on the other hand, involves teachers and principals in the conduct of research for their own intended use. Teachers who ask and seek answers to their own questions in their own settings are more likely to improve their teaching than teachers who read research results in a book (Kemmis and McTaggert, 1988). In action research, the teachers define the research question. Sometimes they are a part of a collaborative team that includes a university researcher and other staff members. Action research programs can be designed in different formats: individual action and reflection, individual action and collaborative reflection, or collaborative action and reflection.

Study Groups meet regularly to discuss a question or topic, or to study and plan topics of common interest. Groups, of no more than six

TABLE 2.3

What to Coach for Cooperative Learning

---

*Elements of Cooperative Learning*
Positive Interdependence
Heterogeneous Grouping
Individual Accountability
Social and Academic Skills Processed
Face to Face Interaction
*Cooperative Strategies/Structures*
Simple Structures (ex: Think-Pair-Share, Round Robin,
Roundtable, Brainstorming, Numbered Heads Together, Mindmapping, etc.)
Complex Structures (ex: Jigsaw, Learning Together, Group Investigation,
Coop-Coop, etc.)
*Students' Learning—Both Social and Academic*
On/off Task
Use and Nonuse of Social Skills (Do students understand the value of using
these social skills?)
Use and Nonuse of Academic Skills (Do students understand the importance
of these skills, and how to apply them?)
Examples of Deep Thinking and Problem-Solving
Examples of Taking Responsibility for Learning
Examples of Attitudes Fostered by CL (ex: love of learning, balance of self and
others, perseverance, etc.)
*Teacher's Role*
Setting the Climate
Planning
Introducing the lesson
Observing groups
Intervening and facilitating
Processing group work
Forming groups
Giving clear directions
Explaining academic and social skills or roles
*Lesson Design*
Length of lesson or parts of lesson
Student readiness for lesson
Lead-up to lesson
Follow-up to lesson
Restructuring the lesson
Practice opportunities
Summary/Synthesis

---

1. Cooper, Carole and Body, Julie. *Collaborative Approaches to Professional Learning and Reflection.* Launceston, Tasmania, Australia: Global Learning Communities, 1995. This resource explains these models in detail, how to implement them, and the benefits of each collaborative reflective practice for professional growth and assessment.

people, investigate what is happening in the broader field of education and then use that information in their own classrooms to implement curricular, instructional, and assessment innovations or collaboratively plan school improvement. Study groups often look at the effects of group size, gender contribution, and status, inclusion of disabled or gifted and talented students, effective group decision-making skills, group cohesion factors, group competition, use of higher order thinking strategies, or any number of practices related to cooperative learning. By formalizing the study process and encouraging teachers to work together, those who might never have been involved in reflective practice often begin to do so. Those teachers who might only work with other teachers to learn a new activity or to socialize become engaged in dialogue about the craft of teaching (Murphy, 1992).

Peer Support Groups are formed by interested people from a school or local geographic area who want to meet regularly to share and generate new ideas, materials, and experiences. They engage in problem-solving and remain current with events and developments in cooperative learning. Participation in peer support groups is usually voluntary. Peer support groups are usually more successful if they do the following:

1. Designate a regular time each month for the meeting;
2. Rotate the meeting place so members can meet in each other's classrooms or schools;
3. Rotate the co-facilitation of the meetings;
4. Select a topic from a list generated in an initial support group meeting;
5. Use a group memory (flip chart) to record decisions;
6. Have each person brings something to share, and all leave with many ideas for their time;
7. Use both large and small groups during the meeting;
8. De-brief the meeting; and
9. Have refreshments.

Professional Dialogue Groups differ from discussion groups because the members explore complex, difficult issues from many points of view. During the group all participants use three processes or group norms:

- They suspend their assumptions and examine and critique to reveal incoherence of thought,
- They regard one another as colleagues, and
- There is a facilitator who holds the context of the dialogue.

Dialogue, therefore, assists in looking at one's assumptions, increases one's ability to hold multiple perspectives and helps one to speak in an authentic voice. Dialogue groups are not decision-making groups; they are simply to help teachers clarify their own thinking on relevant issues. David Bohm (1990) and Peter Senge (1990) have written about dialogue in education and the workplace.

Collegial reflective practices are anchored in the authenticity of the classroom and school and in the view that teachers facilitate their own and others' learning. These approaches put the emphasis on becoming a better teacher and learner, not just on the final product of "good co-operative learning" teacher. They involve both formative and summary information that can facilitate changes in both behavior and thinking patterns. Collaborative approaches to reflection help to expose a teacher's stated and displayed values. In Robert Garmston's words, they help us to "live at the edge of one's competence"(1994, p.10).

## Conditions for Collaboration

For any collaborative model to be truly effective, it is essential that (1) there is a collaborative climate; (2) partners develop personal characteristics that foster teamwork; (3) effective group skills and reflective thinking skills are a part of the content and process, and (4) the principles of adult learning are applied when working together.

### Collaborative Climate

Group members experience a collaborative climate as a feeling that "We care about each other and help each other learn;" "We want you and everyone to be successful;" "It is OK to ask for help and help will be given when asked;" or "Our learning will be better because of each of us than what we could have done alone." This climate does not happen simply because teachers agree to work together to improve each other's practice and learning. It is essential to give the time to build the trust and rapport that helps participants feel comfortable thinking out loud with another, sharing their fears and strengths, having someone else in the classrooms, and admitting mistakes and determining successes. It takes dialogue, team-building, self-disclosure, feedback, common goals, knowing one's responsibilities to the process and to each other, and commitment to carrying those responsibilities out, along with a steadfast commitment to each other's growth. In a collaborative community, everyone is regarded as a teacher and learner; there is equality in the community. In a collaborative group, each person understands and acknowledges that no one individual knows everything, but each person knows something and can contribute in unique ways. No one is as good as all of us. A collaborative climate exists when each member succeeds and learns and assists others to do so.

### Personal Qualities in Partner or Group Members

Most of us want to work with others who love their work and their students, who have personal and professional passion and energy. A sense of humor also helps one persist, be more objective, gain a richer perspective, and appreciate the fun in learning. A person who is prepared, caring, approachable, and fair, and who is able to instill confidence is a good learning partner. Someone who has a knowledge of resources can also extend one's learning. People who are persistent yet patient, and work toward action make good team members.

### Effective Communication Skills and Group Skills

Effective communication and group skills are critical to productive, long-term work together, especially when what is at issue is one's own professional practice. These skills include active listening, questioning, testing assumptions and perceptions, paraphrasing and summarizing, organizing ideas, clearly defining issues, problems, and criteria, seeking alternatives, negotiating and resolving conflicts, monitoring, documenting and evaluating results, acknowledging and appreciating each person's contribution, and adhering to group commitments and ground rules.

Whenever people work together, conflict eventually develops. In fact, it is a poorly functioning group if conflict does not develop; it means that no one cares enough to share honest opinions. Groups invariably encounter the "storming" stage. At that point, it will be necessary to practice conflict resolution principles, such as:

1. People: Separate the people from the problem;
2. Interests: Focus on interests, not positions;
3. Options: Invent options for mutual gain; and
4. Criteria: Insist on using objective criteria (Bernard, 1989).

### Reflective Thinking and Meta-Cognition Skills

Reflection means focusing on thinking and understanding and not just on what you did or are doing. Good learners think about their own thinking; they reflect in action, for action, and about action. They are able to:

1. Recognize relevant patterns in movement, principles, explanations, designs, data and problems;
2. Ask themselves probing questions (open-ended questions that help one to analysis and synthesis of information, and questions they do not know how to answer without probing, mapping, wondering, and researching);
3. Make connections (such as comparing and contrasting, considering differing points of view, looking at things systemically, relating ideas and information, seeing the interdependence of things, generalizing, personalizing, and integrating new data into their understanding and practice); and
4. Articulate their learning in precise and concise ways (summarizing, paraphrasing, grabbing the essence of an issue, illustrating and mapping ideas, putting a complex idea in student terms, being conscious of their actions and how these reflect their thinking).

## Apply the Principles of Adult Learning

For adults, the drive toward competence is linked to their self-worth and efficacy. This is true for children; yet, more so for adults since most adults tell themselves they should already know things or they should be able to easily implement something new. Adults have different concerns, strengths, and needs at different stages of their lives. People new to an idea may experience self-protective concerns. Once a new approach has been tried over time one is ready to experiment and take more independence in molding it to fit one's style and situation. As a teacher does this, she gains in confidence and competence and new concerns take precedence.

We need multiple experiences, time for self-reflection, self-assessment and self-direction. Adults learn when they are actively involved. Adults, like children, vary in their ability to handle cognitive complexity; they see learning both as an opportunity and a risk. What is learned must hold meaning and connect with their current understanding. For adults, development is not automatic. It is a continual process of identity formation and re-formation. Traditional models of staff development generally ignore principles of adult learning. Reflective, interactive approaches do consider the principles of adult learning:

1. Opportunities to try out new practices and to be self-directed in the learning process;
2. Careful and continuous guided reflection and discussion about proposed changes and time to analyze one's own experience, since experience is the richest source of adult learning;

3. Continuity of programs and time for making changes and personal support as well as challenge during the change process; and
4. Provisions for differences in style, time, place, and pace of learning.

These practices allow for the flexibility and conditions described earlier.

## Ways to Implement Collegial Reflective Practices

Reflection improves teacher classroom practices (Costa and Garmston, 1994). Educators do not insist that this be a part of their on-going staff development program because it takes time, but it is important to provide time for reflective practice.

Reflective practices usually require organizational changes that reduce the norms of isolation and invest in teachers as well as in students. Administrators need to see the correlation between teacher's growth and student learning. Parents need to understand that their children need different skills for the twenty-first century than what they needed growing up; therefore, teachers need different knowledge and skills to best facilitate student's needs both now and in the future. Parents can be helped to understand that these changes are based on what we now know about learning and thinking, the conditions for effective professional development, and the change process. This goal requires that schools are re-created as collaborative learning communities, where the focus is on collaboration, rather than isolation or competition, on learning, in contrast to teaching as telling, and on community, where the school builds community with the students, parents and greater community.

In order to have a collaborative learning community, there must be on-going collegial practices. We start by talking about "why schools must change" and having teachers develop individual professional development plans that correspond to the school improvement plans. Then, we assist teachers to choose those reflective practices that fit for them and their conditions. We provide encouragement, modeling, time, and resources.

Other reasons collegial reflective practices are not used are the fear to pursue one's own learning, being seen as incompetent, needing to build relationships that are more than social, and being able to be intimate and vulnerable. Educators make excuses: there is not enough time, interest, facilities, and resources. They do not believe they will "do it right," so they avoid doing the right thing. For educators to continually grow they need to have opportunities to reflect. Currently, we are not seeing real, sustained change in most teachers' classrooms unless they are involved in sustained professional development.

The profession is recognizing that we need new forms and procedures of staff development that are comprehensive, sustained, and based on a new paradigm of learning and thinking, change, and effective professional development practices. Most staff development has taken the form of in-service training for teachers and administrators aimed at equipping them with new classroom strategies and experiences. Research clearly demonstrates that simply providing information and short term experiences result in only a small minority of teachers actually implementing the ideas several months later. Sustained implementation requires much more. We recognize that:

1. Professional growth is achieved through a long-term, planned program of professional development that involves inservice, practice, and reflection.
2. A program destined to create sustained professional growth incorporates: affirmation of current practice, new information, adaptable challenges, transferability of ideas to multiple settings, creation of a learning network among those trying similar ideas, and regular dialogue and reflection time.
3. Professional development should align individual needs with those of the school and system.
4. Professional growth plans are living entities that need to be both guided and adaptable.
5. Teachers should seek professional growth themselves. In the same way that counseling and therapy will not work with a reluctant client, professional growth occurs only in the willing. Creating this willingness is part of the skill of an effective administrator or colleague.
6. Very few people are totally unwilling to change; however, many are afraid. Sustainable professional growth requires the development of trusting relationships in which the people involved are willing to take risks.
7. Teachers can learn how to develop their own present/future maps and clarify personal, professional, and systemic directions in order to know what they want and need in their own development.
8. Teachers need periods of intense guided reflection to assist them to develop and articulate a set of internal learning and teaching principles that will form the basis of their professional growth.
9. Learning is an ongoing and developmental process. Unless on-site support, challenge, and reflective practices are incorporated into the overall school development plan, one of two things typically happens. Either a handful of teachers will benefit and the school

runs the danger of developing "them" and "us" groups, or the idea will die or be replaced by the next "new" idea that happens along.

10. We often learn best by teaching someone else. Teachers need the opportunity to facilitate each others' learning, both within and across schools, and structures need to be created for this to occur.

11. Professional networking is crucial for professional growth. Teachers need the capacity to build supportive and challenging networks within their own schools and across districts and states.

12. People learn and grow differently as individuals, and as part of a team. Each individual has a preferred learning mode and style. A range of possibilities for reflection and collaboration rather than simply one mandated form of self development will more likely meet the needs of all involved.

The professional development approaches of the next decade will not be just workshops; they could be work groups with teachers working together cooperatively to improve teaching and learning, and to build schools into collaborative learning communities. We need to practice what we preach in staff development for cooperative learning, namely give the responsibility for learning to the students, in this case, the adult student. Learning is a continuous, self-directed process constructed through action and reflection (i.e., thinking about our actions and behavior and values). The models in this chapter give educators the opportunities for both action and new ways to learn from their experiences. They provide a foundation from which we can continue to experiment. Even if we fail, we fail forward, ever learning and growing in our craft. These reflective practices provide a foundation for looking at our profession, our school, our colleagues, our students and ourselves.

## References

Bernard, B. (1989). *Working together: Principles of effective collaboration,* Portland, OR: Prevention Resource Center.

Boomer, G. (1986). Keynote Speech at South Australia Principal's Conference, Adelaide, SA.

Costa, A. and Garmston, R. (1994). *Cognitive coaching: A foundation for renaissance schools.* Norwood, MA: Christopher Gordon Publishers.

Joyce, B. and Showers, B. (1982). *Transfer of training: The contribution of coaching,* Eugene, OR: Center for Educational Policy and Management, University of Oregon.

Kemmis, S. and McTaggert, R. (1988). *The action research reader.* Victoria, Australia: Deakin University, p. 29.

Killion, J. and Harrison, C. (1992). The practice of reflection: An essential learning process. *The Developer, National Staff Development Council,* January.

Murphy, C. (1992). Study groups foster schoolwide learning, *Educational Leadership.*

# 3

# THE ROLE OF STAFF DEVELOPERS IN PROMOTING EFFECTIVE TEACHER DECISION-MAKING

*CAROL ROLHEISER AND LAURIE STEVAHN*

Staff development for cooperative learning can take many forms. Formal off-site training as well as informal on-site collaboration, sharing, and problem-solving make unique contributions to a teacher's understanding of the complex nature of cooperative learning. This chapter focuses on formal training programs in cooperative learning and the role of staff developers in effectively leading those programs. A formal program is typically a coherent course of study involving a curriculum conducted in numerous sittings. Effective programs enable teachers to experience cooperative learning first-hand as a group member, reflect on those experiences to strengthen conceptual understanding, and make thoughtful connections to classrooms and schools in an environment conducive to reflection. Teachers are then able to anticipate the challenges that making instructional changes will bring, and foster the kind of cooperative working relationships necessary to meet those challenges.

Whether the program leader is someone inside the school district (such as a staff development specialist, curriculum consultant, teacher, or administrator) or an outside consultant, the leader needs to approach the planning, conducting, and evaluation of the program in a manner that considers the tremendous variation among teacher participants. Such variation includes personal histories, beliefs about students and how they learn, grade level and subject specialization, and differences in schools in terms of resources, support, and student diversity. Teacher success in using cooperative learning depends on a teacher's ability to make effective decisions about using cooperative learning in specific classrooms and specific school settings. Program leaders create training conditions that promote effective teacher decision-making and support transfer of learning for classroom and school use.

There are four interrelated guidelines that direct leaders' decisions and the conduct of training programs for cooperative learning. These are:

1. Teachers must make decisions based on instructional goals and theoretical foundations in cooperative learning;
2. Teachers must "live" cooperative groupwork in formal training programs;
3. Teachers need to make conscious connections between the training and classroom and school contexts;
4. Teachers need to build collaborative school cultures that support change and foster continuous learning.

## Teachers Must Make Decisions Based on Instructional Goals and Theoretical Foundations in Cooperative Learning

The overall purpose of teaching is to affect student learning. The complexity of teaching and learning requires that teachers analyze students' needs, consider options for action based on validated principles, select those actions most likely to foster optimal student learning, and recognize as well as seize unexpected teachable moments. With cooperative learning the number of decisions a teacher makes increases exponentially. Cooperative groupwork is so complex and context specific that it is impossible to conduct it in a "paint-by-numbers" fashion, no matter how simple a particular classroom application may appear to be. Cooperative strategies must be selected, linked, and integrated in context; specifically, with understanding of the development of students in a particular classroom. To promote optimal learning through cooperative strategies, Cohen (1994b) suggests that we address two questions: "What outcomes are desired through cooperative learning?" and "What conditions will mediate the effectiveness of cooperative learning for particular outcomes?" Staff development programs should provide teachers with repeated opportunities to reflect collaboratively on both questions. By doing so, the teacher develops the capacity for considering the range of applications about effective instruction. Collaborative reflection nurtures risk taking and increases the likelihood that critical analysis will become a norm.

Reflection also leads to deeper conceptual understanding which, in turn, increases transfer, long-term learning, and good decision-making about instructional implementation problems (Anderson, Rolheiser, & Bennett, 1995; Hall & Hord, 1987; Hall and Loucks, 1977; Johnson & Johnson, 1994a, 1994b, 1994c). Educators who use cooperative learning successfully do so with fidelity and flexibility. Reflection and critical analysis are the basis of purposeful choices—decisions made by design, not default. Such decisions result from grappling with a range of questions including: "How will students benefit from what I plan to teach?" "Why am I targeting particular goals, objectives, outcomes, content?" "Why am I employing particular instructional strategies and skills?" "How does the content and process of my teaching prepare and enable students to address important societal issues and concerns?" "How will my teaching help students take ownership and responsibility for their learning?" Knowing what you value in teaching and why requires a critical stance as does exercising both artistry and technical competence. The substance for reflection in formal programs needs to be both practical experience and theoretical knowledge.

Theoretical Knowledge

Cooperative group learning is more likely to work in the classroom when instructional decisions are grounded in and guided by research-validated theory. Although a range of cooperative models exist, it is research-based theory that provides the foundation for effectively planning, implementing, analyzing, and modifying classroom and school applications. Cooperative learning training, therefore, must enable educators to comprehend the different theoretical roots of cooperative learning. There are three dimensions of theoretical knowledge that we have found useful for decision-making. These are knowledge of (a) learning theories, (b) research outcomes, and (c) core elements that make groups work.

Learning Theories

Knowledge of learning theories provides a basis for understanding different orientations to research and practice. Each theory is based on different underlying assumptions about motivation and cognition, emphasizes different types of learning outcomes, and places importance on different factors in cooperative interaction. Different cooperative models reflect the various underlying assumptions (see Introduction, this volume, for further discussion). Understanding the assumptions provides a rationale for program leaders to assist teachers in evaluating and selecting models most congruent with their beliefs, prior knowledge, subject matter demands, and desired learning outcomes (see Brody chapter one, this volume, for further discussion).

Social interdependence theory (Johnson & Johnson, 1989) emphasizes the importance of structuring group members' interdependence to support productive cooperative interaction. The theory is that members will cooperate for a goal when each perceives that every members' efforts are required for success. Individual goals are linked in ways such that personal success is possible only when the group is successful. The Learning Together model (Johnson & Johnson, 1994b) is based on social interdependence theory.

Behavioral learning theory focuses more specifically on how group rewards and extrinsic reinforcers influence perceptions of interdependence and motivation to learn. Student Team Learning strategies such as Teams-Games-Tournaments and Student Teams Achievement Divisions (Slavin, 1990) are examples.

Constructivist theory focuses on social construction of knowledge through purposeful talk, and the importance of collaborative arguing and reasoning in resolving cognitive conflict created by puzzling problems. The assumption is that when individuals face a puzzling problem they experience internal conflict and uncertainty. The uncertainty and disequilibrium, in turn, motivate the individuals to interactively grapple with ideas and exchange knowledge in order to resolve the problem. As they do, new conceptual understanding is constructed. The search for a solution becomes a collaborative problem-solving endeavor. Several cooperative models are closely linked to constructivist theory such as academic controversy (Johnson & Johnson, 1989; 1995), complex instruction (Cohen, 1994a, 1994b), group investigation (Sharan & Sharan, 1992), and the Child Development Project (see Watson et., al, chapter 7 of this book). In all of these models student-centered discovery and student-centered knowledge emerge through social interaction.

Cognitive restructuring theory emphasizes the importance of linking information into existing cognitive structures for long-term memory by rehearsing, explaining, and elaborating on the material to be learned (Wittrock, 1978). Explaining to others promotes cognitive restructuring, especially when interactive questioning and responding take place. Examples of models drawing on this theory include Jigsaw (Aronson, 1980; Clarke & Wideman, 1985), cooperative mind mapping (Bennett, Rolheiser, & Stevahn, 1991), many of the thinking skills and information sharing structures (Kagan, 1992), as well as the Build model (Bellanca & Fogarty, 1991).

Research Outcomes

Knowledge of research-validated outcomes is also important for making good decisions because it enables teachers to set well-grounded expectations for student success and carefully monitor student progress. The long history of research in cooperative learning makes it unique among educational innovations. Hundreds of studies conducted primarily in the twentieth century (particularly from the early

1970s to the present) on cooperative learning consistently demonstrate that cooperative learning produces positive effects for students of all ages, in all content areas, across a wide range of tasks (Bossert, 1988; Cohen, 1994b; Johnson & Johnson, 1989; Joyce, Showers, & Rolheiser-Bennett, 1987; Slavin, 1990; Sharan & Sharan, 1992). The predictable and well-documented outcomes include increased achievement, greater retention, enhanced reasoning, increased perspective taking, more on-task behavior, greater intrinsic motivation, higher self-esteem, better attitudes toward school and teachers, greater social support, enhanced use of collaborative skills, and more positive psychological adjustment (Johnson, Johnson, & Holubec, 1993). If students are not attaining a research validated outcome, the teacher needs to adapt the instructional context in ways that will enable students to accomplish that outcome. This requires conceptual understanding of what makes groups work.

Core Elements

Knowledge of core cooperative learning elements is essential for decision-making. Although theories, learning outcomes, and specific cooperative models differ, research on the effectiveness of cooperative group learning points to fundamental elements that define productive cooperative endeavors (Cohen, 1994b; Johnson & Johnson, 1989). The conceptual approach (Johnson & Johnson, 1994b) defines these as: (1) positive interdependence (the perception that one cannot succeed unless all others do), (2) promotive interaction (face-to-face encouragement, support, assistance, and exchange of information, ideas, and resources to facilitate team success), (3) individual accountability (personal responsibility for maximizing the learning of every group member), (4) interpersonal and small group skills (employing communication, leadership, trust-building, and conflict-management skills for optimal group functioning), and (5) group processing (assessing and evaluating teamwork by identifying factors that are enabling team success and planning ways to improve group functioning). Whether teaching for mastery of information, complex thinking, or interpersonal acceptance, systematically structuring those elements into group tasks and cooperative strategies helps ensure that effective cooperative interaction will occur and outcomes will be achieved. The elements also provide a basis for observing interaction between group members, analyzing the effectiveness of interactions, determining adjustments to enable group members to improve their cooperative efforts, and reflecting on changes for continuous improvement. The challenge lies in operationalizing the elements by finding concrete ways to build them into every task, regardless of the cooperative model employed.

Connecting Theory and Practice

Schools tend to be governed by survival and maintenance concerns, making connections to the world of theory often sporadic, unconscious, or non-existent. There are many ways that program leaders can help construct a bridge between theory and practice. One way is by providing time during programs for reading-based activities that connect teachers to professional literature. A group of four individuals, for example, can each read the same article then compare and contrast their varying responses to a set of "Reading Follow-Up" questions (Bennett, Rolheiser, & Stevahn, 1991). Questions we have used to stimulate critical thinking and generate meaningful discussion include:

1. What are the major messages in the reading?
2. What ideas in the reading were most meaningful to you? Why?
3. How might you invite staff, students, or parents to consider these messages/ideas?

Another way to help teachers connect to theoretical knowledge is by conducting a jigsaw (Aronson, 1980) or constructive controversy (Johnson & Johnson, 1995) around an issue such as the use of rewards in cooperative learning. By reading different articles that portray a variety of perspectives on an issue like this, teachers become better informed for their own effective decision-making. We constantly challenge teachers to compare and contrast their own classroom-based analyses to the literature. Doing so helps them meaningfully connect to a broader base, giving them an essential perspective that enriches their own practice (See Schniedewind & Sapon-Shevin, Chapter 10 of this book, for another example of this approach.)

By drawing upon knowledge of social learning theories, research outcomes, and the core elements that make groups work, program leaders also model for teachers the practical value of theory for effective decision-making. Based on our knowledge of the teachers' backgrounds, we draw in theory and research to guide our own decisions about what is appropriate training. We employ academic controversy, for example, when the goal is to help teachers challenge the idea that cooperative groupwork practices may appear to have clear-cut, straightforward answers; in reality there are many underlying issues. By consulting a range of resources, examining research findings, considering unique circumstances in classroom and school contexts, and arguing various perspectives, the controversy process helps a teacher understand complexities inherent in effective instructional choice-making for certain practices that are at issue, and construct a course of action most likely to promote success in his or her context. In this way, the controversy process supportively pushes teachers to critically evaluate prepackaged solutions and, alternatively, construct their own solutions. Knowing that argument in a cooperative controversy can easily turn into competitive debate, we carefully structure the cooperative goal ("Your group goal is to exchange as much information as possible during the controversy in order to mutually construct and agree upon the best course of action at the end"), emphasize and model appropriate social interaction skills (such as "disagreeing in an agreeable way" or "respecting alternative viewpoints"), and observe interaction, reemphasizing the cooperative nature of the task when necessary. Thoroughly processing group functioning by asking group members to reflect and honestly discuss the actions and contributions of each member, strengthens the cooperative experience and promotes future success.

We also encourage teachers to draw on other social learning theories when planning for instruction. A teacher may choose to use a jigsaw strategy to help students study the impact of technology on different aspects of society (e.g., political, social, economic). The teacher does so knowing that the jigsaw procedure will involve students in cognitive restructuring as they translate text and media information into their own words, develop visuals and mnemonics to teach the material to group members, and conduct their presentations. If the teacher observes that some group members are not listening carefully to the presentations of their partners (and therefore are not mastering all of the material), the teacher knows that intervening to strengthen cooperative interaction will help students ensure mastery. Drawing upon theory, the teacher may strengthen positive interdependence by reducing the size of the team, awarding bonus points to all team members when each demonstrates mastery on an individual quiz after the jigsaw, or assigning all teammates interconnected roles during jigsaw presentations (such as interviewer, scribe, quizzer, or encourager). The teacher also may teach the group skill of "checking for understanding" by posting sentence starters, provide specific feedback to groups on their use of the skill during teamwork, and conduct group processing periodically throughout the lesson instead of waiting until the end. With theoretical knowledge, teachers are better equiped to critically analyze cooperative groupwork and modify practice in ways that will be enhancing.

### Teachers Must "Live" Cooperative Groupwork in Formal Training Programs

Experiencing cooperative group work makes theory real. Such experience becomes a springboard for considering the core elements that make groups work and how they can be applied in classroom practice, thereby helping educators to clarify conceptual ambiguity and develop understanding. Program leaders can facilitate two types of cooperative experiences that are important for educators. One is being a member of an ongoing cooperative group that engages in real learning tasks. The other is being a member of a micro-teaching team that cooperatively plans and implements cooperative lessons during training. Both types of experiences provide a number of benefits.

First, personal cooperative experiences help one internalize, value, and understand important dimensions of cooperative learning. One must experience how positive interdependence and social interaction skills contribute to the development of trusting, committed, cohesive relationships among group members, to fully appreciate them. Observing others working cooperatively is illuminating, but cannot replace the feelings, reactions, and insights that are part of one's own experience. What you learn from reflecting on personal experience becomes part of your rationale for why you choose to do what you do.

Second, experience in a cooperative group serves as a model. Analyzing how a program leader structures a cooperative task furthers understanding of how to translate the core elements into concrete actions. This is modelled when leaders and colleagues debrief their own decision-making in planning and implementing the cooperative activity. Another way debriefing can occur is by having small groups of teachers plan an adult cooperative learning lesson and teach it to several other groups. Participants observe the actions and words that were used to structure each core element and debrief their effectiveness.

Third, working in cooperative groups during formal programs becomes the basis for participants predicting classroom needs and difficulties, thinking about adaptations that will be needed for success, and planning applications with options to meet those needs. Following a cooperative activity, we often ask participants: "How could the cooperative strategy you just experienced be applied in your teaching situation? What changes will be necessary for site-based success?"

Fourth, being a member of a cooperative team over time helps establish norms of cooperative interaction. Each time colleagues process and analyze an experience, it contributes to the habits of inquiry and reflection necessary for change. The experiences become building blocks in the establishment of new behavior patterns and relationships. We notice in our programs, a shift from initial requests by teachers for curriculum manuals, step-by-step preplanned lessons, and packaged solutions to requests for time to dialogue with one another in order to craft personal applications and create a range of workable solutions to problems. Teachers learn to trust that through cooperative interaction, clarity for effective decision-making will emerge. We also notice a shift in willingness to engage in controversy. Initial discomfort that teachers often experience when grappling with issues and disagreeing about alternative courses of action in problem solving turns to anticipation that engaging in such experiences will produce deeper insight and understanding. These new norms evolve and become stronger as participants continue to successfully engage in teamwork.

Fifth, the task of making sure that all group members have an action plan for classroom use of cooperative learning increases the probability that it will be tried in each classroom, especially if group follow-up for sharing, support, and problem solving is built into the process. We have participants articulate rationales for using cooperative learning, "go public" with plans of action, and make formal commitments to teammates for ongoing support.

Creating meaningful cooperative experiences for participants means program leaders need to:

1. Choose relevant topics that have meaning; grapple with real issues and problems; use adult language; go beyond the "role play" demonstration;
2. Apply the elements basic to all effective cooperative interaction; carefully and systematically structure those elements into every cooperative activity;
3. Observe participant reactions (especially nonverbal communication); capitalize on "teachable moments" and address needs in meaningful, appropriate, honest ways (with respect and integrity); and
4. Conduct meaningful processing, phrasing questions in ways that promote open, honest, and supportive adult discussion about cooperative interaction and improvement.

### Teachers Need to Make Conscious Connections Between the Training and Classroom and School Contexts

We construct our world by making personally relevant connections, experiencing feelings of excitement, coherence, and success on the one hand or, in the case when we struggle to find connections, experiencing feelings of frustration and confusion. Facilitating teacher transfer from training to classroom requires that staff developers consider how to help participants make these connections and see patterns. One way to foster transfer is to connect personal and professional experiences between the training and the organizational contexts.

Connecting Personal and Professional Experiences

Teachers' personal and professional lives are inseparable. Actively making connections between personal and professional experiences reduces feelings of fragmentation and overload often experienced by teachers when learning something new. Interviews and activities that foster the use of metaphor can encourage participants to draw from their personal experiences to illuminate professional issues. We often structure a cooperative interview focused on friendship (Bennett, Rolheiser, & Stevahn, 1991) to help teachers explore characteristics of personal friendships that also are important in establishing and maintaining cooperative groups in classrooms. We also ask teachers to interview a child, adolescent, or family member about best and/or problematic team experiences. This results in a deeper understanding of the core elements that make groups work. We also use children's picture books or works of art to help teachers gain insight into professional issues. This fosters metaphorical thinking and taps into personal experiences and emotions.

Connecting Training and On-Site Organizational Contexts

Many factors comprise the total context of an educational organization at any level (e.g., school, district, provincial/state), such as the cultural and socio-economic makeup of the student population, the goals of the organization, and the various innovations and programs being implemented to meet those goals. Educators are less likely to experience cooperative learning training as an appendage outside of the normal work day (Fullan, 1995) when the program leader helps them adapt principles and elements of cooperative group learning to the unique characteristics of their environment (e.g., how cooperative learning addresses and supports other needs, concerns, and initiatives such as inclusion, whole language, integrated studies, violence and conflict resolution, at-risk students, and dropout rates (See also, Schniedewind & Sapon-Shevin, chapter 10 of this volume)). Involving teachers in the initial planning and evaluation of professional development programs is one way to foster connections between training and school-based concerns. Teachers should be involved because they want (and need) to have a voice (McBride, Reed, & Dollar, 1994). Involvement begins prior to the formal program and includes plans for follow-up support and evaluation. A teacher steering committee, for example, may work with the program leader to identify needs, jointly determine the content and structure of the cooperative learning training, and make appropriate links to the organizational context. The program leader asks questions to understand the profile of the organization and identify nuances of the context. Questions may include: What initiatives are important right now? In what ways do staff members work with one another? What types of professional development are people involved in? Such questions help the program leader respect the needs and circumstances that exist, and target appropriate connections in training.

Promoting Transfer

Program leaders in cooperative learning need to attend to variables that will promote transfer of cooperative learning into classroom practice. In addition to helping participants make the range of connections presented previously in this chapter, program leaders must also (a) help others to recognize opportunities for adaptation and application, (b) ensure practice in varied contexts, and (c) provide specific support for transfer.

Transfer failures can occur even though learners understand how to adapt a procedure they already know to new situations (Determan & Sternberg, 1993). The problem may be that teachers do not recognize that a tactic they know could be applied to a current situation or task. What often facilitates transfer is the specific suggestion to adapt the previously learned procedures. This is why application and adaptation time during training is so important and why in-class observation and ongoing support back at the school site are necessary.

Program leaders also need to consider the importance of participants practicing new skills in multiple contexts as part of instruction (Determan & Sternberg, 1993). We provide opportunities for teachers to experience a range of cooperative tasks, activities, and lessons in a number of different content areas during long-term professional development programs. We also engage participants in micro-teaching, lesson planning, and cooperative lesson demonstrations. These practices increase the likelihood of transfer by promoting overlearning.

### Teachers Need to Build Collaborative School Cultures That Will Support the Change Process and Foster Continuous Learning

A cooperative learning program leader is on a quest to better understand teachers and schools in order to facilitate ongoing improvement. There are many perspectives from which leaders can understand schools; the cultural perspective is an important one. It focuses on the social construction of organizations (Covey, 1991). Gleave (1994) defines school culture as being "shaped by peoples' unconscious assumptions or taken-for-granted beliefs about school vision, curriculum, instruction, evaluation, and organizational structure. People integrate their conceptions of these cultural elements to create meaning and consistency for themselves."

The realities of a school culture affect the capacity of teachers and administrators to be change agents within that culture. This means helping participants become aware of pervasive cultural aspects that may be barriers to implementing school improvement (e.g., lack of consensus or true collegiality). It also means identifying aspects of the culture that will enhance positive change. We often ask participants to describe and label their school culture by providing a set of characteristics that describe a culture (e.g., balkanization, comfortable collaboration, fragmented individualism, contrived collegiality), (Fullan & Hargreaves, 1991). We then ask them to consider the factors in their school culture that will facilitate and enable their use of cooperative learning (e.g. teacher collegial teams, administrative support), as well as those factors that will hinder use (e.g., teachers working in isolation, strong norms of competition). Illuminating such factors enables problem-solving. We ask groups to determine ways they can overcome the hindering factors, while using the enabling factors for support. The result is a set of practical options participants can use to be change agents in their schools. In this way, participants come to see cooperative learning as a means for affecting school culture by building collaborative work environments, rather than only as an instructional strategy.

Supporting the Change Process

One of the largest educational shifts in recent years is the movement from transmission models of teaching to transactional models (see Chapter 1 of this book for more discussion). Cooperative group learning is part of this shift. It counters the transmission paradigm of learning and tracking that still predominates, and focuses on active involvement of students.

One way program leaders can support career-long professional development and effective school change is by helping teachers develop four capacities for continuous learning (Fullan, 1995). Those capacities are (1) personal vision-building, (2) inquiry, (3) mastery, and (4) collaboration.

*Personal Vision-Building.* Teachers need to articulate what is important to them as educators. At the start of programs, we ask teachers: "When your students leave your classroom at the end of the year, what is one thing you want them to gain?" Later in the program, we have teachers revisit their responses and determine how cooperative group learning can help them achieve those outcomes. Such articulation helps them make connections between the greater purposes they see in their profession and the instructional choices they make on a daily basis.

*Inquiry.* Generating and exploring questions cultivates ownership for learning. The habit of inquiry, however, needs to be nurtured from early teacher preparation and throughout one's career. Program leaders can promote the development of thoughtful inquiry and regular questioning by:

• Sharing their own questions about cooperative learning, and how these have changed over time as they have grown;
• Avoiding a defensive stance when participants raise questions and, instead, taking a proactive stance by modeling critical thinking such as exploring the "positives," "minuses," and "I wonders" after an activity;
• Avoiding definitive answers; rather, exploring a range of responses;
• Having participants create responses for questions rather than just those of the program leader;
• Having participants record questions and seek solutions as homework for sharing at the next meeting.

*Mastery.* Leaders promote participant mastery and competence in cooperative learning by designing programs that include theory, demonstration, practice, and feedback, as well as mechanisms for ongoing support within the school after training (Joyce & Weil, with Showers, 1992). Mastery and competence are not merely outcomes; they are also means through which deeper understanding evolves. This means building into the program design sufficient time to reach a high level of mastery and avoiding one-shot workshops and training that is disconnected from classroom and school contexts.

Mastery of the change process itself is as important as mastery of cooperative learning approaches. The two greatest barriers to change are the lack of awareness regarding the need to change and the lack of the necessary skills to make the change (Fullan, Bennett, & Rolheiser-Bennett, 1990). Program leaders can help teachers become knowledgeable about the change process (e.g., the stages of use and concern, the "implementation dip," the time needed for change) and skilled in managing it. This can be accomplished by including dimensions of change in the training program so that teachers become experts at talking about and dealing with change. Important dimensions include:

1. Understanding the complexity and chaotic nature of change;
2. Understanding personal responses to change;
3. Knowing what factors increase the chances of successful initiation, implementation, and institutionalization of an innovation such as cooperative learning;

4.  Developing capacity to create collaborative work cultures;
5.  Enhancing conflict resolution skills; and
6.  Connecting to an external world of resources, ideas, and practices.

*Collaboration.* Cooperative group learning research indicates that we tend to learn more effectively when we work with others rather than alone. This means that program leaders need to facilitate opportunities for both small-scale collaboration (mentoring, peer coaching) and large-scale (with school district, university, and international networks). Collaborative networks can be fostered, for example, by having teams design and share action plans across schools, and by providing time during the program to study and learn from collaborative experiences. Teachers need time for self-evaluation as well as reflection on group functioning. The goal is to help foster individual teacher inquiry and reflection while also developing capacity for effective peer communication and collegial teamwork.

## Conclusion

In professional development for cooperative learning, teachers must realize that there are no single answers or best answers to situational classroom problems. Teachers need to become relatively comfortable with a state of evolving understanding about cooperative groupwork. Program leaders can facilitate this by consciously structuring activites for discourse and exploration to establish participant norms for reflection. Leaders themselves must practice a reflective approach to crafting formal programs. If our goal is to help teachers think about their practice, then we, as staff developers, have the same responsibility to use and nurture critical reflection to promote better decision-making by teachers. By thinking through the four guidelines presented in this chapter, we can choose more purposefully and act more wisely as staff developers, with the intention that our teachers will do the same in their classrooms. The integrity of cooperative learning and the fostering of continuous learning for everyone depends on the choices we make and the actions we take.

## References

Anderson, S. E., Rolheiser, C., & Bennett, B. (1995). Confronting the challenge of implementing cooperative learning. *Journal of Staff Development, 16*(1), 32–38.

Aronson, E. (1980). Training teachers to use jigsaw learning: A manual for teachers. In S. Sharan, P. Hare, C. D. Webb, & R. Hertz-Lazarowitz (Eds.), *Cooperation in education.* Provo, UT: Brigham Young University Press.

Bellanca, J. & Fogarty, R. (1991). *Blueprints for thinking in the cooperative classroom,* 2nd edition. Palatine, Ill: Skylight Publishing.

Bennett, B., Rolheiser, C., & Stevahn, L. (1991). *Cooperative learning: Where heart meets mind.* Toronto, ON: Educational Connections.

Bossert, S. T. (1988). Cooperative activities in the classroom. *Review of Research in Education,* 15, 225–250.

Clarke, J., & Wideman, R. (1985). *Cooperative learning: The jigsaw strategy.* Scarborough, ON: Scarborough Board of Education.

Cohen, E. G. (1994a). *Designing groupwork* (2nd ed.). NY: Teachers College Press.

Cohen, E. G. (1994b). Restructuring the classroom: Conditions for productive small groups. *Review of Educational Research,* 64(1), 1–35.

Covey, S. (1991). *Principle centered leadership.* New York: Simon and Schuster.

Determan, D. K., & Sternberg, R. J. (Eds.). (1993). *Transfer on trial: Intelligence, cognition, and instruction.* Norwood, NJ: Ablex.

Fullan, M. G. (1995). The limits and the potential of professional development. In T. R. Guskey & M. Huberman (Eds.), *Professional development in education: New paradigms and practices,* pp. 253–267. New York: Teachers College Press.

Fullan, M. G., Bennett, B., & Rolheiser-Bennett, C. (1990). Linking classroom and school improvement. *Educational Leadership,* 47(8), 13–19.

Fullan, M. G., & Hargreaves, A. (1991). *What's Worth Fighting For? Working Together for Your School.* Toronto, ON: Ontario Public School Teachers' Federation.

Gleave, D. (1994). Changing school culture through transactional education. *Journal of Staff Development,* 15(2), 8–11.

Hall, G. E., & Hord, S. (1987). *Change in schools: Facilitating the process.* Albany: State University of New York Press.

Hall, G. E., & Loucks, S. (1977). Developmental model for determining whether the treatment is actually implemented. *American Educational Research Journal,* 14(3), 263–276.

Johnson, D. W., & Johnson, R. T. (1995). *Creative controversy: Intellectual challenge in the classroom* (3rd ed.). Edina, MN: Interaction Book Company.

Johnson, D. W., & Johnson, R. T. (1994a). *Leading the cooperative school* (2nd ed.). Edina, MN: Interaction Book Compnay.

Johnson, D. W., & Johnson, R. T. (1994b). *Learning together and alone: Cooperative, competitive, and individualistic learning* (4th ed.). Edina, MN: Interaction Book Company.

Johnson, D. W., & Johnson, R. T. (1994c). Professional development in co-operative learning: Short-term popularity vs. long-term effectiveness. *Cooperative Learning*, 14(2), 52–54.

Johnson, D. W., Johnson, R. T., & Holubec, E. J. (1993). *Cooperation in the classroom* (6th ed.). Edina, MN: Interaction Book Company.

Johnson, D. W., & Johnson, R. T. (1989). *Cooperation and competition: Theory and research*. Edina, MN: Interaction Book Company.

Joyce, B., Showers, B., & Rolheiser-Bennett, C. (1987). Staff development and student learning: A synthesis of research on models of teaching. *Educational Leadership*, 45(2), 11–23.

Joyce, B., Weil, M., with Showers, B. (1992). *Models of teaching* (4th ed.). Boston, MA: Allyn and Bacon.

Kagan, S. (1992). *Cooperative learning*. San Juan Capistrano, CA: Kagan Cooperative Learning.

McBride, R. E., Reed, J. L., Dollar, J. E. (1994). Teacher attitudes toward staff development: A symbolic relationship at best. *Journal of Staff Development*, 15(2), 36–41.

Sharan, Y., & Sharan, S. (1992). *Expanding cooperative learning through group investigation*. NY: Teachers College Press.

Slavin, R. (1990). *Cooperataive learning: Theory, reserach, and practice*. Boston, MA: Allyn and Bacon.

Waber, B. (1992). *Ira Sleeps Over*. Boston, MA: Houghton-Mifflin.

Wittrock, M. C. (1978). Students' thought processes. In M. C. Wittrock (Ed.), *Handbook of research on teaching* (3rd ed.) (pp. 297–314). New York: Macmillan.

# 4

# STAFF DEVELOPMENT THAT MAKES A DIFFERENCE

## PATRICIA ROY

When the 1970s reform in math curriculum had a negative effect on students' test scores, many felt it was because the underlying assumptions of the "new math" were wrong. However, a math specialist asserted that there was nothing wrong with the new math program; what had been wrong was the inadequate training and development of the teachers who were responsible for implementing the program. Many merely received the textbooks and were not given the conceptual or instructional backgrounds necessary to teach the "new math" effectively. New math did not fail because of a conceptual failure, but because of the failure of staff development.

Early reviews of the implementation of cooperative learning suggest this innovation might be following the same pathway as new math. Many school districts still devote only two or three days a year to staff development. Often, those two or three days begin with a motivational speaker and then a set of hour-long sessions identified by a small staff development committee or the ever-present needs assessment survey. Although the research on what constitutes effective staff development programs is 20 years old, this work does not seem to be used to design development programs that make a difference for the professionals involved nor for their students.[1] To ensure that cooperative learning fulfills its research promise, educators need to apply the components of an effective staff development program when designing ongoing, long-term activities that help teachers use cooperative learning effectively with students.

This chapter includes three sections: the first section describes the components of an effective professional development program. Accompanying the components are descriptions of the organizational/ system features that also need to be considered to reinforce and support effective staff development. The second section discusses the implications of these staff development components for cooperative learning—what effective professional development for cooperative learning includes and what a district or school can plan so that cooperative learning has an impact on student achievement. The third section describes six different models of staff development and how and when those models could be used to help teachers implement cooperative learning effectively.

What are the Components of an Effective Staff Development Program?

Comprehensive Programs

Sparks and Loucks-Horsley (1990) found that programs that make a difference in student outcomes are those that are linked to an overarching school or district goal. Comprehensive staff development aligns topics and formats so that the teachers within the school see how each topic will help them achieve the school's goals and how each topic is related to other topics. A study of three types of school-based professional development programs determined which kind of programs had an impact on student achievement (Olson, 1993). When compared, schools with no interest in development programs, schools with staff development programs that used a random topic *du jour* approach, and schools that had a comprehensive, ongoing program showed great differences. The schools using a comprehensive approach showed the highest impact on student achievement, outscoring both of the other types of schools. These schools demonstrated that a set of new instructional behaviors and skills were aligned with a clear and shared goal for students. Educators understood why the staff development was occurring and why it was important.

Teacher Participation

An old principle of social psychology is that when people are meaningfully involved in making decisions that affect them, the decisions are of higher quality, people are more likely to own and support the decisions, and the decisions are more likely to be put into operation. Teacher participation in designing and implementing staff development is an essential component of an effective program. This means more than assigning a staff development committee to determine topics. Teacher participation can also involve:

- Working with presenters to design topics, activities, and schedules that meet the needs of the staff;
- Conducting parts of the staff development session;

- Helping each other implement new practices through sharing, problem-solving sessions, or peer coaching;
- Providing videotapes of classroom practice; and
- Conducting team building activities or energizers.

When faculty can see staff development as meeting a school or student need, they will be more receptive and open to learning.

*Differentiated Training Opportunities.* For many people, staff development equals workshop. Yet, there are a variety of learning strategies that can be used which will better meet the needs of adult learners. Many educators and researchers are examining and identifying alternative development models which range from action research to individually-guided staff development (Loucks-Horsley, Harding, Arbuckle, Murray, Dubea, and Williams, 1987; Little, 1993). The implication of this work is clear; the standard training format is not equally effective with all teachers and administrators. Adult learners learn best when they can decide which format will best help them accomplish the goal of learning a new instructional method. Just as we do not expect all children to learn in the same way, educators need to decide how they best learn. In the third section I describe six of the most potent models.

Effective Training Programs

Once a staff developer or faculty make the decision to use a training program model, four components must be present for this type of staff development to result in sustained classroom implementation (Joyce, Showers, & Weil, 1993).

1. *Theoretical Understanding.* For teachers to use an innovation well and appropriately, they should understand the theory that undergirds the new practice. Appropriate and effective use involves understanding when to use the new practice as well as how to do it.
2. *Demonstrations.* Participants need to see the new teaching model put into practice by a person who is relatively expert at the model. In fact, some research suggests that there is a need for at least 15–20 demonstrations with different subjects and different students to help teachers learn a new model of teaching (Shalaway, 1985).
3. *Supervised Trials.* Practicing a new innovation and receiving feedback from someone who is knowledgeable is an essential component. While teachers mutually adapt an innovation to meet the unique needs of the classroom, it is also important that the innovation retains its critical attributes. Early trials accompanied by

feedback can help clarify the essential features of the new instructional strategy.

4.   *On-the-Job Coaching.* One of the biggest hurdles to educational train-
     ing is that each person's classroom cannot be replicated for practice
     sessions. Each classroom and set of students is unique and offers a
     variety of opportunities and barriers to implementation. One un-
     derlying assumption of much staff development is that the generic
     skills presented during training programs can be adapted by a new
     learner to meet his/her unique classroom situation. That is a diffi-
     cult assumption given that people at an early stage of learning a
     new approach imitate models and are not knowledgeable enough
     to make appropriate adaptations of the innovation. Classroom
     coaching addresses this dilemma.

Classroom coaching is on-the-job training with the teacher experimenting with the innovation while another person serves as coach, another set of eyes and ears, and not as an evaluator (Joyce, Showers, &
Weil, 1993). The coach can be an outside expert or a peer who has a
shared knowledge base and vocabulary (Sparks, 1983). These early trials must be viewed as experiments that allow the person to fail as well
as be successful. There should be time for the teacher and coach to reflect and analyze classroom use. Early analysis of coaching programs
shows that this component can make the difference in ensuring that
new knowledge gets translated into new classroom practice (Joyce,
Showers, & Weil, 1993).

Executive Control

Educators undertake staff development programs with the assumption that new strategies will benefit student learning. At what
point does a new innovation succeed in increasing student learning outcomes? Joyce, Murphy, Showers, and Murphy (1989) studied this question and found that the innovation positively impacted student learning
when the teacher reaches the executive control level of use. Executive
control is defined as "understanding the purpose and rationale of the
skill and knowing how to adapt it to students, apply it to subject matter, modify or create instructional materials, organize students to use it,
and blend it with other instructional approaches to develop a smooth
and powerful whole" (Joyce, Showers, and Weil, 1993). In other words,
the teacher is able to make decisions easily and effectively about when
to use the innovation and how to use the innovation in the classroom.
The new strategy is no longer an innovation but a natural part of the
teacher's repertoire.

Continuous Improvement

"Staff development is most influential when it is conducted often enough and long enough to ensure progressive gains in knowledge, skill and confidence." (Loucks-Horsley, *et. al*, 1987). According to some researchers, learning a new instructional model will take two to three years of practice before it is used as a natural part of the repertoire. It is unrealistic to hope that a single session conducted at the beginning of a two-three year period would supply all the information and answer all the questions to sustain adoption of a new instructional practice. Teachers go through many stages of use and concern regarding a new innovation (Loucks-Horsley & Hergert, 1985). They do not move automatically from learning about a new approach to implementing it. Sustained learning sessions and time for sharing and problem-solving will more likely support long-term use of a new instructional practice.

## What are the Components of School Culture that Reinforce Effective Staff Development Practices?

Most of the early research on staff development concentrated on the successful practices or the learning progression of the individual teacher in relation to the new instructional strategy. However school and district culture can reinforce staff development activities, or just as easily, can block change. So researchers now widen their lenses in order to examine the organizational context in which professional development occurs. For an effective staff development program to fulfill its potential, there are certain organizational components that must also be considered (see Schmuck chapter 12 of this volume for further discussion).

*Collegiality and Collaboration.* In a study of schools, Little (1982) found that if three norms were present, sustained practice and use of innovations was more likely to occur. Those norms are the norm of continuous improvement, the norm of experimentation, and the norm of collegiality. In the norm of continuous improvement, teachers and administrators believe that learning about teaching is never completed; you never arrive or stop studying effective teaching practices. Rosenholtz (1991) describes a similar norm. She found that teachers in schools who were not growing or changing, believed they had all the information they needed to be good teachers—a belief held even if those teachers were in the first few years of their career.

The norm of experimentation goes hand-in-hand with the norm of continuous improvement: no one is expected to perform as an expert especially when s/he is learning new instructional behaviors. Just as in a scientific experiment, each attempt at using a new strategy does not have to be perfect; one can learn as much from failure as from success. Because it takes two to three years to learn a new instructional method well, it is important that educators understand that initial usage will not be smooth or competent or successful. Unless teachers feel that they can fail—especially with first attempts—continuous improvement cannot exist within a school.

The norm of collegiality is defined as teachers sharing responsibility to help each other learn new instructional behaviors. This norm involves teachers planning instructional materials together, participating in reciprocal classroom observation, talking about teaching practice, and having a shared language about teaching. Collegiality, then, is much more than congeniality and involves moving from independence in the workplace to interdependence. Moving from independence to interdependence involves four stages (Little, 1990): (1) story telling and idea scanning, (2) giving aid and assistance, (3) sharing ideas, lessons, activities, and (4) joint work.

Joint work consists of shared responsibility and decisions based not only on individual needs but on other teachers' needs as well. When a faculty establishes a collective conceptualization of autonomy, teachers see that what happens down the hall or in another classroom affects everyone. Collegiality for its own sake will not necessarily influence instructional behavior (Little & McLaughlin, 1993). Powerful collegiality focuses on supporting the development of new practices and examining current school practices. If collegiality is not focused on supporting change and growth, it can become a way to maintain the status quo.

Collaborative School Culture

Rosenholtz (1991) studied 76 schools and districts and identified those that met her standards for collaboration versus those she described as "stuck"-little movement or growth. Table 4.1 shows how she contrasted the practices and beliefs in these schools:

The belief systems that operate within each school and district affect whether staff development will make a difference for students (see Brody, chapter 1 of this volume for more discussion). If the culture supports the attitude that students cannot learn because they are deficient, then the educators will believe that they do not need to do anything differently—they need a better crop of students! Even the best staff development design will fail if the faculty hold these beliefs.

Growth-Oriented District Staff

Rosenholtz (1991) also studied districts to determine whether there were practices at that level that supported or undermined teacher

TABLE 4.1

Contrasts between Practices and Beliefs

| Stuck | versus | Collaborative |
|---|---|---|
| 1. Teachers swapped stories of a student's poor behavior. | | 1. Teachers problem solve to increase student success. |
| 2. Teacher leaders are involved in union activities or activities not related to schooling. | | 2. Teacher leaders show initiative and willingness to experiment with new ideas and set an example of how to work with students. |
| 3. Teachers describe student problems as behavioral problems. | | 3. Teachers describe student problems as instructional and behavioral. |
| 4. Teachers regard students as the source of problems. | | 4. Teachers regard students as having problems, and teachers try to get to the source. |
| 5. Teachers do not seek help from colleagues. | | 5. Teachers seek help from colleagues, parents, and the principal. |
| 6. Teachers seek help in punishing problem students. | | 6. Teachers seek help in finding ways to help students with their problems. |
| 7. Teachers believe that student learning is not possible with difficult students. | | 7. Teachers believe that learning is possible even for the most difficult students |

collaboration at the school level. Despite the small size of the study, there were a number of similarities in districts that were growing and changing. First, educators in these districts held the belief that teaching is a complex interaction that cannot be simplified into a set of standard operation procedures; good teaching is not factory work but active decision-making and problem-solving. When district level staff hold this belief they tend to rely on delegated authority so that faculty and administration can make decisions to meet their unique needs. These districts included teachers in the following decisions:

1. Selecting key school personnel
2. Setting school goals with principals
3. Allocating fiscal resources
4. Selecting appropriate teaching materials
5. Determining their own inservice needs

When staff and administration are given guidelines with discretion to make decisions, they are held accountable for those decisions. In contrast, "stuck" districts micro-managed the schools, the teachers, and the curriculum and seemed to use more coercive management techniques. Just as a school creates a context for staff development so does the district create a context for schools. Professional development activities are embedded in these cultures, and the beliefs and actions of the school system impact its effectiveness.

## Implications of Effective Staff Development Practices and Organizational Development for Cooperative Learning

When cooperative learning is well structured and appropriately used, the research demonstrates a profound effect on student learning and retention. Yet, there have been many other educational innovations that could boast the same research findings but did not result in increased achievement and retention. Why? The reason may lie in the staff development program design used to help the staff learn and implement the innovation. There are five recommendation for professional development of cooperative learning which follow from the above work.

### Create a Local Need for Cooperative Learning Training That Will Increase the Motivation to Learn

Many schools and districts still select cooperative learning because it is cited by successful schools or it is mentioned in the literature on school change rather than selecting it to meet a particular need. If cooperative learning is one viable approach to a perceived local student need, educators are more likely to embrace learning about it. For example, one school in Arizona began its own development process by jointly agreeing on the skills and behaviors of the ideal student and describing ideal learning conditions. They agreed, as a faculty, that the most effective learning environment for most children was an active, hands-on environment. The principal collected data to determine whether active learning environments were a normal part of the school routine. As he walked around the school, he made notes about the types of learning activities and also gathered data on the amount of teacher-student talk. Throughout the day and at different grade levels, he calculated on-task rates for students. On-task behaviors varied widely from 12 percent to 95 percent. The staff used these data to discuss why students were not on-task and what might be done to involve more students in becoming active learners. One of the outcomes of the discussion was that teachers needed to employ a greater variety of learning activities, and cooperative learning might help teachers create the desired learning atmosphere.

The teachers in that school had established a personal need for implementing cooperative learning. In contrast, a group of middle school teachers in Texas filled out a standard needs assessment survey indicating that cooperative learning was one of their interests. When asked again six months later, they felt they were assigned to the cooperative learning training and did not regard the needs assessment as an indication of personal need. The needs assessment survey had not established a personal or student need for learning cooperative learning and the teachers considered the workshop an imposition, rather than an opportunity to solve problems.

### Effective Development Agendas Include a Balance of Nuts and Bolts With Theoretical Understandings

Teachers appreciate clear, concrete instruction in new instructional strategies. They want to know what to do and how to do it. They value classroom-tested procedures and advice from the field. Yet, teachers must also understand why an instructional strategy is effective and be able to make decisions about the best use of the innovation (NSDC, 1994). Teachers need to reach a level of executive control over the innovation for it to have an impact on students (Joyce, Murphy, Showers, and Murphy, 1989).

Effective professional development of cooperative learning helps teachers understand how to implement cooperative activities in the classroom as well as see connections to the theoretical underpinnings of the model. If educators do not understand underlying theory, it is unlikely they will reach executive control. They might eliminate an essential component of cooperative learning and implement group work, not cooperative work.

For example, during a debriefing three science teachers watched a demonstration of the cooperative structure, "Numbered Heads" (Kagan, 1994). One teacher remarked that this procedure could be done much faster if he indicated who would be called on before the group discussed the answer. The teacher did not understand that positive interdependence was structured into Numbered Heads by having the teacher ask for a response using a random method for choosing speakers. The teacher would have easily made that adaptation without a second thought because he did not fully understand the theory of what makes a group cooperative.

Unfortunately, there is not an agreed upon set of essential components shared among the variety of cooperative learning models. Morton Deutsch (in Strother, 1990), an early pioneer in the exploration of cooperation, provides a meta-view of cooperative learning and suggests three basic ingredients that define cooperative activities. He suggests:

- Students need to develop the motivation and have the opportunity to help one another learn.
- Students need to develop the feeling that they are responsible for and accountable to the group (as well as themselves) for doing their best.
- Students need to acquire the social skills necessary for effective group work.

## Recognize That Effective Classroom Use of Cooperative Learning Will Take Time

According to educational researchers, achieving executive control over cooperative learning takes at least two to three years of consistent and sustained practice (Joyce, Showers, and Weil, 1993). One-shot training sessions will not produce the kind of classroom practice that enhances student learning (NSDC, 1994). There are a series of stages which everyone goes through when they are learning a new behavior—first there is awareness, then there is awkwardness. At the awkward stage, many educators abandon the new practice because it does not feel "right" and change halts. If they continue beyond the awkward stage, the consciously skilled stage comes next.

The last stage is habit or automaticity. During this journey, teachers experience an implementation dip—they get worse before they get better; this dip occurs at the awkward stage. It is a difficult stage for everyone and underscores the need for a norm of experimentation. Teachers need to believe it is all right to have an unsuccessful cooperative lesson—especially when they are just beginning. If new practice is protected, the teacher continues to experiment rather than feel incompetent or believe that cooperative learning cannot work. These feelings can stop implementation. Teachers need to be aware of the change process and accept the opportunity to fail. Failing is normal and a sign that they are truly trying something new.

Allowing time for staff development to develop expert cooperative learning teachers also means that there will be a variety of activities available to help support sustained practice and classroom use. Beginning staff development activities might include a series of traditional training sessions with collegial support groups meeting in-between to share and problem solve. The next year focuses on peer coaching for cooperative learning (see Cooper and Boyd chapter two of this volume). By the third year, some teachers will be ready for action research activities. The measure of the effectiveness of staff development comes from the consistent, appropriate, effective classroom implementation, not the number of teachers participating in "training."

Teacher Collegiality Supports Long-Term Implementation

Collegiality among the staff supports cooperation in the classroom. For cooperative learning to fulfill its potential, the whole school would need to use the strategy appropriately and well. Few districts have the finances to bring in long-term consultation and experts from the outside to sustain the implementation of cooperative groups. But outside experts can increase the capacity of school-based staff to provide support and assistance to each other.

Staff members can support each others' implementation of cooperative learning by becoming members of a support group (see Johnson & Johnson, chapter 11, of this book for further discussion). Support groups meet on a regular basis—once every two to three weeks—to share ideas, create lessons to try, problem solve, and brainstorm alternatives. Support groups do not have to draw teachers from the same grade or content area but members should be willing to support each other's use of cooperative learning.

Peer coaching programs are particularly powerful for supporting continuous improvement of cooperative learning. Peer coaching is a reciprocal observation and feedback cycle that requires the observer to act as another set of eyes and ears for the teacher. The teacher determines the learning goal and the objective of the observation. The peer coach supports rather than evaluates. The intent of peer coaching is to help colleagues learn how to implement cooperative learning by giving technical support and assistance (if asked), providing companionship, facilitating the other person through the change process, examining ways students can be made comfortable with their new roles in cooperative learning, and helping the teacher reach executive control through reflective feedback and discussion. Peer coaching can fulfill the need for classroom coaching which results in effective implementation and higher student achievement (see Cooper & Boyd, chapter 2 of this book for further discussion).

Staff meetings are excellent times to conduct problem-solving sessions in which peers discuss implementation problems with cooperative learning and brainstorm alternative solutions (see Ellis, chapter 13 of this book for detailed examples). This kind of forum for staff can fulfill a number of needs. The culture of most schools hinders teachers from asking for help because it is viewed as a sign of incompetence. If the best teacher begins the process of describing a problem and asking for ideas, the barrier can be slowly broken. Faculty meetings, then, become times to learn from each other and demonstrate that everyone needs help. Problem-solving also fulfills the need for the ongoing support and assistance that cooperative learning requires to ensure successful and effective implementation. Problem-solving acknowledges that learning a new instructional strategy is not easy, that there are common barriers to implementation that are not signs of incompetence, and that there are a variety of ways to solve common problems.

## Appropriate District Level Policies Reinforce Effective Staff Development for Cooperative Learning

Because the district creates a culture just as the school does, the staff developer should examine district practices and policies to ensure support of effective cooperative learning staff development (NSDC, 1994). Faculty should ask these and other questions:

a. Has the district office staff given a clear mandate to the faculty to select professional development activities that meet the unique needs of the school?
b. Has the district office staff established a process for determining school goals that reflect student needs rather than the use of a needs assessment survey?
c. Has the district office staff provided sufficient resources (budget, time, substitutes) so that ongoing staff development activities can occur at the school?
d. Has the district office staff allowed for enough time (two to three years) and set realistic goals concerning the impact of cooperative learning on student achievement?
e. Has the district office staff provided school faculty with information concerning effective staff development practices?
f. Does the district office staff communicate that teaching is a complex activity that requires thoughtful teacher decisions, rather than a standard operating procedures?
g. Does the district office staff delegate authority and trust school staff to make key decisions or do they micro-manage?

## Alternative Models for Training Programs

Educators can make cooperative learning staff development more effective by having alternatives to the standard workshop/training activity. Sparks and Loucks-Horsley (1990) identified several models of staff development, and faculty members can employ each of these models to cooperative learning development.

*Individually-Guided Staff Development.* An individually-guided program formalizes what most teachers do naturally: they read professional magazines, attend courses and conferences, discuss ideas with colleagues, and try new strategies in the classroom. This model of staff development supports the teacher in determining his/her own goal and deciding the best way to reach that goal. An individually-guided program involves four steps:

Step 1.   Determining a goal
Step 2.   Planning learning activities
Step 3.   Doing learning activities
Step 4.   Assessing whether the learning meets the goal

This model is a goal-based approach that allows teachers to use their own learning styles to accomplish a desired outcome that is not determined by seat time or clock hours.

In staff development for cooperative learning, this model can be used after foundation knowledge has been established. Each teacher is asked to determine a goal concerning cooperative learning that s/he would like to accomplish. Some teachers may want to learn how cooperative learning could be integrated with subject areas; others might want to learn how to teach trust-building skills effectively in the classroom. Each person determines his/her own goals regarding cooperative learning and ways to accomplish those activities; it is important to create a goal that can be put into practice.

*Observation/Assessment.* One of the most valuable ways to learn a new instructional model is to practice the method in the presence of a colleague and then reflect on the data collected to determine how it went and how to make it better. Observation and assessment can put into play two powerful forces that increase instructional effectiveness: reflection and analysis. Colleagues provide a powerful resource to each other during observation/assessment. One of the critical elements of success in this approach is that the observer and teacher share a common language and understanding of a specific teaching model. An observation/assessment cycle has four steps: (1) pre-conference to determine a focus and data collection system, (2) observation, (3) analysis of data and, (4) feedback and reflection.

In peer coaching, the teacher determines the focus; in other models the teacher and coach determine the focus. This approach provides ongoing support for the implementation of cooperative learning. Begin by establishing peer coach partners. Among the ways to pair people, include placing a veteran teacher with novice, peer selection, matching schedules, or matching one person's planning period with another's teaching time so the observations can be conducted without substitutes. During the pre-conference phase, the teacher determines a goal related to implementing cooperative learning in the classroom. The goal reflects the critical components of the model of cooperative learning being used in the school.

For example, if the teacher is concerned about the level of trust among cooperative group members, the observer would gather data reflecting the level of trust among students. During the pre-conference the teacher and observer identify the behaviors that demonstrate trust and a lack of trust. Group observation forms are created which use these behaviors. In the observation phase, the observer tallies the number of times trusting or untrustworthy behaviors are heard or seen. The observer spends three to five minutes with each group. In the post-observation reflection and analysis, the data are shared, the observer offers descriptive feedback, and the teacher analyzes student behavior. The teacher considers appropriate next steps and can ask the observer for additional ideas or solutions.

*Development/Improvement Process.* Engagement of a school staff in curriculum development, program development, or systematic school improvement processes defines the next model of staff development. New skills, behaviors, attitudes, and knowledge are developed in order to complete the school-based projects. Reading, discussion, observation, or training can be used to acquire the needed skills. The components of this process include:

- Problem Identification: strengths and weaknesses of the school or of student outcomes are identified.
- Solution to Problem: the faculty and administration determine appropriate solutions to the problems.
- Acquiring Needed Skills: the faculty determine the information, skills, or attitudes needed in order to implement the solution.
- Installing Solution: the faculty and administration implement a new program or product designed to solve the original problem.
- Evaluation: staff members evaluate the effectiveness of the solution and examine whether any other problems occurred as a result of the solution.

Cooperative learning can be the answer to a variety of school-based problems. For example, one high school eliminated tracking because of the negative effects of tracking on students reported in the research. Administrators created heterogeneous classroom rosters. It quickly became clear that the solution included more than merely placing students together in the classroom. The faculty and administration found that teachers did not know how to address the span of achievement levels present in the classroom. Small teacher committees reviewed the research on the procedures other schools implemented when they untracked. After reviewing the literature, the faculty determined that they needed to learn more about differentiated instruction and cooperative learning. The Complex Instruction model from Stanford University held great promise for helping address the needs of all students (see Lotan, Cohen, & Morphew, chapter six of this volume). The faculty and administration organized study sessions to learn about Complex Instruction. Interdisciplinary groups of teachers developed a new curriculum appropriate to the heterogeneous classroom.

*Training.* Effective training programs include the following elements: (a) theoretical understandings of the model, (b) classroom demonstrations of the model, (c) supervised practice with expert feedback, and (d) classroom coaching. Changes in classroom behaviors are more likely to occur when all these elements are present.

An effective training program for cooperative learning includes the four elements. First, teachers learn the theory that undergirds cooperative learning through activities, readings/discussions, and presentations. Positive interdependence and individual accountability receive special emphasis. Participants experience activities that clarify the difference between groups and cooperative groups. The activity involves reviewing descriptions of group activities and labeling the essential elements. There are many ways to understand underlying theory, and one of the most effective strategies is to debrief experiential activities.

Second, there are multiple demonstrations of cooperative learning in content areas and grade levels. Demonstrations include workshop participants simulating cooperative learning activities, viewing videotapes of actual cooperative lessons, or having a group of students complete a cooperative activity. The number and type of demonstrations increases when there are a wide range of participants so that each person has a model that closely resembles his/her working environment.

Third, participants develop cooperative activities, practice delivering the lessons, and receive feedback during the training program. Micro-teaching provides the avenue to accomplish these activities. Small groups of participants develop mini-cooperative learning lessons in which other class members participate. The remainder of the class provides descriptive feedback on the lesson, and everyone engages in determining how the process could be applied to other content.

Fourth, in-between the ongoing training sessions, peer coaching occurs. Topics presented during training sessions become the focus of peer coaching activities. For example, if the workshop session focused on developing class building or team building activities, the coaching partners might develop a trust building activity and conduct it in the classroom. The observer collects data on student reaction to the activity and records student processing statements.

*Inquiry.* Inquiry models of staff development begin with teachers asking questions about their own instructional practices and finding objective answers to those questions. Inquiry methods are similar to action research procedures. The process involves (a) determining a problem of interest, (b) exploring ways to collect data concerning the problem, (c) analyzing and interpreting the data, (d) determining changes, (e) implementing changes, and (f) evaluating how the changes impact the problem. Individuals, small groups, or whole faculty can use inquiry methods.

One way the inquiry method applies to cooperative learning involves focusing on questions about the effectiveness of group activities. Small groups of teachers who are using cooperative learning begin by asking questions about cooperative groups and finding possible solutions. For example, one group wondered how to handle a dominant group member who controls the group and does all the work. The teachers identify data that would help solve the problem and divide the data collection tasks. One person talks to the school's counselor about strategies for dealing with dominating people. A second person reviews books on cooperative learning for any advice about handling this group problem. A third person observes cooperative groups to determine how frequently a dominating member happens and ways other group members handle the problem. The fourth person reviews her workshop notes concerning dealing with difficult people. The group decides they need two weeks to gather the data.

When the group reconvenes, they review all the data and discuss implications. After examining classroom data, they determine that the problem is not extensive—usually one or two groups out of ten had a dominant member. They examine strategies for addressing this problem and identify three worth trying. The first two use participation chips to monitor the amount of time each member contributed ideas, and collecting participation data while the group worked. Then the teacher discusses with the class reasons why equal participation is a key condition of effective groups, sharing the collected data with them. Next groups brainstorm ways to solve the problem of unequal contributions.

A third strategy involves teaching conflict resolution strategies to group members to keep the dominant member from taking over the group. Each teacher decides which strategy or combination of strategies s/he would try when the problem occurs in the classroom. The action research group also decides to ask students to give feedback on how they felt about the strategies.

In three weeks, the group meets again to discuss the use of the strategies. They share student responses and their own feelings about how well each strategy worked. They decide that they need to establish from the beginning that equal participation is a critical component of working in a small group. The group of teachers decides to plan how they can help students understand and define cooperative learning in that way.

*Study Groups.* Study groups are a new model of staff development that came from work designed to alter the culture of schools. Joyce and Showers (1988) felt that the isolation of the classroom and the lack of professional exchange among educators worked against instructional change occurring in most classrooms. Study groups' objectives focus on working together to support the implementation of new instructional practices (Roy, 1994). Study groups meet on a regular schedule of one hour every one or two weeks. Sometimes study groups read and discuss the same materials; other times group members determine what information they need to help them become proficient in a specific instructional model. Study groups also employ many other processes such as an inquiry or action research.

Staff development for cooperative learning could use study groups in many different ways. For example, one school established a goal that teachers use cooperative learning activities. Three years were spent developing those faculty skills through formal training, peer coaching, and support groups. Due to changes in staff, there were six new teachers who were not as familiar with cooperative learning. Because cooperative learning continued as an important instructional strategy for the school, the six teachers became a study group to learn more about cooperative learning. They selected a text with accompanying study guide that provided discussion questions, activities, and projects. The group meets weekly for an hour and completes activities or holds discussion. They also create the agenda items for the next meeting. Responsibility for assembling the materials and the agenda rotates among group members. As a part of their development, they pair with teachers at the same grade level who use cooperative learning successfully. Study group members observe cooperative lessons and later begin peer coaching activities with veteran teachers.

Teachers Establish Local Need for Cooperative Learning

In many schools, staff development involves finding a presenter and arranging training sessions. This kind of activity assumes that teachers will be motivated and ready to learn. Sadly, that is a huge assumption. Effective staff development creates a need for teachers and administrators to learn a new set of skills. A data-based goal setting process can create the need for cooperative learning. This process involves four steps:

*Clarify the Students' Ideal Skills and Behaviors.* What should a child be able to know and do as a result of being a student in this school? A mission statement should answer that question. Often, the mission statement is nothing more than platitudes or vague statements. An effective mission statement is a decision-making tool. This process of clarifying students' ideal skills and behaviors takes a long time if sincere discussion and disagreement occur. It provides the blueprint and the standard for determining whether the school is accomplishing its goals for students. For example, one school felt that one essential student skill was working well with others, especially people from different cultures and backgrounds.

*Assess Current Accomplishment of Student Goals.* The mission statement determines the data collection items. The data demonstrate the current success or failure of the student goals. For example, to assess how well students currently work well with others, teachers form small, heterogeneous groups of students and ask them to complete a problem-solving task together. The teachers develop an observation form to tally important cooperative skills. Students' ability to work with others is rated according to a pre-established rubric.

*Interpret Data.* The patterns, not anomalies, are identified in the data. The analysis includes determining successes and needs and developing a student-based improvement goal. Teachers review the observational data on students' ability to work together. They find that students wanted to complete the task. They also find that a majority of the student groups had high achievers dominate the interaction and that male and female members make unequal numbers of contributions. Encouraging others to participate hardly occurred within the student groups. As a result, teachers wrote this student goal: "Student behavior in heterogeneous groups will be characterized by equal participation, encouraging others to participate, and listening to everyone's ideas."

*Select Priority Student Goals.* There are usually more student goals available than the staff has time or energy to work on, so the faculty decides which goals are a priority for them. There are many group decision-making techniques to help people arrive at consensus on priorities. Time for discussion, advocating, and clarifying is crucial so that the staff supports the goals and views them as appropriate for the school and students. Merely voting on goals does not result in consensus. The faculty needs to rank and discuss all student goals until a few reach prominence.

*Determine Staff Development Outcomes.* In the next step, the staff development committee determines whether professional development is necessary to accomplish the goal. To accomplish the student goal of equal participation, encouraging, and listening during group activity, the staff identifies what information, resources, or behaviors they need to help students accomplish this goal. For example, the staff may decide to learn more about status expectations and Complex Instruction and how to create curriculum that is appropriate for heterogeneous groups.

*Determine Which Staff Development Model(s) Best Accomplish the Goal.* An earlier section described six different models of staff development. A staff committee could determine which of the six models or combinations of the models to use to accomplish their staff development goal. Next they might create study groups that read about aspects of a chosen specific cooperative learning strategy. These groups would also view videotapes and examine sample curriculums. Once teachers have created a strong information base, study groups become action research groups and experiment with new strategies and curriculum and determine if these new procedures make a difference for students. When people make decisions, they are more likely to feel ownership for them and are committed to put the decisions into practice. Using this data-based goal setting process can create a feeling of commitment to and ownership for staff development activities.

## Conclusion

Staff development that does not change classroom practices is like a parachute that opens after the second bounce! For cooperative learning to fulfill its promise, it must be used appropriately and wisely with children in the classroom. There are several ways to develop cooperative learning, but each method needs as a goal to change teachers' instructional behaviors. To accomplish that goal, professional development must be realistic, long-term, and continuous with support through collegial interactions and strong administrative leadership. Students will benefit from cooperative learning if teachers use the instructional strategy appropriately and effectively.

## Notes

1. This chapter appeared in a slightly different version in *Cooperative Learning,* a publication of the International Association for the Study of Cooperation in Education, volume 16 (2) 1996. Copyright 1996 IASCE. Adapted by permission.

## References

Joyce, B., Murphy, C., Showers, B. & Murphy, J. (1989, November). School renewal as cultural change. *Educational Leadership,* 47 (2), 70–77.

Joyce, B. & Showers, B. (1988). *Student achievement through staff development.* New York: Longman.

Joyce, B., Showers, B., & Weil, M. (1993). *Models of teaching.* Englewood Cliffs, NJ: Prentice-Hall, Inc.

Kagan, S. (1994). *Cooperative learning.* San Juan Capistrano, CA: Kagan Cooperative Learning.

Little, J. & McLaughlin, M. (1993). *Teachers' work: Individuals, colleagues, and contexts.* Columbia University: Teachers College Press.

Little, J. (1990). The persistence of privacy: Autonomy and initiative in teachers' professional relations. *Teachers College Record* 91 (4), 509–536.

Little, J. (1982). Norms of collegiality and experimentation: Work-place conditions of school success. *American Educational Research Journal,* 19(3), 325–340.

Loucks-Horsley, S., Harding, C., Arbuckle, M., Murray, L., Dubea, C., & Williams, M. (1987). *Continuing to learn: A guidebook for teacher development.* Andover, MA: Regional Laboratory for Educational Improvement of the Northeast and Island, and the National Staff Development Council.

Loucks-Horsley, S. & Hergert, L. (1985). *An action guide to school improvement.* Alexandria, VA: Association for Supervision and Curriculum Development.

Maeroff, Gene. (1994, May–June). Start the revolution without me. *Teacher Magazine,* p. 39.

National Staff Development Council. (1994). *Standards for staff development: Middle level edition.* Oxford, OH: National Staff Development Council

Olson, Lynne. (1993, February 10). Student gains, intensive restructuring linked, study finds. *Education Week,* p. 5.

Rosenholtz, S. (1991). *Teachers' workplace: The social organization of schools.* Columbia University: Teachers College Press.

Roy, P. (1994). *A primer on study groups.* Wilmington, DE: Patricia Roy Company.

Shalaway, T. S. (1985). Peer coaching: Does it work? *R & D Notes,* Washington, D.C.: National Institute of Education.

Sparks, Dennis and Loucks-Horsley, Susan. (1990). *Five models of staff development.* Oxford, OH: National Staff Development Council.

Sparks, G. (1983). Synthesis of research on staff development for effective teaching, *Educational Leadership,* 42 (6), 65–72.

Strother, D. (1990). Cooperative learning: Fad or foundation for learning? *Kappan,* 72(2), 158–162.

# PART II

## LESSONS FROM THE FIELD: APPROACHES TO COOPERATIVE LEARNING AND IMPLICATIONS FOR PROFESSIONAL DEVELOPMENT

ॐ

# 5

## Staff Development and the Structural Approach to Cooperative Learning

### Spencer Kagan and Miguel Kagan

### Introduction

All approaches[1] to cooperative learning share a number of characteristics with regard to educational philosophy and practice. Most importantly, cooperative learning approaches all attempt to create promotive social interaction among students about content, with the aim of facilitating academic achievement, thinking skills, and improving social relations and social skills. The theory and methods of cooperative learning constitute the most complex set of educational innovations ever devised. Different cooperative learning approaches emphasize different basic principles and different methods, leading not only to differences in classroom practices but also to differing approaches to staff development (Davidson, 1994; Sharan, 1994).

The Structural Approach to cooperative learning is distinct from other approaches to cooperative learning in both its classroom practices and its approach to staff development. There are six keys central to the structural approach: 1) structures; 2) basic principles; 3) teambuilding and classbuilding; 4) teams; 5) management; and 6) social skills. Staff development in the structural approach therefore strives to provide teachers fluency in all six areas. These six keys to cooperative learning have been described in detail elsewhere (Kagan, 1993; Kagan & Kagan, 1994). Here we will focus on two of the six keys that most distinguish the structural approach from other approaches to cooperative learning: 1) structures, and 2) basic principles. We will examine the nature of structures and the basic principles central to the structural approach; why the structural approach emphasizes structures and the basic principles in staff development; and how structures and basic principles are being taught in teacher training. We will also preview some staff development models currently being employed in the training of the structural approach, and what schools have done to restructure their staff meetings.

## Structures

### What Are Structures?

Structures[2] are ways of organizing the social interaction among students in a classroom. Structures are distinct from content. If a teacher stands before the class telling students about the meaning of democracy, the content is 'the meaning of democracy,' and the structure is 'teacher talk.' The same content could be treated very differently, as when a teacher has students seated in teams of four and says, "Talk it over in your teams—What is the essence of democracy?" In this latter scenario, the content is still "the meaning of democracy," but the structure is a "team discussion."

Learning is a function of the interaction of two important factors, the content (the *what* of learning) and the structure (the *how* of learning). In the structural approach we refer often to what we call the fundamental formula of teaching:

$$\text{Structure} + \text{Content} = \text{Activity}$$

At any one moment in the classroom while teaching is in progress, there is always some content, and the content is being delivered by some structure. The combination of a structure and content is called an activity. Each activity has a different learning potential. In our example above, very different learnings will transpire if the teacher uses a Team Discussion with the democracy content than if the teacher uses Teacher Talk to address the same content. Changing the structure will change what is learned just as surely as changing the content. Many teachers emphasize content and fail to focus on the importance of structure. The structural approach attempts to correct that imbalance.

It is possible to distinguish dozens of structures, each with predictable and very different learning outcomes in the academic, cognitive, and social domains (Kagan, 1993; Kagan, 1990). A list of cooperative structures and their domain of usefulness is provided in a manual (Robertson, Kagan, Kagan & Warner, 1995). In the structural approach we become very differentiated regarding cooperative learning structures. We examine each structure for its usefulness in each of six domains of usefulness: Teambuilding, Classbuilding, Mastery, Thinking Skills, Information Sharing, and Communication Building. Some structures are very useful in mastering facts (e.g., the Flashcard Game); others in organizing information (e.g., Team Word-Webbing); others in generating ideas (e.g., 4-S Brainstorming); and yet others in reviewing and checking for understanding (e.g., Numbered Heads Together).

Even within domains of usefulness we become quite differentiated. Let's examine just two. Among the mastery oriented structures are the Flashcard Game and Pairs Check. In the Flashcard Game students work in pairs trying to "win back" their own flashcards (items they need to master) from a partner. The Flashcard Game is very efficient for memorizing information as it maximizes time on task, provides repeated immediate reinforcement and supportive feedback, and presents facts in a game-like fashion that motivates students. The Flashcard Game, however, is not particularly efficient when students are attempting to learn a new skill such as how to diagram a sentence, or how to carry out a math algorithm. Pairs Check is a far more efficient structure for skill acquisition. In Pairs Check each student in turn, works through a problem while a partner coaches with pencil and paper or with manipulatives. The emphasis in Pairs Check is accurately carrying out all the steps of a skill; the emphasis in the Flashcard Game is memorization of facts. Skill acquisition is facilitated in Pairs Check by the coaching built into the structure as well as the "self-talk" students engage in as they talk through the steps of a problem; memorization is facilitated in the Flashcard Game by the repeated trials on the same items. Different structures are designed to facilitate different types of learning and in the structural approach, teachers are trained to become quite differentiated about the domain of usefulness of each structure, so they can make wiser choices when structuring the interaction of students in their classrooms. The goal: teachers are empowered with knowledge of a wide range of structures so at any moment in the classroom they can choose the most efficient structure to build the learning experience they wish to create.

Why Teach Structures?

There are a variety of reasons to include structures as a component of staff development in cooperative learning. When teachers learn how to use a variety of cooperative learning structures they are empowered to reach various educational objectives. Structures provide rich and varied learning experiences for students; structures facilitate the implementation of cooperative learning; and structures make teaching and learning more fun.

Structures Empower Teachers

As educators, we are faced with a range of educational objectives. Teaching is much more than simply imparting knowledge to our students. Students need to learn to be critical and creative thinkers, how to share information with others, communicate effectively with others, solve problems, make decisions, reach consensus, and get along with others. No single structure can accomplish this breadth of educational objectives. We think of structures as tools; different structures are differentially effective in achieving different goals. The more tools a teacher has, the better prepared that teacher is to construct learning experiences which efficiently reach the range of learning objectives. A teacher well versed in the use of many different tools can select the proper tool or structure and more efficiently and effectively achieve the learning objective.

Structures Provide Varied Learning Experiences

Students come to school with different cultural backgrounds, values, learning styles, and intelligences. No one structure can adequately accommodate such diversity. To insure equity in education, we must use a variety of teaching methods to accommodate all students. More structures provide students with a wider range of learning experiences. If every teacher uses the same structure every day, he or she is limiting his or her students' learning potential. To truly educate all students and prepare them to be successful members of an increasingly pluralistic society, we must provide rich and varied learning experiences—different structures provide that richness.

Structures Facilitate the Implementation of Cooperative Learning

The structural approach provides discrete, bite-sized learning units for teachers. Learning the intricacies of the theory and methods of cooperative learning may be overwhelming; learning one new structure is relatively easy for teachers. Teachers often state that the structural approach is easy compared to other approaches. This is so for two reasons: 1) It is more difficult to plan a cooperative learning lesson than to include cooperative learning structures in existing lessons. Approaches that would have teachers only apply abstract principles in designing cooperative learning lessons can result in difficult lesson planning; the inclusion of co-op structures into existing lessons is far easier. 2) Teachers can acquire the structures one-at-a-time. After teachers have learned a structure well, they are encouraged to learn another one. The structures amount to a curriculum for teachers. To support the concept of structures as a curriculum for teachers, a personal survey based on the structures in Kagan (1993) is administered. Linking structures to form multi-structural lessons comes naturally to teachers who learn the structures well, one at a time. The domain of usefulness of each structure is also acquired naturally through experience. Teachers are encouraged to experiment with the structures, play with them, and discover what they are and are not useful for.

## Structures Make Teaching and Learning Fun

Using many different structures makes teaching and learning more fun. If variety is the spice of life, structures are saffron and paprika for the classroom. Structures cultivate creativity in both teachers and students. Teachers extend and expand their teaching repertoire as they find fresh new alternatives for reaching their objectives. Almost all students are delighted to participate in engaging and exciting learning experiences. Teaching and learning are then characterized by novelty and exhilaration, rather than by monotony and tediousness.

## How Structures Are Taught

The teaching of cooperative learning structures varies depending on the needs and experiences of the staff. However, when introducing a new structure, the following eight steps have been found to be very successful for teaching structures. The steps are not always taught in the same order. The steps are detailed in a *Co-op Facilitators' Handbook* (Kagan & Robertson, 1992) and include the following:

1. Experience. Teachers experience the structure as if they were a student in a classroom.
2. Variations. Teachers experience and discuss variations on the structure.
3. Management & Social Skills. The facilitator provides and models management techniques and social skills methods associated with the structure. For example, in Pairs Check, students learn to ask for and offer help politely; in Team Interview, in addition to interviewing skills, students learn to manage the time so everyone participates equally and all teams finish at the same time.
4. Content. The facilitator provides academic content ideas with the structure, priming the pump for teachers' own generation of content applications.
5. Applications. Teachers generate and record academic content ideas appropriate to their own classrooms, using a structured recording sheet.
6. Rationale. Teachers derive the rationale for the structure. The rationale includes: benefits of using the structure; the domain of usefulness of the structure—when it is appropriate and when it is not appropriate; and how the structure incorporates the basic principles (PIES). Teachers perform a PIES Analysis (see below) for each

new structure to better understand the structure and gain a deeper understanding of PIES with each new structure.

7.   Workshop Practice. Teachers practice the structure, role-playing using it in their classroom, and receiving supportive coaching.

8.   Individual Accountability. A plan is created in which each participant is held accountable for practice of the structure. These plans can include journals, peer coaching, videos, and/or visitations.

The most powerful way to teach structures is experientially. After teachers experience and process a structure, they can see immediately how they could incorporate it into their existing teaching practices. Building a repertoire of structures is the first major aim of the structural approach. A second aim is to provide teachers with fluency in the basic principles central to the structural approach.

## Basic Principles

### What Are PIES?

The acronym PIES stands for the four basic principles of cooperative learning in the structural approach: Positive Interdependence, Individual Accountability, Equal Participation, and Simultaneous Interaction.[3] To the extent these basic principles are in place in a classroom, students tutor and encourage each other, carry out assignments, participate equally, and participate actively much of the time. In short, when the four basic principles of cooperative learning (PIES) are incorporated in a lesson, learning and other positive outcomes are more likely to occur. However, if the principles are left out, positive outcomes will not necessarily occur.

The presence of each of the four basic principles can be determined by asking simple questions that focus on the presence or absence of the critical attributes of each principle.

*Positive Interdependence.* To determine if positive interdependence exists, we ask: *Does a gain for one student result in a gain for another?* If so, two powerful outcomes result: Students are more likely to help and tutor each other (after all, if I help him, I am also helping myself); and students encourage each other, developing peer norms in favor of achievement. Whenever we can answer "Yes!" to this first critical question, we know positive interdependence exists.

To distinguish strong from weak positive interdependence we ask a second question: *Is cooperation necessary?* If cooperation is necessary, that is, if students cannot reach their goals without working together at least part of the time, strong positive interdependence exists. When strong positive interdependence exists, students perceive the need to co-operate. Strong positive interdependence can be created in a variety of ways, including division of labor and team goals that cannot be reached by one student working alone. The sense of a shared goal that no one student can reach alone provides a powerful sense of interdependence which motivates cooperation, tutoring, and mutual encouragement.

If a gain for one is likely to result in a gain for another, but students can accomplish their goals without help, then cooperation is not necessary and we have weak positive interdependence. Where there is weak positive interdependence cooperation, tutoring, and mutual encouragement are not as likely as when there is strong positive interdependence.

*Individual Accountability.* The presence of the second principle is determined by asking: *Is individual public performance required?* If students are required to show someone else (a fellow student, a team, the class, the teacher) what they can do on their own, they are individually accountable for their learning. Individual accountability can be created by a quiz, by students asking each other questions, or by an individual performance in which there is an audience, even of one other. When students take a quiz they know their teacher will know what they have and have not learned—thus they feel they will be held accountable for their learning. When individual accountability exists, students are motivated to learn.

*Equal Participation.* As the name suggests, the critical question here is, *How equal is the participation among classmates?* Equal participation can be created by assigning each student an equal part of a project, by calling on all students equally, and by structuring learning tasks so that everyone has the same amount of participation time. Understanding the Equality Principle leads to restructuring of cooperative learning. For example, if a teacher calls for a Team Discussion, it is likely that some but not all students will discuss the topic, or at least there will be a very unequal amount of "air time" for each student. In contrast, if a teacher calls for a RoundRobin, each student in turn will share. To take another example, a Pair Discussion often leads to the brighter or more verbal student doing most or all of the talking. A Timed Pair Share in which each student has a minute to share his or her ideas while the other listens, leads to equal participation. As teachers learn to respect the Equality Principle, they begin to substitute Timed Pair Shares for Pair Discussions and RoundRobins for Team Discussions, at least part of the time.

*Simultaneous Interaction.* With this fourth principle we ask, *How many students are active participants at any one moment?* The greater number of active participants at any one moment, the greater the amount of learning. The transformation that occurs in a classroom by applying the simultaneity principle is dramatic: If we want each student to be an active participant sharing his or her ideas for one minute, it would take over 30 minutes if we call on the students one at a time; four minutes if we have them share for a minute each in groups of four; and only two minutes if they share with a partner. The time savings occurs because students are participating simultaneously. At any one moment only one out of 30 talks in the whole-class structure; one out of four in a team discussion; and one out of two in a pair discussion. Simultaneous interaction can be created by using teams rather than whole class structures, and by using pair work within teams.

## Why Teach PIES?

Understanding and using PIES is empowering. The teaching and learning of PIES allows teachers to derive definitive answers to important issues such as optimum team size, and whether to use group grades. Understanding PIES empowers teachers to select the most appropriate structures; deepens the understanding and commitment of teachers to structures and cooperative learning; provides a framework to engage in a powerful ongoing self-evaluation and improvement process; and provides a common language and value system allowing teachers and administrators to communicate effectively about cooperative learning.

## Addressing Critical Issues

An understanding of PIES allows teachers to derive definitive answers to important issues in cooperative learning. Lets examine two examples.

*The Team Size Issue.* The principle of positive interdependence indicates that we often want students working together toward a common goal. An issue naturally arises: how many students should work together on each team?

The simultaneity principle suggests that we most often choose teams of four. If we form teams of six, at any one moment during a RoundRobin or a Team Discussion only one out of six students in the class is an active participant. In contrast, with teams of four, one-fourth rather than one-sixth of the students in the class become active participants at any one moment. (In teams of six, it takes six minutes to do a RoundRobin; with teams of four, it takes only four minutes to accomplish the same task.)

With regard to the basic principles, teams of three or five are not as good as teams of four because, during pair work in a team of three, one student is left out, violating the equality principle. A team of five reduces the opportunity for equal participation compared to a team of four. Leaving any one student out violates the equal participation principle. If we reduced team size to just two members, we would lose much of the positive interdependence that occurs as a group interacts. The simultaneity principle, however, tells us we should do pair work often because it is optimum for maximizing the number of students active at any one moment—one out of every two. To best satisfy the basic principles, we select teams of four and often have students pair up within their teams to work in pairs.

*The Group Grade Issue.* If we assign students a project and grade the project so that each student on the team receives the same grade, based on the quality of the project, we violate the principle of individual accountability. If we give out grades based on the quality of the team's end-product without assessing who did what, there is no individual public performance required of all students. In fact, in that kind of situation students often elect to have one or two high achievers on the team do most or all of the work. Without required individual public performance, there is no motivation for some students to learn or achieve.[4] Individual grades should be based exclusively on what individual students do alone. Individual accountability can be created for team projects or team reports in a number of ways, including: having students take an individual quiz, write an individual essay on what they learned, create a contribution to their portfolio, or create an individual performance evaluation. Note: It is fine to give groups feedback (written or oral, from teacher, class, or other teams) on group projects or presentations, but feedback to groups should not be confused with evaluation of individuals and should not contribute to an individual's grade.

There are other reasons as well that we should never grade individual students based on the performance of their group (Kagan, 1995). Group grades communicate to students a message opposite that which ought to be communicated: When we use group grades, we communicate to students that their grade is not just a function of how hard they work or how much they learn. We communicate to students that to an important extent their grade is out of their own control; we give them reason not to try.

Group grades are simply unfair. Two identical students—identical with regard to their ability, effort, and performance—will receive different grades, depending on who their teammates happen to be. This results in report card grades which are partially a function of chance rather than ability or effort, a situation which is indefensible.

Choosing Appropriate Structures

There are dozens of cooperative learning structures that have been defined and described in detail (Kagan, 1993; Kagan, Robertson, & Kagan, 1995; Robertson, Kagan, Kagan, and Warner, 1995). A knowledge of PIES enables teachers to distinguish unstructured group work from cooperative learning and allows teachers to select the most appropriate structure for the given learning objective.

Group Work Versus Cooperative Learning

Simply placing students in a group and telling them to work together on some curriculum problem without providing a structure for the students to work within is group work. It does not ensure positive interdependence or individual accountability and does not necessarily result in equal participation and simultaneous interaction. In the structural approach we distinguish cooperative learning from group work through PIES; we take PIES as the defining characteristics of cooperative learning. In the structural approach, if any one of the four basic principles is not implemented, students are not doing cooperative learning. Without structuring the interaction of students, it is unlikely that cooperative learning will result. If a teacher wants to implement the basic principles, choosing group work is wishful thinking. The basic principles will not necessarily be implemented if we do not structure for them.

Pair Discussion Versus RallyRobin

How can teachers select the most appropriate structure for a given topic? Let's contrast two structures: Pair Discussion and RallyRobin. If we call for pairs to discuss a topic, and examine the interaction carefully, we will discover that in many pairs one person is doing all the talking, violating the principle of equal participation. There is nothing in the structure of a pair discussion that creates equal participation. It is a structure, therefore, that should be used only occasionally. Often, too, if we ask students to repeat the ideas suggested by their partners following a pair discussion, we find they have not been listening well. We can remedy both of these problems by calling for a RallyRobin in the pairs, with a RallyRecorder: students repeatedly take turns suggesting ideas (equal participation), each one recording the idea suggested by his or her partner (individual accountability for listening). A Timed Pair Share (each student speaks for one minute to a partner) followed by students recording their partner's ideas is another structure that creates equal participation and individual accountability for listening.

## Teams Report Versus Teams Compare

For another contrast, let's contrast Teams Report and Teams Compare. The teams have ideas to share. If we call on one team at a time to share, a structure called Teams Report, we violate the simultaneity principle because there is only one active participant in the classroom at any one moment—the one student who speaks for the team. Instead we might use one of the many simultaneous sharing structures, a Teams Compare, in which teams pair off, and each team in turn presents to the partner team. When using simultaneous sharing structures, at any one moment there are many active participants, not just a few, and everyone shares in a fraction of the time it would take if they did so one at a time.

## Deepening Understanding and Commitment to Cooperative Learning

Structures are the perfect starting point for teachers getting into cooperative learning. They are easy to learn, fun to use, and have proven very successful. Without an understanding of PIES, however, structures may be seen as trivial techniques. An understanding of PIES provides the rationale for learning and using structures. Established cooperative learning structures such as Pairs Compare, Inside/Outside Circle, and Three-Step Interview (Kagan, 1993) each incorporate all four of the PIES principles. PIES are "built-into" all of the basic structures teachers learn in the structural approach. Teachers learn to avoid using group or pair discussions because those structures result in unequal participation and a lack of individual accountability. Because all four of the principles are embedded in strong cooperative learning structures, implementation of the principles is made easy as teachers master strong cooperative learning structures: a teacher needs only to use strong cooperative learning structures in order to ensure that principles are implemented. The teacher who sees that structures are tools for making PIES happen shows a deeper commitment to the structures and will be less likely to modify a structure in a way that reduces the implementation of PIES.

## Self-Evaluation and Self-Improvement

The PIES Analysis can be used in many ways, to help in the coaching and/or evaluation process. In the structural approach, we use a PIES Analysis as an aid in self-evaluation—as part of an ongoing self-improvement process. PIES becomes most powerful when it becomes part of an ongoing self-evaluation process that teachers engage in during a lesson. If a cooperative learning lesson is not going well, often it is because one of the four basic principles is not being implemented. As we become fluent in PIES, we have a framework for evaluating and adjusting as we teach. Fluency in PIES is facilitated if teachers frequently sit down after a lesson and ask themselves the four critical questions. Once this process becomes habitual, the PIES Analysis becomes internalized so that at any one moment during the teaching process the teacher is adjusting the lesson to maximize positive interdependence, individual accountability, equal participation, and simultaneous interaction. As this process takes over RallyRobins begin to replace Pair Discussions; Pairs Compare replaces Group Discussions; and Simultaneous Sharing replaces Sequential Sharing. The classroom becomes more active, and the positive outcomes of cooperative learning are shared more equally among all students.

*Common Language.* The PIES framework provides a common language and value system that allows teachers and administrators to communicate effectively about cooperative learning. Teachers and administrators can easily and objectively evaluate lessons and provide concrete suggestions for improving cooperative learning.

## How PIES Are Taught

Staff training on PIES, like structures, is experientially based. During training, teachers experience a structure or structures and then perform a PIES Analysis. A PIES Analysis is simply an examination of the structure for its inclusion or exclusion of the basic principles of cooperative learning. To serve as an example, we will do a PIES Analysis of a traditional classroom structure and one of a cooperative structure (this analysis explains why cooperative learning produces outcomes superior to traditional approaches). To do a PIES Analysis, we answer the basic questions associated with each of the four basic principles.

## PIES in the Traditional Classroom

A common traditional classroom structure is the whole-class question-answer scenario: a teacher is checking for understanding following a lecture or homework assignment. First the teacher asks a question, some students raise their hands, the teacher calls on one student, the others lower their hands, the student called upon gives an answer; finally the teacher either praises or provides a correction opportunity.

*Positive Interdependence.* There is some positive interdependence in the traditional classroom because a correct answer by the student who answers may help other students cement their own learning. But there is also some negative interdependence, since a gain for one is a loss for others: As the students compete to be called upon by the teacher, a gain for one (being called upon) is a loss for the others (missing the opportunity to be called upon). That is why the non-selected students make a sound of disappointment as they lower their hands after the teacher has called upon a classmate. Further, because students who raise their hands want the opportunity for teacher and peer approval for their answers, as well as the opportunity to formulate and articulate their own thoughts, some students are actually glad when a fellow student misses a question. A loss for one student is a potential gain for another, because when a student fails, other students gain a renewed opportunity to be called upon and receive approval for their answer. The traditional structure sets one student against another and creates peer norms against achievement. The student who always gets the answers right often is labeled ("nerd," "geek," "brown nose") and ostracized by the others. They realize that the gains of the high achiever decrease the probability of their own recognition and participation.

*Individual Accountability.* Students in the traditional classroom know there is no required individual public performance. They know that if they do not wish to be held accountable, they need only not raise their hand. In this situation, some students can and do "drop out" mentally. They sit in class, but know it is safe to pay little attention to the game being played between the teacher and the higher achieving students.

*Equal Participation.* A subset of high-achieving students almost always raises their hands while the lowest achieving students seldom or never do. The traditional classroom thus violates the equality principle.

*Simultaneous Interaction.* In a classroom of 30 students, only one out of 30 is an active participant at any one moment as the teacher calls on students one at a time. Because students are speaking one at a time, to give each student in this setting one minute of active participation time takes far more than half an hour because it takes time to ask each question, listen to each answer, and to provide approval or correction following each answer. To have students speak one at a time violates the simultaneity principle and leads to an unacceptably low level of active participation.

PIES in the Cooperative Classroom

If the goal is to check for understanding, review, and create some active involvement, the traditional whole class question-answer structure is but one of many possible ways to structure interaction among students. A favorite cooperative learning alternative is Numbered Heads Together.

The students in teams each have a number. After a question is posed by the teacher, the students "put their heads together" to talk over the question and make sure everyone on the team has an answer. Following the "heads together" step, the teacher randomly calls a number, and the student with that number shares her/his response. Sometimes the sharing is by one student only; sometimes by all the students with that number, as in a Blackboard Share (one student from each team simultaneously writes a response on the blackboard). A range of variations on Numbered Heads Together is possible (Kagan & Robertson, 1992).

*Positive Interdependence.* If the structure is Numbered Heads Together, students know that if a teammate has a good thought or answer, it will help the whole team during the Heads Together time of the structure as well as during the response phase. Thus a gain for one is a gain for others and teammates hope each one achieves well. Students know that when a number is called, a good performance by their teammate with that number will reflect well on their team. Therefore, they encourage and tutor each other during the "heads together" time. Peer norms develop favoring achievement and helping.

*Individual Accountability.* Each student knows he or she will be called upon randomly one fourth of the time, and at that point teammates cannot help. Thus a required individual performance is "built into" the structure.

*Equal Participation.* In Numbered Heads Together, each student's number is called about equally, leading to an equal opportunity for response. Because students have had a chance to discuss their answers in teams before being made individually accountable, they seldom elect not to raise their hands. Participation is not entirely equal, however, because during the "heads together" time of Numbered Heads Together, some students might be more active than others. Nevertheless, overall the participation in Numbered Heads Together is far more equal than in the traditional whole-class question-answer structure.

*Simultaneous Interaction.* If teams of four are used, at least one out of four students is an active participant at any one moment as the team discusses their thoughts. If simultaneous response modes are used (such as slates or response cards) in the last step of Numbered Heads Together, simultaneously one student from each team responds so there are eight students rather than one actively involved (in a class of 32).

## Staff Development Models

The learning of structures and PIES can occur in many contexts, including one-day workshops, curriculum-specific cooperative learning workshops, and multi-day institutes of various kinds. Wide-scale implementation, however, does not result without a differentiated, long-term site-based plan.

### Model I. Individual Trainings

Although wide-spread implementation occurs only with a multifaceted site-based plan, individual teachers profit from attending workshops and training institutes. If their school is not involved in a site-based plan, teachers are encouraged to find at least one other grade-alike or content-alike partner so that they can coach and support each other between trainings.

### Model II. Site-Based Trainings

Each school or district creates its own training and implementation plan. Some districts have coordinated efforts across schools (adopting similar training plans across sites, with training teams from different sites meeting to plan trainings, divide the labor, and coordinate efforts) whereas other districts have encouraged unique and different training plans for each site. Some of the most important elements of successful peer-based trainings have been as follows.

*Three-Year Plan.* Sites adopt a three year plan in which a site-based training team commits to three years. In the first year site based facilitators learn the six keys, and a range of structures well. In the second year they lead a Structure-A-Month Club (SAM Club), described below, at the site. In the third year they facilitate new leaders who assume responsibility for the continuance of the SAM Club.

*Site-Level Facilitators.* Training of teachers at a site in co-op structures and PIES is led by facilitators (teachers, resource teachers, or administrators) who have had at least one year of training and practice in the structural approach. Ideally, the facilitator team has made a three year commitment, the first year of which is dedicated to acquiring competence in the structures and in the ability to train others in the structures. Competence is fostered in part by borrowing classrooms at various grade levels to practice new structures. In that way, in the following year when a Structure-A-Month club at the site is instituted, the site level facilitators can train with genuine authority.

*Structure-A-Month Clubs.* One of the most powerful components of staff development in the structural approach is the Structure-A-Month Club or SAM Club as it is called at some sites. Teachers at a site all concentrate on adding the same new structure to their repertoire each month. Many teachers may use far more than one structure that month, but each teacher in the Structure-A-Month Club makes a commitment to practice the same structure each month and to problem solve, share successes, model for each other, and develop and share variations on the same structure. Because all teachers are adopting the same structure, it provides them with a common experience and language, contributing to the culture of the school as a cooperative learning school.

The assumption is that any new instructional practice must be applied many times before unconscious competence is acquired. If the new structure is practiced enough during the month, it will never be forgotten, and when the second structure is adopted the first will continue to be used. Thus over the school year, a number of structures will be added to each teacher's "toolbox of structures."

Model III. Site-Based, Expert-Assisted Trainings

Many administrators want each teacher to receive initial training from experts in the field rather than from peers. One solution has been to send members of a site to workshops or institutes as a kick-off for the site-based implementation plan. Another solution has been to bring in expert trainers for school- and district-wide trainings that are an integral part of the site-based plans. In some cases the expert involvement has been limited to a one-day awareness session to generate interest and support for the site-level plan. In other cases the expert involvement has been very extensive including any number of the following: training in peer coaching, expert coaching of site-based facilitator teams, conducting monthly workshops coordinated with the Structure-A-Month plan, demonstration lessons, leading parent involvement meetings, and special sessions for special groups such as teacher aides and language specialists in schools and districts.

Model IV. District-Wide Trainings

The most impressive implementations of the structural approach as measured by both quality and quantity of implementation have come as a consequence of sophisticated multi-year, multi-faceted, district-wide plans. These plans have taken different forms, including in some cases monthly expert-led workshops attended by teachers from various sites, with peer and administrative coaching and support between workshops. Some districts have full- or part-time expert staff dedicated to training and supporting training in the structural approach. In several very large districts in the United States and Canada, after several years of training in the structural approach, most teachers use a range of co-op structures; perhaps more importantly, they are continuing to expand their repertoires through within-district trainings.

## Restructuring Staff Meetings

Schools deeply involved in the structural approach have applied the structures and PIES to restructuring staff meetings. The typical staff meeting is plagued by the same problems as the traditional classroom with lack of positive interdependence among staff, lack of individual accountability for participation and contributions, unequal participation, and lack of simultaneous interaction.

After applying the structural approach, staff meetings little resemble what they once were. Staff use classbuilding and teambuilding structures to build positive interdependence, and teams are formed to allow more equal and simultaneous interaction. The staff meeting becomes a powerful work place in which various carefully selected teams work simultaneously, each toward the goal it has chosen. The staff members feel empowered, acting as active program developers rather than passive pawns in a plan developed by others (see Ellis, chapter 13 of this book, for more discussion).

## Conclusion

PIES and structures are two distinguishing features of the structural approach to cooperative learning. They go hand-in-hand: understanding and implementation of one facilitates an understanding and implementation of the other. Structures are methods to ensure that PIES take place in a classroom. Implementation of PIES and structures ensures good cooperative learning and, therefore, a range of positive outcomes in the classroom. PIES and structures constitute a cooperative learning curriculum for teachers. Because the structures are discrete, they facilitate both the teaching and the learning of cooperative learning for teachers as well as students.

## Notes

1. We are greatful to Laurie Robertson, Director, Kagan Cooperative Learning Consulting, for her helpful input. Laurie has been responsible for developing and implementing the Expert-Assisted and District-Wide training models described in the last section of this chapter. Laurie has been personally responsible for training more teachers and trainers in the structural approach than anyone.

2. The structures described in this chapter were developed by the first author and are explained in depth in his book, *Cooperative Learning* (Kagan 1993).

3. The notion that there are four basic principles of cooperative learning was first developed by Miguel and Spencer Kagan, and set out in their book, *Advanced Cooperative Learning* (Kagan & Kagan, 1992). The Acronym PIES was first developed by participants in the 1993 Facilitators Institute in Newport Beach, California.

## References

Davidson, Neil. (1994.) Cooperative and collaborative learning: An integrative perspective. In Thousand, Jacqueline; Villa, Richard; and Nevin, Ann. *Creativity and collaborative learning: A practical guide to empowering students and teachers.* Baltimore, MD: Paul H. Brookes Co., Pp. 13–30.

Kagan, Miguel; Robertson, Laurie; & Kagan, Spencer. (1995) *Cooperative learning structures for classbuilding.* Kagan Cooperative Learning, San Juan Capistrano, CA.

Kagan, Spencer. (1993) *Cooperative learning.* Kagan Cooperative Learning, San Juan Capistrano, CA.

Kagan, Spencer. (1995) Group grades miss the mark. *Educational Leadership,* 52 (8), 68–71.

Kagan, Spencer. (1989–90) The structural approach to cooperative learning. *Educational Leadership,* 47(4), 12–15.

Kagan, S. & Kagan, M. (1992) *Advanced cooperative learning.* Kagan Cooperative Learning, San Juan Capistrano, CA.

Kagan, S. & Kagan, M. (1994) The structural approach: 6 keys to cooperative learning. In Sharan, Shlomo. *Handbook of Cooperative Learning Methods.* Greenwood Press: Westport, Connecticut, 115–133.

Kagan, S. & Robertson, L.(1992) *The co-op facilitators' handbook.* Kagan Cooperative Learning, San Juan Capistrano, CA.

Kagan, S. & Robertson, L. (1992) *Numbered heads together: The structure in depth.* A Video Production of Kagan Cooperative Learning, San Juan Capistrano, CA. 1992.

Robertson, Laurie; Kagan, Miguel; Kagan, Spencer; & Warner, Liz. (1995) *Cooperative learning: The instructor's manual.* Kagan Cooperative Learning, San Juan Capistrano, CA. 1995.

Sharan, Shlomo. (1994) *Handbook of cooperative learning methods.* Greenwood Press: Westport, Connecticut, 1994.

# 6

## Beyond the Workshop: Evidence from Complex Instruction

### Rachel Lotan, Elizabeth Cohen, and Christopher Morphew

When sociologists of education think about staff development for cooperative learning, they begin, not with a discussion of feelings, attitudes, or beliefs, but with an analysis of the type of groupwork that the teacher, the principal, and the staff developer have set out to implement. Sociologists then continue by examining the organizational factors that promote or inhibit implementation. As sociologists of education, we have two major goals in writing this chapter. First, we wish to illustrate the utility of a sociological approach to the professional development of teachers. Second, we would like to share with other staff developers our research findings on the relationship between the implementation of complex instruction, and systematic follow-up and feedback from staff developers as well as support from principals and colleagues. Complex instruction is a pedagogical approach in which groupwork is an essential component.

Cooperative learning methods vary from simple to complex, from limited in scope to demanding in effort and resources. When instructional methods are complex and demanding, they cannot be reduced to a recipe or to step-by-step instructions. Rather, teachers need to develop more general, theoretical ways to understand what their task has become; as they learn to implement these more demanding methods, teachers need someone who observes their work with an expert eye and who provides sound feedback. Furthermore, complex and demanding instruction requires the active involvement of colleagues and tangible support from the principal. It is neither possible, nor is it advisable to work with teachers in isolation, without considering the context of their school.

More and Less Demanding Methods of Cooperative Learning

For an analysis of various methods of cooperative learning, let us start with the nature of the tasks that the group of students are carrying out. In the less demanding methods, groups are doing the same task and students go through the task in roughly the same manner and at about the same pace. Such tasks often have one right answer; usually there are a limited number of ways to arrive at that answer. Frequently, these tasks are paper-and-pencil or reading-and-discussion; they come from textbooks, worksheets, or similar parts of the standard, available curriculum. They do not require a variety of materials, sources of information, or manipulatives. The teaching objectives are typically comprehension of text, application of an algorithm, or mastery of factual material and information. Collaborative seatwork is an example of such a relatively simple method: the teacher might ask groups of students to solve a simple math problem, to answer a comprehension question on a reading assignment, or to go over the material that has just been taught. Buzz groups, like collaborative seatwork, have a similarly simple structure in that all groups address the same question. Even when the groups do not come up with the same answer, they typically proceed at a uniform pace, without the need for additional materials or special preparation by the teacher.

In contrast to these routine tasks are intrinsically interesting, open-ended, discovery-oriented, investigative tasks—those that involve innovative problem-solving, original and creative thinking, mechanical ingenuity, artistic refinement, dramatic poise, or musical delivery. Such tasks require a variety of resources, manipulatives for science experiments, visuals, audio or video tapes, and other primary sources of information. When tasks are varied and open-ended, groups proceed by different paths, using a variety of materials and a wide range of problem-solving strategies. These demanding, multi-dimensional tasks are true group tasks—one person cannot possibly complete the job by himself or herself in a limited amount of time, i.e., one or even two class periods. With true group tasks, it becomes necessary for people to exchange ideas, propose alternatives, investigate possible solutions, and actively contribute to the work of the group.

Rarely can such rich group tasks be found in conventional curricular materials. They need to be either expressly created for cooperative learning, as with complex instruction or, as in group investigation, the students, with the assistance of the teacher, develop a particular topic for their group.

More demanding tasks are characteristic of more demanding methods of cooperative learning. In such methods, when the teaching objective is the development of higher-order thinking skills, the developers try to foster group interaction to support the social construction of knowledge. Research on complex instruction has consistently shown that under conditions of a true group task with an "ill-structured solution," the extent to which group members talk and work together is directly predictive of learning gains (Cohen, 1994a). Interaction is not a direct predictor of learning gains during collaborative seatwork (Webb, 1983; 1991).

Differences in characteristics of the learning tasks produce marked differences in the role of the teacher while the groups are operating. When student tasks are less demanding, the teacher may retain the role of direct supervisor, diligently checking to see that all groups are completing the tasks in a timely and efficient manner. The main challenge for the teacher is to make sure that those who need help do indeed receive it, and that those who know the answers explain them to those who do not.

In contrast, when the groups are working on more challenging and uncertain tasks, direct supervision becomes impractical. In this situation, the teacher needs to delegate authority to the groups so that the members can go about finding a solution to their problem in their own way. Even when the students make mistakes, there is no need for direct intervention—for the group learns from its mistakes.

With these complex tasks, if interaction is the key to learning, then it is incumbent upon the teacher to foster and to optimize the interaction in the groups. Interrupting the groups with direct instruction or hovering over the groups will cut down on the interaction (Cohen, 1994b; Cohen, Lotan, & Leechor, 1989). Instead of directly supervising, the teacher listens and observes, decides whether or not intervention is inevitable for groups that are floundering, looks at group behavior and collects information on intellectual and social problems as well as on ways in which the groups may have solved these problems. When the objective is the development of higher-order thinking skills, the teacher also has a challenging intellectual agenda. Through pre-training and group processing, the teacher prepares students to operate on a high cognitive level, to explicate their ideas, to deliberate, to consider additional perspectives, and to justify their arguments.

## Nature of the Task and Role of the Teacher in Complex Instruction

Complex instruction uses a demanding and non-routine type of cooperative learning as an essential component of its set of instructional strategies recommended for teaching in heterogeneous classrooms. In complex instruction, each small group of students works on a different task, using different resource materials or manipulatives.

These learning tasks are specifically designed for teachers who use complex instruction. Completion of these tasks by the students requires many different intellectual abilities: hypothesizing, estimating, explaining, analyzing, drawing, measuring, expressing one's ideas dramatically, and using language persuasively are just a few of them. Tasks are also open-ended and uncertain so as to stimulate and enhance the interaction; they are organized around a big idea or a central concept. Because the goal of instruction is a deep understanding of abstract concepts and the development of higher-order thinking skills, rotations through the different tasks provide students with multiple opportunities to grasp the central concept or the big idea.

Instead of the teacher acting as supervisor, constantly telling students what to do and how to proceed, the teacher delegates authority to the students and students take responsibility for completing the task. Each student plays a different role in the group (e.g., facilitator, reporter, materials manager, harmonizer, safety officer) and these roles rotate so that eventually each and every student plays each and every role. Cooperative norms learned by the students in an initial, skill-building phase, help them to assume responsibility for themselves and for others in their group. Teachers hold students accountable for creating a group product as well as for completing their individual reports (for a detailed description of complex instruction, see Cohen and Lotan (1997).

When the teacher delegates authority, she or he does so by distributing activity cards that contain instructions for the task, by not hovering over groups, by holding groups accountable for the group product and individuals responsible for playing their roles and using the cooperative norms, and by insisting on the completion of individual reports. Intervening only when absolutely necessary, the teacher can now turn her attention to stimulating and extending students' thinking, and making connections. Most importantly, the teacher equalizes participation among members by treating status problems that arise in groups. For example, the teacher may observe a group that is following the lead of Susan, a popular class member. However, Susan has paid no attention to the activity card and the group is quite confused. In the meantime, Luis, who is totally neglected by his peers, quietly reads the activity card and thoughtfully assembles the materials to build a solid structure. After standing by and carefully observing the group for a while, the teacher intervenes by pointing out that Luis is doing something very useful: he is following the diagram on the card, moving from diagram to real structure, an important intellectual skill and one that makes him a key resource for the group. In doing so, the teacher is using a status treatment: she assigns competence (for more detail on status treatments, see Cohen 1994b). There is no standard way of playing this teacher role; under no circumstances can it be reduced to a set of routine procedures.

Relationship Between Task Complexity and Role of the Teacher

Sociologically speaking, when cooperative learning is a complex and demanding classroom technology, the teacher is constantly making non-routine decisions. Rather than following a pre-formulated plan or set of directions, the teacher's actions depend on careful observation and consideration of multiple factors, including the underlying theory of what makes groups work; how students learn difficult new skills and novel ideas in group settings; how status problems operate to impede interaction and learning, and how to treat these problems.

These analytical distinctions between methods do not imply that there are better and worse ways of doing cooperative learning. Which model teachers use depends on their teaching objectives; highly-skilled teachers who possess rich pedagogical repertoires use different models at different times. Moreover, the distinctions are not of the "either-or" variety. Many versions of cooperative learning would fall somewhere in the middle on the continuum of complexity we have just described.

The central point of this analysis is that as learning tasks become more uncertain and demanding for students, teachers need to use new and different strategies. These strategies are not learned through a program of routine, step-by step responses; they reflect reliance upon a more abstract and profound body of knowledge. Like an engineer who is solving a technical problem, these understandings enable the teacher to make non-routine, analytical decisions by taking into account different alternatives, immediate outcomes, and long-term consequences (Lotan, 1985). For example, after observing the students in a particular group, the teacher might decide to push and deepen their learning by making a connection to another situation or context, to a previous unit or activity; he or she might decide to reinforce cooperative behaviors or to comment on the use of roles. The teacher might decide to address the group as a whole or provide feedback to an individual student. Finally, the teacher might decide to move on to the next group without saying anything at all. The implementation of these new strategies and understandings will require extensive practice and systematic feedback, much more than is available in an average workshop or in-service training without follow-up in the classroom.

Demanding Cooperative Learning Methods and School Organization

These features of the more demanding cooperative learning methods have clear implications for the school as an organization.

Groupwork that is dependent on an array of manipulatives, special curricular materials, or library sources necessitates both money and help with acquisition, organization, and storage. Just as the uncertainty of the task for students requires that they talk and work together, the uncertainty around implementation of a complex classroom technology requires that teachers have the time to talk and work together as well. Teachers need release time for planning, for reviewing their understanding of the subject matter, and for practical problem-solving. Thus, the principal and the other teachers of the school must participate in staff development so that work arrangements of the school change to accommodate this new, more challenging method of instruction.

## Staff Development for Complex Instruction

Our model of staff development consists of a two-week workshop in the summer, a follow-up day in mid-January, and three individual, formative feedback meetings between the teacher and a staff developer during the academic year. Data for the feedback are collected through systematic observations of the teachers' classrooms, conducted prior to the meetings.

### Initial Workshop

The sessions of the summer workshop provide opportunities for the teachers for active learning, for developing a conceptual understanding of the underlying theory and research on complex instruction, and for making decisions based on a healthy combination of theory and practice. During the first week, teachers learn about the theoretical principles and the empirical findings in complex instruction classrooms; they also experience the skill-building exercises they will use with their students. Instruction during the workshop mirrors complex instruction in the classroom. Generally, after a brief introduction to the concepts, the teachers break into groups to practice what they've just learned. The groups present their products in a wrap-up, and the instructor provides feedback and makes connections to the central concepts.

During the second week of the workshop, the practicum week, teachers experiment with the new strategies by planning and carrying out a complex instruction lesson in a classroom situation, with school-aged students, with micro-teaching, or if staff development takes place during the school year, in the teacher's own classroom. While the teachers implement the lesson, a staff developer observes the lesson using the observation instruments and another staff member makes a videotape of the lesson, collecting data to be used for the teacher to consider while reflecting upon her teaching. The observations and the videotape serve as opportunities for the teachers to analyze real-life, messy classroom situations, identify missed opportunities and practice recognizing groupwork situations that demand special attention. While at first these are frightening, even threatening experiences for the teachers, they gradually become accustomed to "opening the classroom door," interacting with colleagues and honestly talking about their difficulties with implementing new ways of teaching. As one teacher commented: "At first, I was nervous a bit, but came to enjoy the opportunity to talk about myself and my teaching. We discussed the fact that this is the first opportunity to really talk about teaching. The annual principal observation required is a 15-minute perfunctory visit. I think there should be more of this." (Interview, June 1983).

Unlike much staff development, theory and research play a central role in our work with the teachers. For example, we emphasize our research findings about the positive relationship between interaction and learning, on the one hand, and the negative relationship between direct supervision and interaction on the other. Teachers come to understand the importance of fostering interaction and they are careful not to make any adjustments that would cut down on the amount of student interaction. Teachers have considerable autonomy to make changes and adaptations as they see necessary—as long as these do not infringe upon the level of student interaction and as long as they continue paying attention to status problems.

The day-long meeting in the winter provides the teachers and the staff with an opportunity to revisit and further reinforce the strategies for treating status problems, introduced and dealt with extensively during the summer. We found that it takes about three to four months for teachers to become comfortable with managing and organizing the classroom for complex instruction: introducing students to the cooperative norms and to the roles, delegating authority, and having students understand and get used to the routines of groupwork. Only after they reach a certain comfort level are teachers ready to tackle the most difficult challenge of groupwork: working towards equalizing the participation of high- and low-status students. On the follow-up day in winter, teachers also share with the staff and with their colleagues some of the inventions and adaptations they developed to meet the needs of their particular student body.

Follow-up in the Classroom

Probably the most exacting and expensive feature of our model of staff development is the consistent follow-up in the classroom during the academic year. It is based on the ideas about authority and evaluation developed by Dornbusch and Scott (1975), who showed that if workers perceive evaluations of their work as soundly based, they will put out more effort to obtain more favorable evaluations. Important dimensions of a soundly-based evaluation are clarity and legitimacy of the criteria and the standards upon which the evaluations are based, and adequacy of the sampling of the worker's performance by the evaluator. We also use the work of Gonzales (1982) to argue that specificity of the feedback helps the teacher to perceive the evaluation as soundly based. Feedback is specific when the teachers know exactly what they have done well and what they need to do to improve their implementation. "Mrs. Putney was observed and received feedback. She remarked: 'I wouldn't have minded if the feedback sessions had been more frequent and earlier in the year. They were extremely useful because they were so specific. I got a very clear picture of what was going on. I now have a much clearer idea of what it is that I said at the beginning of the year and how I've changed . . . I can see the same principles apply with us (teachers) and the children. That is, the more specific feedback you get, the better you understand'" (Ellis and Lotan, 1997).

We consider these feedback sessions as a teaching and learning device, intended to further teachers' conceptual understanding and knowledge about complex instruction. These sessions are opportunities to diagnose problems that arise during implementation, to propose solutions and then evaluate them, to reinforce the linkages between the theoretical framework and the research findings on the one hand, and the teacher's actual classroom experiences on the other. This is how one teacher described the process: "All the pieces of the puzzle don't make sense at first. But afterwards, when you go out and implement it, it makes sense . . . Feedback is important so you know whether you are doing what the program is asking you to do and whether children are reaping the benefits. And you are reminded of some things you could do to better implement it" (Ellis and Lotan, 1991).

Ideally, we aim to meet with each teacher for three feedback sessions, each based on a set of systematic observations collected during at least three separate classroom visits. While conducting these observations, trained observers use two kinds of instruments: one, the whole class instrument, is used to record the activity patterns of the students while at the learning stations, and the other, the teacher observation instrument, to record categories of teacher talk either during orientation and/or wrap-up or during groupwork time. The following categories of teacher talk are recorded on the teacher observation instrument: facilitates students' work, disciplines, informs or defines, asks factual questions, stimulates higher-order thinking, makes connections, gives specific feedback, talks about multiple abilities, assigns competence, talks about roles, talks about cooperation and norms (for an example of these observation instruments see Cohen and Lotan (1997), appendices A and B).

One complete set of observations consists of a) six observations of the students using the whole class instruments (two observations are taken during each visit), b) at least 30 minutes (ten minutes per visit) of teacher talk during orientation/ wrap-up, and c) at least 30 minutes of teacher talk while students are in groups. The data collected are summarized in bar charts and they serve as the basis for discussion and problem-solving during the feedback session. Ms. C.A., an elementary school teacher remarked: "The feedback sessions were helpful because I saw a lot of the problems I was having. I was beginning to feel real frustrated and I could see in the graphs why: because my facilitation was way too high, and talking and thinking was too low. I was beginning to facilitate too much instead of letting them do their own job. So I know it helped me a lot. A real lot." (Interview, 6/86).

Teachers have ample opportunity to interpret these data, and they have the background to do so. After a problem has been identified, the developer and the teacher discuss possible solutions. The bar graphs provide an excellent way for teachers to document and follow their own progress from one feedback session to the next. "The sessions were extremely useful. For example, in my first stage, in the very first stage of the process of implementing the philosophy, I was very concerned about the management system that I was going to set up, and the structure, and making sure my students understood their roles. So after my first feedback, I observed that I really needed to focus in on multiple abilities, so, okay . . . The graph showed where I was putting in a lot of energy and where I needed to now balance it out. In that respect, I was able to see my area of need or where is my next stage . . . There were no discipline problems, and that was wonderful to see. Basically, what it did, it just helped me to actually see what had been done, it reinforced my positive feelings about what was going on, and it helped me to develop a focus point for the next stage." (Interview, 6/86).

The teachers themselves learn how to use the observation instruments during the summer workshop. The instruments are a useful tool for observing colleagues, student teachers, or teacher aides. These same instruments are also used to measure classroom implementation for purposes of research and program evaluation. This is an important component of the feedback process because it provides clarity about the criteria underlying classroom observations. Based on our research, we have established clear standards for gauging the quality of the implementation. For example, we found that in classrooms in which less than 35 percent of the students are observed talking and working together, the average achievement gains are not up to par. Therefore, we advise teachers to refine their management system to be sure and pass this threshold.

## Organizational Support

To participate in our program, schools must send a team that includes teachers and administrators. At least two teachers from a grade level or from the same department should attend the summer workshop together. In some cases, resource teachers or other specialists are part of the team; they can learn how to do classroom observations and can help collect data for feedback.

The principals attend a day-long session in the spring before the summer workshop for the teachers. In this session, principals watch a videotape of parts of a complex instruction lesson, and learn from the program staff and from principals who have had experience with complex instruction what kind of organizational help and instructional leadership is necessary to make the program a success. We urge principals to attend the summer workshop along with the teachers, or at minimum to be present on the days when their faculty are teaching in the practicum. During the workshop, we also arrange special meetings of teachers and administrators from each of the schools, to tackle the practical and logistical problems that the teachers might already have foreseen, such as getting materials, finding adequate space and furniture for teaching or storing materials, or setting aside time for joint planning.

## Research Evidence from Complex Instruction

To find out if a method of staff development is effective one needs to open the door and look into the classroom. As explained above, we collect two kinds of data: a) systematic observations of the teachers' talk before and after groupwork (i.e., during orientation and wrap-up), and while the students are at the learning stations, and b) systematic observations of the students' activities while in groups. For example, to know whether the work with the teacher has been effective in helping her adopt a non-routine role, the staff developer counts the frequency of non-routine behaviors that are essential to the method of cooperative learning he or she wants to implement. In the case of complex instruction, we count the rate per ten minutes of the teacher asking higher-order questions, carrying out status treatments, or making connections. Because our objective is to foster student interaction, we count the number of students talking and working together during groupwork. We found that this measure was the single best predictor of learning gains, both at the elementary and at the middle school level.

To obtain measures of how much organizational support teachers receive, we ask the teachers themselves. (The principal's perceptions might or might not coincide with those of the teachers.) At the end of the academic year, we ask them about different features of the organizational support at their school: for example, how much help they received with acquiring and organizing the materials necessary for complex instruction, how many times the principal visited their classroom to observe the groupwork, and the extent to which other teachers and the principal expected them to follow through and implement complex instruction after the initial workshop.

We also ask the teachers how they felt about the feedback they received from our staff: How clear were the criteria and the standards on which the feedback was based? To what extent was the feedback sufficiently specific so that they knew how to improve their implementation? To what extent did the observers gain an adequate picture of the implementation in their classrooms? We then examine the relationship between these measures of organizational support and features of the implementation of complex instruction in the classroom.

Findings

We have organized the presentation of findings according to important features of cooperative-learning-in-action. We have done so to highlight the ways in which the manner of staff development predicts the character of what goes on in the classroom. The three dimensions we have chosen to emphasize are those that particularly concern staff developers of the more demanding methods of cooperative learning: 1) non-routine behaviors of the teacher, 2) the amount of interaction of students while working in groups, and 3) the amount of time teachers devote to groupwork as well as the number of curriculum units covered during cooperative learning.

The data we are discussing come from classrooms of teachers at the elementary and middle school levels. The population of students at these schools was multiracial and multilingual. All the teachers in our sample experienced the two-week summer workshop and the classroom follow-up. Some of the teachers from the middle school sample were in their second year of implementation at the time that the classroom and questionnaire data were collected. The teachers in the elementary grades were using Finding Out/Descubrimiento, a bilingual (Spanish-English) curriculum designed to develop thinking skills through the application of math and science concepts. (For a more detailed presentation of the data, see Cohen and Lotan (1997), Chapters 14 and 15.)

Non-Routine Behaviors

In earlier research, Lotan (1985) found that a measure of conceptual understanding of the underlying principles that the teacher gained from the summer workshop and through the feedback process, was significantly positively-related to her use of non-routine behaviors during implementation of Finding Out/Descubrimiento and when students worked in groups. These non-routine behaviors included giving specific feedback to individuals and groups, stimulating and extending students' thinking, and treating status problems. Swanson (1993) found that among pre-service teachers, a measure of conceptual understanding dealing with the theory underlying status treatments was a strong predictor of one of the most challenging non-routine behaviors: their ability to implement status treatments in response to a videotaped classroom situation.

Another powerful predictor of non-routine behaviors is our system of feedback to teachers on their classroom implementation. Ellis (1987), and Ellis and Lotan (1997) found that the number of feedback meetings between a teacher and a staff developer predicted the frequency of non-routine behaviors in the classroom of elementary teachers and the number of feedback sessions was positively related to the teacher's level of conceptual understanding.

A central component of complex instruction is the use of status treatments by the teachers. As staff developers, we focus much of our attention and energy on teaching teachers how to identify low-status behavior, how to design multiple-ability orientations, and how to assign competence to low-status students (for a detailed description of status treatments and their consequences, see Cohen, 1994b, and Cohen and Lotan, 1995).

The more soundly based the teachers perceived the feedback system to be, the more frequently we observed them using the status treatments. We also found that teachers who were in their second year of complex instruction had higher rates of using status treatments, suggesting that it may take time before teachers use this skill more frequently. An additional finding confirms the challenge of learning this strategy: teachers who reported working and worrying more about the use of status treatments carried them out more frequently. A final predictor in this analysis was the amount of release time that teachers were given to work on complex instruction: those teachers who reported having had more release time used status treatments more frequently.

In another analysis of the frequency of status treatments, we found evidence of other organizational variables. A climate of expectations that teachers would follow through and implement after initial training was a significant predictor of the use of status treatments. In addition, a measure of the teachers' perception of the adequacy of school resources for implementation of complex instruction (space and furniture, curricular materials, and release time) was also a significant predictor of the use of status treatments.

For a more general analysis of non-routine teaching behaviors at the middle school level, we combined status treatments, talking about students' thinking, and making connections (among activities, among units, and among real-life events and classroom activities) and examined the predictors of this variable. Once again, the climate of expectations and the amount of release time were significant predictors. In this sample of middle school classrooms, we also found that the level of management problems was a negative predictor of the teachers' use of non-routine behaviors. Some of the teachers in the middle school sample clearly had more severe management problems than teachers at the elementary level. These teachers were hardly able to carry out the newer and more pedagogically challenging ways of relating to students. The teachers were too busy trying to get the groups to stay on task, or had given up altogether. Teachers with a higher percentage of students observed off-task showed lower rates of non-routine behaviors.[1]

Do the principal's actions have any direct effects on the teacher's mastery of non-routine behaviors in a classroom innovation? Obviously, the strength of variables such as release time and adequacy of school resources implies the action of the administration in allocating necessary funds and in coordinating release time. Beyond this purely administrative role, some principals act as instructional leaders. They inform themselves about complex instruction by attending the summer workshop; they communicate their expectations to the teachers to follow through and implement complex instruction after the initial workshop; they frequently visit the classrooms of teachers who are in their first year of implementation; they talk with the teachers, trying to be helpful in solving problems.

On the average, elementary school teachers gave more favorable reports on their principals than middle school teachers. Nevertheless, some middle school principals in our sample took a keen interest in the new form of cooperative learning, and gave direct, personal support to the teachers. As we had predicted, teachers who had higher scores on the index of principals and teachers talking and working together had markedly higher rates of non-routine behaviors. This finding was present in the middle school data, but not in the elementary school data. Apart from the principal as instructional leader, the principal's role as coordinator of resources was important in a number of these analyses of non-routine behavior.

Student Interaction

As mentioned above, the percentage of students observed talking and working together during groupwork is the best predictor of learning gains at the classroom level, and the best indicator for the quality of implementation. At the elementary level, three factors were significantly correlated with the percentage of students talking and working together: teachers' perceptions of the soundness of the feedback, the reported climate of expectations for implementation, and teachers' reports of the adequacy of resources for complex instruction.

In an analysis using several predictors at once, we found connections between the measure of students talking and working together and measures of teachers talking and working together. Colleagues' expectations that one implement the program were a direct precursor of student interaction, along with the perception that the feedback from the staff developer was soundly based. It is not surprising to find that those teachers who report a high level of cooperation among teachers at their school also perceive that their colleagues expect them to implement.

The parallel analysis at the middle school showed that a general index of feedback (that took into account the number of feedback sessions and the perceived soundness) was a direct predictor of the level of student interaction. However, this analysis of student interaction was complicated by the more complex social structure among the adolescents in middle school classrooms. We found, for example, that two classes taught by the same teacher, at the same grade level, using the same curricular materials, could have significantly different percentages of students talking and working together. This difference was sensitive to the way popularity (i.e., peer status) and academic status were related to each other in a given classroom. Peer dynamics could act to depress or raise the level of social interaction in a way that had little to do with the variables concerning staff development and organizational support (for an analysis of student interaction at the middle school level, see Cohen, Lotan, and Holthuis, 1995).

Quantity of Implementation

How consistently do teachers use groupwork? To what extent is cooperative learning an integral part of the teacher's instructional repertoire rather than a device for Friday afternoon's fun and games?

We were more successful in estimating the amount of time students worked in groups at learning stations and the number of curriculum units covered in the elementary grades than we were in the middle schools. With the variability in subject matter and in the length of class periods, and with the more pronounced concern of middle school teachers with curriculum coverage, we were dissatisfied with our questions measuring these variables at the middle school.

Analysis of what we termed "quantity" of implementation proved particularly fruitful in the elementary level sample. The analysis showed the simultaneous effects of the principal's role as instructional leader and coordinator of resources. The index of principal and teachers talking and working together had a direct effect on the number of units of Finding Out/Descubrimiento completed. This relationship between the principal and the teachers had an additional, indirect effect. The more principals and teachers worked together, the more influential the teachers perceived themselves to be in their schools. A sense of influence, in turn, predicted the amount of time teachers had students working in groups. This association between reports of working with the principal and an increased sense of influence suggests a more collegial, rather than a hierarchical relationship. The principals were probably asking for and taking advice from the teachers on what they, the principals, could do to be more helpful and supportive. Just as talking and working together leads to learning for the students, talking and working together with the principal fosters productivity among the teachers—especially when the conversations are truly two-way and equal-status.

The effect of the principal's role as coordinator of resources was an indirect one. Those teachers who reported talking and working with their principals more also said that they received more organizational help with curriculum materials and consumables. Because many different manipulatives were needed for each activity and for each unit, the issue of materials was a central one for the Finding Out/Descubrimiento curriculum. Someone had to collect, organize, and often replenish these materials so that a set could be readily available for each learning station. This task was too much for a single, unassisted teacher. Reporting satisfactory help with organizing materials was a predictor of a report by the teachers that resources (i.e, the supply of materials, adequate teaching space, and time to plan and prepare) were adequate. The index of adequate resources was a direct predictor of the amount of time students spent in groups, at the learning stations. There was good reason why we found this connection in the data. Some teachers were unable to implement more units because of lack of materials (e.g., batteries, test tubes, consumables like flour, or sugar) or lack of time to prepare for implementation. Thus, the number of units completed was partially dependent on how well the organization, i.e., the school, supported complex instruction in the classroom.

## Discussion and Review of Findings

We summarize the findings in terms of the main factors that are of concern to the staff developer. These factors showed significant connections with more than one important aspect of cooperative learning-in-action (see Table 6.1). Moreover, these factors had observable correlates in a number of independent studies of complex instruction at the elementary and middle school levels.

## Feedback

The frequency and the perceived soundness of feedback to teachers from the staff developers predicted the rate of non-routine behaviors at the elementary school and the rate of the most difficult of these new teacher behaviors, use of status treatments, at the middle school. Feedback was also linked to the amount of observed student interaction in groups at both levels. We can infer from the predictive power of feedback within these samples that if the workshop had no follow-up at all, the level of non-routine behaviors and student interaction would be dramatically lower.

### Organizational Support

The organizational context of the school had many important consequences for implementation. The adequacy of space and curricular materials as well as time for planning and preparing for implementation are crucial, yet frequently overlooked prerequisites for the more demanding types of cooperative learning. Help with acquisition and organization of the curricular materials, the manipulatives, and the consumables is a closely related factor. In most cases, provision of these resources takes money, but in all cases it requires the administrators' attention and skills of coordination. Adequacy of resources was a predictor of non-routine behaviors (as was organizational help) such as status treatments at the middle school and of the amount of student interaction at the elementary level. The following is what one principal said about helping his teachers with materials: "I made sure that each teacher had a materials-and-supply budget where they could purchase items. In this building, it's highly unusual; money is allocated by de-

TABLE 6.1

Antecedents of Important Dimensions of Cooperative Learning in Action

| Antecedents | Elementary School Level | Middle School Level |
|---|---|---|
| Feedback & follow up | Non-routine behaviors of teachers<br>Conceptual understanding of knowledge base by teachers<br>Amount of student interaction in small groups | Status treatments used by teachers<br>Amount of student interaction in small groups |
| Organizational support as perceived by teachers<br>• adequacy of resources<br>• help with organizing materials & manipulatives | Amount of student interaction in small groups | Status treatments used by teachers |
| Climate of expectations for implementation held by:<br>• colleagues<br>• principal<br>• staff developers | Amount of student interaction | Non-routine teaching behaviors |
| Role of Principal<br>• is informed<br>• works with teacher/visits classrooms<br>• communicates expectations | Number of units covered | Non-routine teaching behaviors |

For a more detailed presentation of the data, see Cohen and Lotan, (1997), Chapters 14 and 15.

partments, not by teachers. What happened is that I said: 'Complex instruction will have a materials budget of . . . , and if you need it, see me, we'll access it, see the school secretary, don't worry about it.' The other aspect that was interesting and a little bit unusual is that normally we run everything through the standard P.O. route. With emergencies, the teachers would go out, buy, and we'd reimburse. That's discouraged by the district, but for complex instruction teachers, if you need to go out and buy, we'll pay for it later. And that's important, because it cuts through the level of bureaucracy which is, send it down to Purchasing and let Accounting bill it" (Interview, 6/19/92).

Climate of Expectations

Implementation of new and complex instructional strategies is a demanding process for teachers. A climate of expectations for implementation held by colleagues, the principal, and the staff developers was clearly instrumental in helping teachers over the initial hesitations and hurdles of the first year of implementation. These expectations were a predictor of non-routine behaviors at the middle school and of the level of student interaction at the elementary school. M.S., a middle school principal, talked about the organizational support for complex instruction at her school: "First off, the fact that (Stanford's) support is in place, that they (the teachers) know that they (the Stanford staff) are coming out, it just gives that structure so that they say 'I need to be doing this.' The other thing is, we have teams of teachers so that the teachers can support each other and they can work together to get ready for Stanford coming out, to get their lessons ready, and I think that helps also. So it gives a sense of structure, they know that they're coming just about once a month, they know that they will be getting feedback from them, they know that they've got to get a lesson ready. It forces them to implement the concepts and implement the curriculum . . . When they come out, it is a pleasurable experience for the teachers. They don't see it as somebody checking up on them or evaluating them. They see it as somebody there to support them, give them feedback . . . As we are getting things from them to help us provide better instruction and more appropriate curriculum for our kids, we're also helping Stanford learn about how children learn and how teachers teach." (Interview, 6/16/92).

Role of the Principal

Finally, like so many other scholars of educational change, we found that the role of the principal is critical. When their principals are informed about complex instruction, work with the teachers, and communicate their expectations to persevere and implement, then middle school teachers exhibit more non-routine behaviors, and elementary school teachers cover more units of curriculum with cooperative learning. This is how M.S., the middle school principal we quoted earlier, described her role: "One role that I played is just letting my staff know that I was supportive of this (complex instruction), this was a vision of mine. I set that tone, and then provided a lot of opportunity for dialogue in staff development days as we began getting ready about the components of complex instruction. So that was one way. Then, of course, in addition, I've got to find ways to support Donna and Marianne (not their real names), to free them up to be teacher leaders, so I set monies aside for that , whatever way . . . They were the ones who wrote the sixth grade curriculum, and I certainly don't expect them to do all that on weekends, so we provide for these times substitutes for them to come in and they're working in here down the hall. I provide space for them to work together, provide materials for them; they have a computer down there, so I support them in that kind of way. And then I mentioned the collaboration time for staff, and I try to get into the classrooms as much as I can and just champion the whole cause. It's exciting to see, it's always exciting to see complex instruction lessons. There are times when I talk to communities . . . we made a presentation at our board meeting about complex instruction, our relationship with the staff at Stanford. I talk about it at open houses, back-to-school night and parent meetings of any sort. I write about it in our newsletter—just to keep people in the community informed that this is happening" (Interview, 6/16/92).

### Differences Between Elementary and Middle School Levels

Although the effects of feedback were consistent regardless of school level, we reported some differences in the way that the organizational context affected the classroom at the two levels of schooling in our sample. How seriously should we take these differences? Some of the differences were due to problems of measurement of the quantity of implementation at the middle school level. Other differences were due to the special effects of peer group dynamics on the amount of observable student interaction among middle school students. As most educators know, peer dynamics are much more powerful and complicated factors in the middle grades than they are at the elementary level.

There are undoubtedly some real differences in the organizational context at the two levels. Middle schools appear to be even more loosely organized than elementary schools. Teachers at the middle schools reported less support on all our measures than teachers at the elementary schools. However, the middle school principals who were strong and active instructional leaders had important effects on the implementation of cooperative learning.

### Implications

Many of us who work with teachers on the development of difficult new skills for cooperative learning can benefit from what we have learned. For teachers to master these skills, most of which require non-routine behaviors, we must provide a conceptual framework from the very beginning. By a conceptual framework we do not mean the use of vague abstractions that teachers rightfully resist, but general propositions that permit teachers to reason and reflect about action in the classroom. For example, a conceptual framework might include a way to understand how working in a group affects learning, how the teacher's authority changes with the introduction of groupwork, and why inequalities develop within groups. With such a framework, teachers can make adaptations necessary for particular settings and specific classroom populations without destroying those features of cooperative learning that produce the desired outcomes.

This research has presented powerful evidence for the effects of a feedback system perceived by the teachers as soundly based. The features of this system, i.e., adequate sampling of the teacher's performance, clear criteria and standards for what constitutes quality implementation, and specificity provide a basis for the staff developer to evaluate techniques of classroom follow-up. For example, peer coaching is a lower-cost alternative to the staff developer repeatedly visiting a teacher's classroom and conducting systematic observations by himself or herself. But how well does peer coaching used in the first year of program implementation measure up? Do colleagues have the release time to make multiple observations? Are the criteria that the colleague is using completely clear to both parties? And how is the feedback provided? As general praise or criticism? As a rating on a scale? Neither of these common alternatives gives the teacher specific information on what went particularly well or how to improve her implementation. Many of the peer coaching methods currently in use do not meet the criteria of soundly-based feedback. This is not to say that colleagues are unimportant. Lotan (1989) found that after the first year of implementation, collegial feedback that was similar to the model described in this chapter, produced superior implementation in subsequent years.

When the methods of cooperative learning are more complex and demanding, staff development must mean more than working with individual teachers from different schools. Because the teachers will need support with materials, release time for planning and working with other teachers, and the right kind of space and furniture for groupwork, the administration of the school must have an early involvement and a commitment to the success of the new strategy. As a matter of fact, a preliminary examination of the school context may suggest that the school is unsuitable for a particularly demanding program. If the principal is only superficially committed, if there are competing projects and programs that also require extensive resources and administrative attention, or if the principal has little respect for the teachers (or the teachers for the principal), one would do well to find another school.

If, on the other hand, the school seems an excellent candidate in terms of its ability to furnish resources and instructional leadership, then a team should be selected from that school. This team should include a group of teachers who will have some planning time together. If they form a cohesive group, they can help each other during that difficult first year, by establishing a climate of expectations and mutual encouragement. In subsequent years, they can provide collegial support through systematic observation and collegial feedback. Some teachers may wish to continue to deepen their expertise and may choose to become teacher trainers or mentors to other teachers.

The team includes the principal. In addition to attending the summer workshop, principals will need special preparation and support for their role as coordinator and supplier of resources and their role as instructional leader.

For instructional models to grow and develop, communication between teachers and developers of innovations is crucial. Developers should take the education of teachers very seriously and address the issue of the development of teacher's understanding. Teachers, on the other hand, are to be given the opportunity to share with the developers the adaptations they have invented. If legitimate, they could be incorporated into the innovation, making it richer, more flexible, and more powerful. Evaluations of the innovation by the developers and incorporation of newly discovered findings into the implementation and training models also make the innovation more powerful. In that sense, complex instruction is a good example of a program that shows growth over time and has developed into an integrative and innovative instructional approach rather than a specific and limited curriculum.

In conclusion, the staff developer who wishes to work with teachers on one of the more challenging methods of cooperative learning must work with teams of teachers and with their schools. The more challenging the cooperative learning approach, the more organizational support will be necessary. Just as students learn more by talking and working together, so do teachers—as they talk with staff developers, with each other, and with their principals. If we, as staff developers are to be effective in bringing about changes in the classrooms, we must expand our concept of staff development to include cooperative working relationships in the schools.

## Notes

1. Sometimes a principal will urge a teacher to become involved with complex instruction because that teacher "needs help." According to our findings on the level of student disengagement and our long and painful experience with teachers who had problems controlling their classroom even with

whole-class instruction, this is not a good idea. Such teachers cannot delegate authority when they do not have authority in the first place. We have found that it is almost impossible to help these teachers with the underlying class-room management problems through groupwork. As a matter of fact, group-work exacerbates existing problems with classroom control.

## References

Cohen, E. G. & Lotan, R. A. (Eds.) (1997). *Working for equity in heterogeneous class-rooms: Sociological theory in action.* New York: Teachers College Press.

Cohen, E. G. (1994a) Restructuring the classroom: Conditions for productive small groups. *Review of educational research.* 64, 1–35.

———. (1994b) *Designing groupwork: Strategies for heterogeneous classrooms:* 2nd edition. New York: Teachers College Press.

Cohen, E. G., Lotan, R. A. & Holthuis, N. (1995). Talking and working together: Conditions for learning in complex instruction. In Maureen T. Hallinan (ed.) *Restructuring schools: Promising practices and policies.* New York: Plenum Press.

Cohen, E. G., Lotan, R. A., & Leechor, C. (1989) Can classrooms learn? *Sociology of Education,* 62, 75–94.

Cohen, E. G., Lotan, R. A., Whitcomb, J. A., Balderrama, M. V., Cossey, R., & Swanson, P. E. (1994). Complex instruction: Higher-order thinking in heterogeneous classrooms. In S. Sharan (Ed.) *Handbook of cooperative learn-ing methods.* (pp. 82–96). Westport, CT: Greenwood Press.

Cohen, E. G. & Lotan, R. A., (Spring, 1995). Producing equal-status interaction in heterogeneous classrooms. *American Educational Research Journal.,* Vol-ume 32, Number 1, pp.99–120.

Dornbusch, S. & Scott, W. R. (1975). *Evaluation and exercise of authority.* San Fran-cisco: Jossey Bass.

Ellis, N. (1987). *Collaborative interaction and logistical support for teacher change.* Unpublished doctoral dissertation. Stanford, CA: Stanford University.

Ellis, N. & Lotan, R. A. (1997). Teachers as learners: Feedback, conceptual understanding, and implementation, In Cohen, E. G. & Lotan, R. A. (Eds.). *Working for equity in heterogeneous classrooms: Sociological theory in action,* Chapter 14. New York: Teachers College Press..

Gonzales, J. (1982). *Instructor evaluations and academic effort: The chicano in college.* Unpublished doctoral dissertation. Stanford, CA: Stanford University.

Lotan, R. A. (1985). Understanding the theories: Training teachers for implementation of complex instructional technology, Unpublished doctoral dissertation. Stanford, CA: Stanford University.

Lotan, R. A. (1989). Collegial Feedback: Necessary condition for successful program continuation. Paper presented at annual meeting of the Sociology of Education Association, Asilomar, CA.

Swanson, P. E. (1993). *Linking theory to practice: Strategies for preservice education.* Unpublished doctoral dissertation. Stanford, CA: Stanford University.

Webb, N. (1983). Predicting learning from student interaction: Defining the interaction variable. *Educational Psychologist, 18,* 33–41.

Webb, N. (1991). Task-related verbal interaction and mathematics learning in small groups. *Journal of Research in Mathematics Education, 22,* 366–389.

# 7

## A Social Constructivist Approach to Cooperative Learning and Staff Development: Ideas from the Child Development Project

*Marilyn Watson, Sylvia Kendzior, Stefan Dasho, Stanley Rutherford, and Daniel Solomon*

For the past sixteen years, the staff of the Child Development Project (CDP) has been working to develop and implement a comprehensive approach to elementary school education that is designed to promote children's ethical, social, and intellectual development (Solomon, Watson, Battistich, Schaps, Tuck, Solomon, Cooper, & Ritchey, 1985; Solomon, Watson, Battistich, Schaps, & Delucchi, 1992). The program seeks to create a "Caring Community of Learners"—a learning environment in which students have close and caring relationships with their peers and teachers; are engaged in challenging, relevant, learner-centered curriculum; and learn about and practice prosocial values such as kindness, helpfulness, personal responsibility, and respect for others. Cooperative learning is a key component of the program.

CDP's model of cooperative learning and our approach to helping teachers learn this model has evolved over the years (Watson, Solomon, Dasho, Shwartz, & Kendzior, 1994). At first CDP cooperative learning was composed of elements from models developed by Elizabeth Cohen, (1994, see chapter six of this book); David and Roger Johnson (1984, see chapter 11 of this book); and Shlomo and Yael Sharan (1976, 1992). During our work over the years with hundreds of teachers in hundreds of classrooms, however, we developed our own model which is more consistent with and better supports our own overriding agenda, namely our explicit focus on fostering students' ethical development, our view of learning as an inherently social process involving the construction of meaning, our belief that children need to be motivated intrinsically, and our theory that this intrinsic motivation to learn and uphold the values of the school will only develop if children see their classroom and school as a caring community.

For most teachers, we have discovered, learning CDP's approach to cooperative learning requires a new set of teaching behaviors, new understandings about children and how they learn and are motivated to learn, and a broader educational goal, one that explicitly focuses on helping children become caring, fair, and responsible people as well as good learners. Learning new behaviors and approaches to teaching, however, is an extremely challenging task that requires time, commitment, repeated practice, and a network of support, encouragement, and feedback—a workshop or two is not nearly enough. Yet very few schools or districts seem willing or financially able to provide on-site assistance and support for this intense level of staff development, and without it, a good technique, poorly implemented, can lead to disillusionment and frustration for both teachers and students and negate any kind of possible benefits. Battistich, Solomon, and Delucchi (1993) observed extensively and queried students in 18 elementary classrooms and found that the social and academic benefits of cooperative learning occurred *only* when student interaction in the cooperative groups was high quality—that is, where students were friendly, helpful, considerate, and collaborative—but that frequent group work was associated with *poorer* outcomes when the quality of interaction was low.

The problem then becomes how to provide teachers with effective staff development and sustained support to enable them to implement cooperative learning well.

In this chapter, we present 1) a brief description of CDP's model of cooperative learning, 2) a summary of research findings concerning the implementation and effects of CDP, and 3) a description of CDP's approach to staff development to support continued teacher learning.

## The CDP Model of Cooperative Learning

CDP's model of cooperative learning builds on the foundation of several other models. Where we depart from other models is our explicit emphasis on teaching prosocial values and building a caring schoolwide and classroom community, our social constructivist approach to cooperative learning activities, and our focus on fostering children's intrinsic motivation to learn.

The Importance of Community—A Schoolwide and Classroom Culture of Caring

To operate effectively, CDP's approach to learning requires a total classroom and schoolwide context in which students are immersed in a culture of caring, an environment where the values of fairness, helpfulness, respect, and responsibility are taught and experienced. Along with other aspects of CDP, cooperative learning activities are designed to foster these values and to provide students with opportunities to explore and practice them. These activities are carefully constructed and managed to promote cooperation, build trusting child-child connections, help students develop a sense of classroom unity, and, of course, advance their academic learning.

This emphasis on building a caring community is central to CDP's efforts (see Dalton & Watson, 1997). Research conducted by the Developmental Studies Center has shown that there are strong positive relationships between students' sense of the school or classroom as a community and many of their personal and social qualities (e.g., social competence, concern for others, conflict resolution skill, sense of autonomy); as well as their academic orientations and performance (e.g., liking for school, achievement motivation, reading comprehension) (see more in section 2, below; also see Battistich, Solomon, Watson, & Schaps, 1994; Solomon & Battistich, 1993; and Solomon, Watson, Battistich, Schaps, & Delucchi, 1992).

A Social Constructivist Approach to Cooperative Learning

New understandings about learning based on studies of children's social and intellectual development posit that learning is greatly influenced by a child's developmental level and social/cultural context—his or her background, experiences, and personal interest (Bruer, 1993; Rogoff, 1990; Tharp & Gallimore, 1988). Further, learning involves a complex and active process of constructing, challenging, and reconstructing one's understanding of how things work and what things mean (Piaget, 1934; Sigel & Cocking, 1977). This "social constructivist" view of learning encourages "teaching for understanding"—a hands-on approach to learning that requires an environment in which trial-and-error experimentation and interaction with fellow learners assisted by a teacher allows each child to build his or her own understanding.

CDP uses a social constructivist approach in all of its learning activities, and, like other constructivist educators, for example, Yael and Shlomo Sharan (1992), has forged a mutually-reinforcing alliance between constructivism and cooperative learning. We have found that small cooperative learning groups provide an ideal, safe, fertile environment for students to explore their own understanding, challenge each other's thinking, exchange ideas, and arrive at new understandings—processes that are central to a constructivist approach.

We design all of our cooperative lessons to help facilitate student engagement with the learning process. Teachers offer introductions to each lesson to motivate students by helping them see how the lesson is relevant to their lives and how it relates to and builds on their prior knowledge and experience. Each lesson is structured in an open-ended manner to allow students to engage the activity differently depending on their unique experiences, skills, and levels of development. Teachers try to help students understand that learning is often a trial-and-error process, that it's okay to make "mistakes," and that it's important to help, encourage, and support each other in this effort. Collaboration, not competition, is the goal.

Specific social learning goals—such as being courteous listeners, dividing up the work fairly, respecting other's ideas—are part of each cooperative lesson, and teachers usually discuss these goals as part of the introduction to the activity. Teachers help students to think about how they can work together in ways that are consistent with these goals. For example teachers might say, "In this activity each of you will probably have lots of different ideas; how can you be sure that in your group everyone's ideas are heard and treated with respect? Was this a problem the last time you worked together? What did you do about it?" Then at the conclusion of the activity, teachers invite students to reflect on and share what they learned about both the subject matter under consideration and how their groups performed with respect to the social goals. A teacher might ask "How did the work go? Do you think everyone was treated fairly in your group? What did you do to make sure that everyone got a chance to participate?" The teacher's goal is to help students construct their own understanding of complex social concepts in the same way that they are helped to build understanding in the academic realm.

In keeping with this goal, we encourage teachers to form learning groups that are heterogeneous with respect to gender, race, knowledge, and skill levels, in order to create situations that challenge students' abilities to collaborate and stimulate their thinking by exposing them to differing perspectives. We discourage allowing students to select their own groups, which may create exclusion, perpetuate homogenous cliques, or create situations in which there is little challenge to promote social learning.

Similarly, we discourage assigning roles or specific tasks for students within each group, such as "recorder," "facilitator," "materials manager," and so forth. We have learned from our experience that assigning roles tends to reduce the degree of interaction among students and interferes with their autonomy in shaping the task and their approach to it. Further, setting up situations in which students have to think about and grapple with what it means to divide a task fairly and to give each group member a meaningful chance to participate is precisely what helps promote their ethical and social understanding. (CDP teachers do sometimes assign roles for students when they are first introducing them to cooperative learning to offer ideas on how work can be divided and shared, but later ask students to assume responsibility for deciding how to accomplish the task.)

## A Focus on Intrinsic Motivation

Fostering children's intrinsic motivation to become life-long learners and caring, responsible citizens is central to CDP. We want to help children develop a personal commitment to their own learning so that learning becomes a meaningful, self-motivated endeavor, and a personal commitment to prosocial values (not just a mimicking of prosocial behavior to please the teacher, for example). To this end, learning activities are designed to be inherently interesting and relevant to students and are open-ended enough to engage children of different skill and ability levels. We encourage teachers to take a "child-centered" approach to teaching, which includes addressing in developmentally-appropriate ways students' needs for autonomy, belonging, and competence (Deci & Ryan, 1985).

A major tenet of CDP is the assumption that students will be motivated to act responsibly, to support their classroom and school community, and to learn the skills and acquire the knowledge that are valued by that community, when their basic psychological needs are being met by that community. Autonomy, belonging, and competence are three central psychological needs all children (and adults) have; some teachers have dubbed these the "New ABC's." Children need to feel that they have a measure of autonomy and control over their lives, and they are valued members of their community, hence have a feeling of belonging. They also need to feel that they have the skills to do worthwhile things and the ability to accomplish worthwhile things; in short, have a sense of their own competence. We pay strict attention to these needs. We try to:

1.  Offer children a voice and choice in their learning activities and in determining how their classroom should operate to provide them with a measure of autonomy;
2.  Build an inclusive classroom community in which each child is valued and cared for so that each will have a sense of belonging; and
3.  Give students opportunities to be successful learners, and contribute to and assume meaningful, responsible roles in their classroom and school community to promote their sense of competence (for a more comprehensive discussion of the model, see Watson, Solomon, Dasho, Shwartz, and Kendzior, 1994; for its use with young children see Watson, Hildebrandt, & Solomon, 1988).

## Summary of Research Findings Concerning CDP

CDP cooperative learning is part of a comprehensive approach to education, and is not intended to operate in isolation; it requires a consistent and supporting environment; i.e., a classroom (and preferably a school) that operates by similar principles and with similar concerns and emphases. The evaluation of CDP has therefore been conducted on CDP in total, not just cooperative learning exclusively.

### Evaluation of the CDP Program, Grades K–6

CDP was first developed and evaluated in a suburban California community, and the following summary describes that evaluation. A further effort was recently completed in six school districts spread throughout the country (publication forthcoming). The evaluation had two major foci: an assessment of implementation of the program in the classrooms, and an assessment of its effects on participating students.

This first effort to pilot and longitudinally evaluate the CDP program occurred in San Ramon, California, beginning in the 1982–83 school year, and continuing through 1988–89. There we worked closely with teachers in three program schools one grade level at a time to develop and implement the program, and followed a cohort of students receiving the program from kindergarten through sixth grade, and then into eighth grade in a two-year follow-up assessment in intermediate school. The evaluation also included teachers and students in three comparison schools that were similar to the program schools in terms of various demographic characteristics and scores on a series of assessments conducted the year before the start of the program.

To see how well the program was being implemented in the classrooms, we trained observers to use an observation system specifically designed to assess such implementation. Data from repeated visits made to each participating classroom each year showed large differences between the program and comparison classrooms, with program teachers scoring higher on all the various indices of program implementation, including their use of the CDP approach to cooperative learning.

We assessed the effects of the program on students' interpersonal behavior, attitudes, academic and interpersonal motivation, moral reasoning, and academic performance—using interviews, small-group activities, questionnaires (from third grade up), and achievement tests.

Over the seven years of this longitudinal evaluation, we found consistent, repeated differences favoring the program students in several areas:

- Students' behavior toward one another in classrooms was more positive and considerate;
- Students got along better and worked better with their classmates, and were less lonely in school;
- Students showed better understanding of others, and greater ability to solve interpersonal problems and conflicts;
- Students showed greater commitment to democratic values;
- Students were more likely to see their classrooms as communities, and this sense of community was itself related to a broad set of other positive characteristics among students (e.g., self-esteem, social competence, empathy, achievement motivation, reading comprehension), and also helped to enhance a number of the effects mentioned above.

Although both groups scored at the same high level on standardized achievement tests, the program students scored higher on a performance-based measure of higher-order reading comprehension given at sixth grade.

## Follow-up Study on Students in Grades 7 and 8

Students from four of the schools, two program and two comparison, entered the same intermediate school for seventh and eighth grades. We assessed these students during those two years with questionnaires and teacher ratings, focusing on the group of 50–57 students who had been with the project all the way back to kindergarten.

Despite the more regimented and restricted atmosphere of this intermediate school compared to the elementary schools previously attended, we found that there were a number of differences that still favored the program students. One or two years after the end of their program experience, the program students:

- Scored higher on measures of conflict resolution skill and self-esteem,
- Were more involved in extracurricular activities,
- Were rated by their teachers as more assertive and popular, and
- Had friends who were more involved in positive activities.

We also found better outcomes in the intermediate school assessments for program students who had had better implementation experience in elementary school (as assessed by the observations). They
were rated more positively by teachers, scored higher on measures of
moral reasoning, and had higher grade-point averages.

The results in San Ramon demonstrated that the CDP program
could be well-implemented in public elementary schools, and that it
was effective in bringing about many of the positive effects for students
that we had envisioned, relating to each of the three focal areas—social,
ethical, and intellectual development (see Battistich, Solomon, Watson,
Solomon, & Schaps, 1989; Solomon, Battistich, & Watson 1993; Solomon,
Watson, Battistich, Schaps, & Delucchi 1992; Solomon, Watson, Delucchi, Schaps, & Battistich 1989; and Solomon, Watson, Schaps, Battistich,
& Solomon 1990).

## CDP's Approach to Staff Development

The principles and strategies that form the basis of CDP's approach to the education of children—the importance of developing a
caring community of learners, a social constructivist approach to learning, the use of cooperative learning strategies, the fostering of intrinsic
motivation—also form the basis of CDP's approach to staff development. CDP's staff development materials, workshops, and on-going
support structure are intentionally and specifically designed to provide
a model for teachers of what we hope the classroom learning experience
will be like for children.

Ultimately, CDP is a program designed to effect whole-school
change. Purposeful, deep change, of course, is never easy; it never occurs overnight; it's often accompanied by disagreement and resistance;
and its challenges are magnified when the context is the whole school,
not just an individual teacher or classroom (Fullan, 1993). This kind of
change requires a consistent, clearly defined and focused, long-term
effort to develop an environment that fosters trust, encourages risk-
taking, understands and condones the need for trial-and-error exploration, promotes dialogue, and provides the materials and logistical
help teachers need to pursue their own personal growth and learning.
CDP's model of staff development attempts to address these needs.

The following considers, first, some of the principles that underlie our staff development effort and, second, the specific components of CDP's "infrastructure" to support whole school change. It is literally impossible to talk in isolation about our staff development for cooperative learning, since cooperative learning strategies are an all-pervasive, integral, inseparable part of the entire CDP program.

Four Principles Underlie CDP's Approach to Staff Development:

### Creating a Caring Community Where Everyone Is a Learner

We believe that the Caring Community of Learners should embrace everyone in the school community—students, teachers, staff, parents, extended families, even neighbors. Just as students need to be immersed in a community of warm, trusting, caring relationships to promote their desire and ability to learn, so do teachers. Just as it's essential to foster children's intrinsic motivation to become life-long learners and caring, responsible citizens, so too is it essential to help foster teachers' intrinsic motivation to be life-long learners and to realize their full potential as role models of caring, responsible adults. We therefore place a major emphasis on giving teachers opportunities to be learners, and helping them to understand the significant impact they have on their students as role models of what it means to be motivated and excited about learning. The teacher who is no longer actively engaged in his or her own learning is a teacher whose class suffers profoundly as a result—not just because he/she may be using outdated, less effective methods, for example, but because the spirit of discovery and the energy to explore may have been lost, leaving students with no one to inspire them, motivate them, and show them how exciting learning can be.

### A Social Constructivist Approach to Staff Development

As with children's learning, we emphasize a social constructivist approach to adult learning. All our staff development efforts are based on the understanding that learning is constructed through personal understanding and is based on personal experiences; is nonlinear, idiosyncratic, and requires trial-and-error "messing around;" and is often enhanced by the exchange of ideas and the challenging of perceptions. We therefore structure our workshops to tap into each teacher's personal experience, challenge them with new ideas, provide opportunities for them to discuss and explore these ideas, and ultimately help them to construct their own understanding and approach to teaching by making CDP "their own."

Many teachers were educated and trained in the tradition that teaching is primarily "telling," and learning is primarily "remembering." Many teachers still operate on this assumption and structure their student's learning activities starting with an I'll-tell-what-you-need-to-know lecture or reading assignment followed by a now-you-tell-it-back-to-me test. Social constructivist learning theory, while not denying the value and helpfulness of "direct instruction," emphasizes that most learning is a much more active and complex process that is enhanced by engagement in active problem-solving, discussion, theorizing, analysis—a process of trying it out to see if it works, rethinking it, then trying it out again.

Teachers expand their understanding of what the learning process is all about by an ongoing process that engages them in constructivist learning experiences and invites them to reflect on their own learning. We ask workshop participants to share their thoughts about learning, discuss and compare their ideas, and thereby discover for themselves that different people learn in different, often highly individual ways, and usually have distinct preferences about how they like to go about it. This exploration, of course, provides insights into what constitutes effective and engaging approaches to teaching—knowledge that teachers then take back to their classrooms, "mess around" with, work with, modify, and try again.

### The Use of Cooperative Learning Strategies

We make extensive use of cooperative learning activities in our workshops—frequent partner work, small group discussion and focus groups, unity building activities, and so forth. These activities are used to model CDP's approach to cooperative learning for students and to further our strategy of helping teachers build their skills at working together collaboratively to build a Caring Community of Learners.

Our staff development program encourages teachers to work together in cooperative partnerships during the school year to further their own professional growth and learning. We call this "Collegial Study and Support," and believe that it helps teachers to break through the feeling of being an isolated adult struggling alone in a classroom of children, and is an effective way to support long-term, on-going change in classrooms and schools (see more about Collegial Study and Support below).

### The Fostering of Intrinsic Motivation

Most teachers care deeply about children, are personally motivated to be the best teachers they can, and realize that continued learning is essential for them to further develop their skills and knowledge.

They are therefore intrinsically motivated to learn, and we try to tap into and foster this intrinsic motivation in order to help them grow and develop professionally.

Teachers, like all of us, perform at their best and learn at their best when their basic needs for autonomy, belonging, and competence are being met, and so, just as we do for children, we try to address these needs.

*Autonomy.* Every teacher needs to feel that she is an autonomous being who has a measure of control over what she does and how she does it. We therefore offer no extrinsic inducements to teachers to use cooperative strategies, and we discourage principals from doing so. Such inducements are either unnecessary or ultimately harmful. If, in the teacher's professional judgment, cooperative learning is a valuable teaching strategy, then extrinsic inducements will not be necessary. If, on the other hand, the teacher does not believe that cooperative learning will benefit his students, then any extrinsic inducement, if effective, will deprive the teacher of the autonomy to act on his own beliefs. Our commitment to the importance of teacher autonomy also guides our workshop design. For example, workshops frequently include time for teachers to join focus groups on topics of their own choosing, and other voluntary collegial opportunities.

*Belonging.* Every teacher needs to feel that he is valued by his peers and is a respected member of his community, hence has a feeling of belonging. If teachers fear that making mistakes will lead them to be less valued by their peers, or if they feel the need to hide their uncertainties or "teaching disasters" in order not to be rejected, they will not take the risks necessary to learn dramatically different approaches to teaching. Therefore, we consciously work to increase the likelihood that teachers will like and respect one another and view one another as helpful colleagues rather than as competitors. Similarly, we discourage principals from using social comparisons as a way of motivating their staff, and try to get them to eliminate activities in which teachers compete with one another. In workshops, we try to foster a sense of belonging by engaging in unity-building activities and by having an open discussion to establish norms for working together. We also try hard to listen carefully to and treat with respect the faculty and staff who do not share our beliefs or who actively resist our staff development efforts.

Careful attention to building or maintaining teachers' respect and liking for one another is especially important in whole school change efforts involving teacher collaboration. When teachers work closely together on the same goals they become more aware of their differences and frequently divisions arise and "camps" develop around, for example, the role of instruction in discrete skills or the role of extrinsic rewards and consequences (Murphy, 1991). Such divisions make it less safe for teachers to take the risks they need to take to learn new ideas and skills and therefore can undermine the entire staff development effort. It is easier to prevent these camps from becoming entrenched if the teachers have personal reasons for liking and respecting one another.

*Competence.* Every teacher needs to feel that she possesses the skills and knowledge to be efficacious in her teaching efforts, and therefore has a sense of her own competence. In workshops we acknowledge participants' competence by drawing extensively on each teacher's knowledge, experience, and abilities in, for example, focus groups where participants exchange ideas and share their learning with each other. We also try to help teachers achieve reasonable success at the start of their learning by providing them with detailed lesson guides designed to scaffold their initial efforts at classroom implementation. We have classroom teachers on our staff development team who can describe their own, sometimes disastrous initial efforts, in order to help others see that failures do not mean incompetence.

Autonomy, belonging, and competence are powerful human needs, and by acknowledging and addressing them the CDP staff tries to optimize the conditions that allow teachers to take responsibility for their learning and pursue it individually and through cooperative efforts.

## CDP's Staff Development "Infrastructure" to Support School Change

Creating a Caring Community of Learners and fostering teachers' growth and development, especially if they are moving from a transmission or curriculum-centered approach to a more constructivist, learner-centered one, requires time, practice, on-going support and encouragement, and schoolwide commitment (see chapter one of this book for discussion of this paradigm). Workshops are only the tip of the iceberg; real change requires a permanent infrastructure of ongoing support. The iceberg, in fact, is CDP's metaphor for staff development—a structure of considerable depth with multiple levels of learning and support, much of it "beneath the surface."

### CDP's Staff Development "Iceberg"

We recently worked with six different school districts over a three year period to implement and evaluate the CDP program. Our staff development work includes various strata of support to promote teacher learning and schoolwide change, as follows:

- *CDP staff development workshops;* the visible tip of the iceberg;
- *On-site assistance from experienced practitioners;* help from a mixture of both CDP staff developers and an on-site group of teachers and staff developers who have had more extensive training and experience with cooperative learning and other aspects of the CDP program;
- *An established program in each school of collaborative Study and Support partnerships;* teachers working in cooperative pairs or groups, who meet periodically to support each other in their learning efforts, share ideas and plans, view a video of classroom practice and discuss its relationship to their classroom work, read and discuss an article, and so forth;
- *CDP teaching materials;* detailed classroom activity guides, such as CDP's cooperative learning lesson formats, unity-builders, and literature-based curriculum designed to support the initial use of new teaching techniques; and, finally,
- *Individual commitment to learning through actual classroom practice, planning, and reflection; the deepest level of learning.*

This model may continue to evolve as we expand to greater numbers of schools (and as schools, of course, develop their own hybrid of this design), but the idea that staff development is not just a series of workshops, but a continual, everyday process of engagement, reflection, sharing, discussion, and cooperative effort will remain central to CDP's approach to professional growth and schoolwide change.

The following is a more detailed examination of each of the strata of CDP's staff development infrastructure.

CDP Staff Development Workshops

We spread our workshops over three years—a five-day institute each of the three summers, and three to four one-day workshops during the course of the three school years. These institutes and workshops typically include the following types of activities:

*Unity Building Activities.* These are fun, non-threatening, purposeful whole group activities in which participants mix randomly with each other, meet or get to know each other better, and share ideas or experiences or feelings related in some way to the topic of the day's workshop. These activities mirror CDP unity-building activities for children.

*Partner Work.* We make extensive use of partner problem-solving and discussion throughout all of our workshops. Some activities are specifically designed to engage partners in interviewing each other to learn the other's ideas and techniques for doing things or to work together on a specific problem and generate shared ideas. Sometimes partners engage in a "partner reading" activity, during which they read an instructional text and discuss it; how they go about doing this is left to each partnership, but the idea is to get participants to approach reading and reflecting on the reading as a cooperative activity, rather than an exclusively individual one. These types of partner work mirror CDP's suggestions for children's partner work in the classroom and provide teachers with ideas to use with their students along with some actual experience in what partner work is like.

*Small Group Discussions.* Much of the work of each workshop is conducted in four-to-six member discussion and focus groups. These small groups are ideal vehicles for participants to engage in constructivist learning. Groups are invited to share ideas about ways to implement the techniques and strategies that are introduced in the workshops; discuss information provided during presentations or in videotapes of CDP classrooms; discuss topics of mutual interest, problem-solve, exchange ideas, and share knowledge, experience, and concerns. These group activities also have specific social goals—respect for others' ideas, shared participation, careful listening—just as do CDP's cooperative activities for children.

*Role-Play/Practice Sessions.* Applying the techniques and gaining practical experience in the learning/teaching strategies is essential if teachers are going to be able to use these strategies effectively in their classrooms. During role-playing sessions teachers take turns facilitating discussions or conducting cooperative learning wrap-up sessions. We have also created a series of videotapes of CDP teachers and students engaged in learning activities in actual classrooms and use these to provide teachers with a look at CDP teaching techniques in practice, and as concrete stimuli to spark discussion.

*Direct Instruction Presentations.* Direct instruction provides participants with an overview or introduction to certain topics, specific ideas about learning theories and techniques, and is a way to consolidate or summarize topics. Presentations are often augmented by written materials, and are usually followed by opportunities for either personal reflection or application of the concepts or techniques.

*Co-planning Activities.* There is considerable time at each workshop for partners (Study and Support Partners, for example, or two teachers who teach the same grade level) to engage in lesson or activity planning. This gives them a chance to work out specific ways they want to implement various CDP strategies. These planning activities help participants to gain experience and develop skills in partner work, which will help them in future Collegial Study and Support activities.

*Reflection Time.* At the end of each activity or at the end of the day participants often reflect on what they have just learned either in partner or small group discussion or individual journal writing. Reflection is an important part of the learning process—a way to consolidate and review new ideas and fit them into one's personal structure of understanding.

On-site Assistance by Experienced Practitioners

To provide on-site assistance and encouragement in our recent project, we worked for an initial year with the principal of each school and a small group of volunteer teachers and staff developers to create an on-site support and staff development team, called the "Implementation Team." We provided on-site coaching and support to this volunteer group about four times during the year. The Implementation Team was intended to provide support to fellow teachers, but we found that most teachers are not eager to have anyone come into their classroom to "help them change," let alone a colleague. In order to reach more teachers at the classroom level, we now use a process we call "fish-bowl coaching." CDP staff developers worked with a volunteer teacher to co-plan, co-teach, and debrief a CDP lesson while a small group of other teachers observe and join in a final debriefing discussion.

Although the Implementation Team members in our projects have done little actual coaching, they have made valuable contributions to the overall staff development effort. Their enthusiasm and personal successes have gradually encouraged more and more of their colleagues to apply the principles and pedagogical techniques in their classrooms. Their voices are heard in corridor and teachers lounge conversations. Some have grown quite comfortable having peers drop in on CDP lessons in their classrooms. They have shaped and changed workshops and materials to meet local needs and conditions.

Collegial Study and Support

A key aspect of our staff development program is an on-going support structure (other than coaching) to help teachers continue their own learning and professional growth. In each CDP school, teachers are teamed with a colleague (usually, but not always, with a teacher of the same grade level) to form a Collegial Study and Support team. The initial goal was to provide each teacher with a supportive colleague who would act as a sounding board and with whom he or she might discuss common issues, share ideas, explore solutions to problems, read and discuss articles, co-plan lessons, and so forth. We envisioned teachers meeting weekly, exchanging periodic visits to each others' classrooms to observe each other at work, and then afterwards sharing their observations in a supportive, non-judgmental way. In reality, regular Collegial Study and Support has been very difficult to make happen and it has taken a somewhat different shape at each CDP school.

Collegial Study and Support is based on several assumptions about the nature of school change, schools, and learning. If schools are to be learning places for children they must become learning organizations for all members of the community (Fullan, 1993). There are ways for teachers to find time to work and learn together (Raywid, 1993) and teachers can learn much by exploring their different reactions to the same observed lesson, article, or video tape. If teachers have a regular forum to exchange ideas and viewpoints, they will inevitably challenge each others' thinking, and spur each other to new levels of understanding and skill.

Such collegial learning conversations have not been a part of most teachers' professional experiences and finding the time in overloaded work schedules is very difficult. We therefore developed outlines to guide various types of partner learning experiences, e.g., viewing a video tape, reading an article, co-planning a lesson, and so on. We also worked with principals to encourage them to help teachers find the time for Collegial Study and Support work.

As mentioned above, this support work has taken many different forms. Some schools have found that triads rather than partnerships work better for them. Some schools have gotten grants so that they can hire substitutes to free up teachers' time to engage in Study and Support activities. In others, teachers met weekly an hour before school started. Some schools have created Collegial Study and Support programs that also include monthly brown-bag meetings of the whole school staff; others incorporated some partner time as part of regular staff meetings. In other schools, teachers have preferred to meet for two hours bi-weekly. In two schools, periodic voluntary after-school meetings for which teachers receive a stipend substitute for collegial study and support. Gradually, the number of teachers engaging in Collegial Study and Support increased. The process itself became less formal, and a growing number of teachers reported that their "collegial conversations" not only reduced their feeling of isolation, but became an essential part of their learning and professional development.

CDP Teaching Materials

We have developed 250 cooperative learning activities that teachers can use to guide their classroom practice (see *Blueprints for a Collaborative Classroom*, 1997). Teachers have the unenviable task of having to learn while they perform, and they have to develop a degree of "automaticity" in what they do. Teachers have to teach, observe, respond to a complex set of stimuli, and make quick, yet well-reasoned judgments, and the greater their ease and facility with basic classroom procedures, the better they will be able to focus on the content of the lesson and the quality of student interactions.

For teachers and students who are accustomed to the more traditional method of working individually on learning tasks, cooperative learning can be intimidating and difficult to adjust to. In particular, cooperative activities can be extremely disquieting for students who are used to competitive environments where each student's work is judged and graded and each project is his or her "own." Most teachers have to contend with their students' discomfort as well as their own, so we suggest that teachers incorporate cooperative learning techniques into their teaching repertoire slowly and carefully. CDP cooperative learning activities are designed to help teachers and students experience successes and build on those successes, and to provide teachers with frameworks within which they can develop their own understanding and expertise.

These learning activities are built on recognizable "formats," so teachers can give students new assignments that fit within the structure they have used before. Teachers and students can thereby build on their previous experiences and develop a sense of competence and automaticity. For example, in lessons that follow an interview format, students take turns interviewing their partners about specific topics; in lessons that follow a "Mind Mapping" format, students create a visual representation of what they know about a topic, showing major ideas or events, interesting or important details, and relationships among them. Each format can be repeated over and over with new content. For each format suggestions are offered for preparing students for the academic, social, and ethical challenges likely to arise as they engage in the activity (see Figure 7.1). Gradually students and teachers acquire proficiency at working within the format structure, which enables everybody to focus better on the content of the lesson and the quality of their interpersonal interactions.

FIGURE 7.1

Mind Mapping

**JOINT IDEAS**

*Organizing Ideas*

# Mind Mapping

A MIND MAP displays what a person or group knows about a subject and, like a conventional map, can show them where they are and where they might go next in their explorations. Less formal than standard outlining techniques, mind maps are visual tools that help students gain some control over a lot of discrete pieces of information. These graphic representations of knowledge—students' perceptions of a topic's "big" ideas and related groups and subsets of ideas—are especially useful as a first step in a unit of study to identify students' prior knowledge or as a culminating activity to celebrate all that students have learned. And as a cooperative activity, when students work together on mind maps they learn from each other's insights, appreciate their own and each other's learning, and practice their collaborative skills.

## WHY TO USE

- to develop students' ability to think systematically and relationally
- to help students connect details to broader ideas and concepts
- to help students represent what they know or have learned

## WHEN TO USE

- when all students are likely to know something about the topic and can contribute to the process
- when the topic is open-ended and students can benefit from hearing different points of view
- when you want insight into how students are identifying and connecting the "big" and "little" ideas in a topic
- at the beginning of a unit of study
- as the culmination of a unit of study
- prior to producing a product representing student knowledge, such as a dramatization, a report, or a mural

## HOW TO DO

The Mind Mapping blueprint asks students to

- brainstorm categories of information to include on the map
- write these on the map and show how they connect
- say ideas that they think should be included on the map
- discuss which category of information the idea connects to
- agree on where to put the idea
- record the idea on the map
- change categories or create new ones as necessary

*Blueprints for a Collaborative Classroom: Joint Ideas.* Reprinted with permission.

In time, teachers find they want and feel capable of making their own adaptations. Ultimately most teachers develop a repertoire of their own lessons and units that bear the imprint of their unique personalities and tastes.

## Individual Commitment to Learning Through Actual Classroom Practice, Planning, and Reflection

The deepest and most meaningful level of learning for teachers occurs in the classroom. Nothing replaces the actual experience of teaching and working with students. Through our support system of workshops, on-site assistance, collegial study and support, and teaching materials, we try to assist teachers in their efforts, but ultimately it is teachers themselves who are responsible for their own teaching and their own learning. We can, however, help teachers reflect on their own experiences in the classroom. We have developed a Reflection Guide for Teachers that offers a set of "principles" for creating classrooms that support the ethical, social, and intellectual development of all students. It includes examples of what teachers can do to put these principles into practice, and examples of behavior by students that indicate whether the teacher's efforts are being successful. The reflection guide offers a summary of ways that teachers can implement the CDP program and can assess their success at doing so, while helping them develop a mindful and reflective approach to what they do in the classroom as a way to advance their own learning.

## Summary

The goal of CDP is to help teachers and administrators create classrooms and schools that foster the ethical and social as well as the intellectual development of all children. Several conditions are essential to such classrooms and schools:

1. Warm, supportive, stable, caring relationships;
2. An explicit focus on ethical and social issues;
3. An honoring of intrinsic motivation;
4. A social constructivist pedagogy.

Creating these same conditions is also important for staff development. We work to build a climate of mutual respect among the teachers, staff, principals, and our staff development team. We have developed a reading and language arts curriculum, and approaches to classroom management and cooperative learning that explicitly address ethical and social as well as intellectual development. We avoid the use of extrinsic motivators and encourage principals to avoid them in favor of seeking ways to convince teachers that the above four principles can work with their students, that they can successfully apply them, and that when they do so their professional goals will be better realized. Finally, we have developed materials, workshop activities, and support structures designed to assist teachers in the construction of new goals, new skills, and new understandings about teaching and learning.

## References

Battistich, V., Solomon, D., & Delucchi, K. (1993). Interaction processes and student outcomes in cooperative learning groups. *The Elementary School Journal*. 94, 19–32.

Battistich, V., Solomon, D., Watson, M., & Schaps, E. (1994). *Students and teachers in caring classroom and school communities.* Paper presented at the Annual meetings of the American Educational Research Association, New Orleans.

Battistich, V., Solomon, D., Watson, M., Solomon, J., & Schaps, E. (1989). Effects of a program to enhance prosocial behavior on children's social problem-solving skills and strategies. *Journal of Applied Developmental Psychology*, 10, 147–169.

Battistich, V., Watson, M., Solomon, D., Schaps, E., & Solomon, J. (1991). The child development project: A comprehensive program for the development of prosocial character. In W. M. Kurtines & J. L. Gewirtz (Eds.), *Handbook of moral behavior and development: Vol. 3. Application.* New York: Erlbaum.

Bruer, J. (1993). *Schools for thought.* Cambridge: MIT Press.

Cohen, E. G. (1994). *Designing groupwork: Strategies for the heterogeneous classroom.* New York; Teachers College Press.

Dalton, J., & Watson, M. S. (1997). *Among friends: Cooperative classrooms where caring and learning prevail.* Oakland, CA: Developmental Studies Center.

Deci, E. L., and Ryan, R. M. (1985) *Intrinsic motivation and self-determination in human behavior.* New York: Plenum Press, 1985.

Developmental Studies Center (1997). Blueprints for a collaborative classroom. Oakland, CA: Developmental Studies Center.

Fullan, M. G. (1993). *Change forces.* Falmer Press.

Johnson, D. W., & Johnson, R. T. (1984). *Cooperation in the classroom.* Edina, MN: Interaction Book Company.

Johnson, D. W., & Johnson, R. T. (1989). *Cooperation and competition: Theory and research.* Edina, MN: Interaction Book Company.

Johnson, D. W., Maruyama, G., Johnson, R. T, Nelson, D., & Skon, L. (1981). Effects of cooperative, competitive, and individualistic goal structures on achievement: A Meta-analysis. *Psychological Bulletin,* 89, 47–62.

Murphy, C. (1991). Lessons from a journey into change. Educational Leadership. (May), 63–67.

Piaget, J. (1934). *The construction of reality in the child.* London: Routledge and Kegan Paul.

Raywid, M. (1993). Finding time for collaboration. *Educational Leadership.* 50, 30–34.

Rogoff, B. (1990). *Apprenticeship in thinking: Cognitive development in social context.* New York: Oxford University Press.

Sharan, S. (1980). Cooperative learning in small groups: Recent methods and effects on achievement, attitudes and ethnic relations. *Review of Educational research,* 50, 241–271.

Sharan, S., & Sharan, Y. (1976). *Small-group teaching.* Englewood Cliffs, NJ: Educational Technology Publications.

Sharan, S., & Sharan, Y. (1992). *Expanding cooperative learning through group investigation.* NY: Teachers College Press.

Sigel, I., & Cocking, R. (1977). *Cognitive development from childhood to adolescence: A constructivist perspective.* New York: Holt, Rinehart, & Winston.

Slavin, R. E. (1983a). *Cooperative learning.* New York: Longman.

Slavin, R. E. (1983b). When does cooperative learning increase student achievement? *Psychological Bulletin,* 94, 429–445.

Solomon, D., & Battistich, V. *Students in caring school and classroom communities.* Annual meetings of the American Psychological Association, Toronto, August, 1993.

Solomon, D., Watson, M., Battistich, V., Schaps, E., & Delucchi, K. (1992). Creating a caring community: Educational practices that promote children's prosocial development. In F. K. Oser, A. Dick, & J. L. Patry (Eds.), *Effective and responsible teaching: The new synthesis.* San Francisco: Jossey-Bass.

Solomon, D., Battistich, V., & Watson, M. *A Longitudinal investigation of the effects of a school intervention program on children's social development.* Annual meetings of the Society for Research in Child Development, New Orleans, March, 1993.

Solomon, D., Watson, M., Delucchi, K., Schaps, E., & Battistich, V. (1988). Enhancing children's prosocial behavior in the classroom. *American Educational Research Journal, 25,* 527–554.

Solomon, D., Watson, M., Schaps, E., Battistich, V., & Solomon, J. (1990). Cooperative learning as part of a comprehensive program designed to promote prosocial development. In S. Sharan (Ed.), *Cooperative learning: Theory and research.* New York: Praeger.

Solomon, D., Watson, M., Battistich, V., Schaps, E., Tuck, P., Solomon, J., Cooper, C., & Ritchey, W. (1985). A program to promote interpersonal consideration and cooperation in children. In R. Slavin, S. Sharan, S. Kagan, R. Hertz-Lazarowitz, C. Webb, & R. Schmuck (Eds.), *Learning to cooperate, cooperating to learn.* New York: Plenum.

Tharp, R. G., & Gallimore, R. (1988). *Rousing minds to life: Teaching, learning, and schooling in social context.* New York: Cambridge University Press.

Vygotsky, L. (1962). *Thought and language.* Cambridge, MA: MIT Press.

Watson, M., Hildebrandt, C., & Solomon, D. (1988). Cooperative learning as a means of promoting prosocial development among kindergarten and early primary grade children. *International Journal of Social Education, 3,* 34–47.

Watson, M., Solomon, D., Battistich, V., Schaps, E., & Solomon, J. (1989). The child development project: Combining traditional and developmental approaches to values education. In L. Nucci (Ed.), *Moral development and character education: A dialogue.* Berkeley, CA: McCutchan.

Watson, M., Solomon, D., Dasho, S., Shwartz, P., & Kendzior, S. (1994). CDP cooperative learning: Working together to construct social, ethical, and intellectual understanding. In S. Sharan (Ed.). *Handbook of cooperative learning methods.* Westport, Conn.: Greenwood Publishing Group.

# 8

## PREPARING TEACHERS AND STUDENTS FOR COOPERATIVE WORK: BUILDING COMMUNICATION AND HELPING SKILLS

### SYDNEY FARIVAR AND NOREEN WEBB

Group work is a powerful instructional methodology. We define group work as students working together interdependently on a clearly assigned task in a group small enough that everyone can participate (adapted from Cohen, 1986). Our definition of group work is very general and is meant to cut across the many forms of group work used in classrooms today, whether called cooperative learning, collaborative learning, peer-directed learning, small-group learning, or just small group work. Regardless of the specific method of group work used, students need to learn how to work effectively with other students, and teachers need to be able to prepare their students for small group work.

This chapter describes a cooperative learning program that focuses on building students' small-group communication and helping skills, and how four middle school teachers were prepared over the course of a semester to implement the program in their mathematics classrooms. The following sections describe the theoretical and empirical basis for the cooperative learning program, the sequence of activities that made up the instructional program implemented in classrooms, the school site and teacher participants in this particular project, how teachers were prepared to implement the program, effects on teachers and students, and dilemmas we faced during the course of preparing teachers and our reflections about preparing teachers for such a program in the future.

### Theoretical and Empirical Basis for Cooperative Learning Program

The theoretical basis for the instructional program implemented in this project was that students learn by interacting with others. They internalize social processes that occur in small groups and use them to shape and reconstruct their own understanding. One way that students can use social processes to shape their understanding is through helping one another. But the nature of the help exchanged is important: elaborated help, such as detailed step-by-step descriptions of how to solve a problem, is more likely to be beneficial for learning than is non-elaborated help, such as only the answer to a problem without any description of how to solve it.

From a theoretical perspective, both the help-giver and the help-receiver may benefit from elaborated help much more than from non-elaborated help. Giving explanations encourages the explainer to clarify, restructure, and reorganize the material in new ways to make it understandable to others, which in turn helps the explainer to understand it better (Bargh & Schul, 1980). Giving non-elaborated help, such as only the numerical answer to a mathematics problem, may not always involve cognitive restructuring or clarifying on the part of the helper, and so may have less impact on the help-giver's understanding. Receiving explanations can help the receiver by filling in gaps in his or her understanding, correcting misconceptions, and strengthening connections between new information and previous learning (Mayer, 1984; Wittrock, 1990). Receiving non-elaborated help has little benefit for help-receivers because it does not enable them to correct their misconceptions or lack of understanding.

Most of the empirical research on the relationship between helping behavior and learning in small groups has found that giving and receiving elaborated help are more strongly positively related to achievement than are giving and receiving non-elaborated help (see King, 1992; Peterson, Janicki, & Swing, 1981; Webb & Palincsar, 1996, reviews by Webb, 1989, 1991). Moreover, receiving non-elaborated help often is negatively related to achievement, suggesting that it may be detrimental for learning.

The main focus of our cooperative learning program is to encourage students to exchange elaborated help rather than non-elaborated help. As will be described in more detail below, students are taught the difference between elaborated and non-elaborated help and are given specific guidelines about how to be effective help-givers. Students are also given guidance in effective help-seeking so that they would be more likely to receive elaborated help than non-elaborated help (Nelson-Le Gall, 1992).

Giving and seeking elaborated help are sophisticated skills that cannot be developed in isolation. Developing such high-level interaction skills presupposes that students possess basic communication and small-group social skills, that they feel comfortable interacting with others in small groups, and that cooperative and prosocial norms are in place to encourage positive and beneficial interaction. At a minimum, building effective help-giving and help-seeking skills assumes that students can listen to others, allow and encourage others to participate, and can resolve disagreements in constructive ways. Without such basic communication and social skills, students may try to bully others, dominate group work without listening to others or letting them participate, sit back and let others do all of the work, or criticize others in hurtful ways. All of these detrimental processes would short-circuit any attempts to engage in effective helping.

To help prepare students to work with others, many cooperative learning methods include activities to establish norms for cooperative behavior in the classroom and to help students develop and practice communication skills (e.g., Learning Together, Johnson, Johnson, Holubec, & Roy, 1984; Group Investigation, Sharan & Sharan, 1976 & 1992; Co-op Co-op, Kagan, 1992). Some entire classroom instruction or school-wide programs emphasize cooperative norms and prosocial development, for example, the Child Development Program developed in San Ramon, California (Solomon, et.al, 1985; Solomon, Watson, Schaps, Battistich, & Solomon; 1990; also see Watson, et.al., chapter 7 of this book), Cohen, Lotan, and Catanzarite's (1990) adaptation of *Finding Out/Descubrimiento* (DeAvila & Duncan, 1980, see Lotan, Cohen & Morphew chapter 6 of this book), and Kagan's (1992, see also Kagan & Kagan chapter 5 of this book) structural program of cooperative learning.

Recognizing that development of effective helping skills depends upon laying a groundwork of effective communication skills and prosocial norms and behavior, we integrate into a single instructional program preparation for group work (developing basic communications and small-group social skills and building small-group cohesion), fine-tuning communication and cooperation skills, and developing effective helping skills (focusing on elaborated help).

## The Instructional Program: Sequence and Activities

The cooperative learning program consisted of three sequential stages: Preparation for Group Work, Fine-Tuning Communication and Cooperation Skills, and Sharpening Explaining Skills. Each stage is designed to last for about three weeks during which time cooperative learning activities take place alongside classroom work on the subject matter.

The first stage of the sequence (Preparation for Group Work) begins with activities to make students feel that they are a part of the class, via class inclusion and class building, and part of a group, via teambuilding. Classbuilding activities help students become acquainted with each other, learn classmates' names and interests, and feel comfortable in their class. Teambuilding activities help students become acquainted with members of their small groups, learn commonalities with their teammates, feel comfortable, and develop cohesion in their group. In addition, students are prepared for group work with activities that help them learn to work with others, including social skills (e.g., listening attentively, working with classmates without putting them down, speaking politely without yelling), and communication and cooperation skills especially important for effective small-group work (e.g., sharing ideas and information, promoting equal participation by everyone, interacting constructively and positively, checking each other's understanding, understanding the difference between cooperation, competition, and working individually, and promoting equal participation by everyone; see Farivar & Webb, *Helping Behavior Activities Handbook*, (1991), for a description of the activities used in the program).

The second stage (Fine-Tuning Communication and Cooperation Skills) focuses on fine-tuning students' communication skills and introduced helping skills. Fine-tuning communication and cooperation skills includes activities to help students understand the value of two-way communication, learn how to share the talking and directing, learn to use teammates as resources, and work as a group without depending on the teacher. Activities for developing students' helping skills begin with discussions of research findings on the value of helping behavior and the kinds of helping behavior most highly related to promote learning. Based on class discussions, students and teachers work together to make charts of behavior that students could use when they needed help and when they gave help (see Tables 8.1 and 8.2). The behaviors emphasize the processes of understanding and solving problems rather than merely getting the right answers. This stage also includes "debriefing" activities in which students fill out a checklist to help them evaluate their helping behavior, and discuss in small groups or whole classrooms their experiences in their groups.

The activities in the third stage (Sharpening Explaining Skills) develop students' helping skills still further by focusing on distinctions among different kinds of help, emphasizing explanations over briefer and less-informative responses. The primary activity, described below, consists of skits for students to role play and discuss that contrast effective and ineffective explanations of how to solve math problems (adapted from Swing & Peterson, 1982). Skits for "effective" helping

TABLE 8.1

Chart of Behaviors for Students Who Need Help

| Behavior | Example |
|---|---|
| *Problem*: Groups design their own restaurant menus with prices for entrees, desserts, and drinks. They each select a meal, and estimate the total cost for their entire group, including 8.5 percent sales tax and 15 percent tip. | |
| 1. Recognize that you need help. | "I don't understand how to calculate sales tax." |
| 2. Decide to get help from another student. | "I'm going to ask someone for help" |
| 3. Choose someone to help you. | "I think Maria could help me" |
| 4. Ask for help | "Could you help me with sales tax?" |
| 5. Ask clear and precise questions. | "Our group's bill is $24.00. Why don't we just add $0.85 to $24.00 for the sales tax?" |
| 6. Keep asking until you understand | "So if the bill was $50.00, are you saying that the sales tax would be 8.5 percent of $50.00?" |

From "Helping and Getting Help—Essential Skills for Effective Group Problem Solving" by Sydney Farivar and Noreen M. Webb, 1994, *Arithmetic Teacher*, 41, p. 522. Copyright 1994 by the National Council of Teachers of Mathematics. Reprinted by permission.

show one student explaining to another student the steps in solving a problem, giving the other student a chance to try to solve the problem, correcting the other student's errors with explanations of what should be done and why, asking follow-up questions to make sure that the other student truly understands, and giving praise for work well done. Skits for "ineffective" helping show one student giving another student only the answer to the problem without describing the solution process, telling the other student to hurry up, and telling the other student to concentrate on getting the answer rather than understanding how to solve the problem. Students also practice checking each others' work and giving explanations to teammates.

Although the division of the cooperative learning program into these three stages seems reasonable and is logistically feasible, the sequence of activities could be segmented in other ways. The main principles for implementing this program in the classroom are that activities be clustered in stages to give students opportunities to learn, practice,

TABLE 8.2

Chart of Behaviors for Students Who Give Help

| Behavior | Example |
|---|---|
| 1. Notice when other students need help. | Look around your group to see if anyone needs help. |
| 2. Tell other students to ask you if they need help. | "If you need help, ask me." |
| 3. When someone asks for help, help him or her. | "Sure I'll help you. What don't you understand?" |
| 4. Be a good listener. | Let your teammate explain what he or she doesn't understand. |
| 5. Give explanation instead of the answer. | "8.5% is not the same as $0.85. The sales tax is not the same amount of money for every bill. The bigger the bill is, the bigger the tax will be. So here we have to figure out 8.5% of $24.00. 10% of $24.00 is $2.40, so the sales tax will be a little less than that." |
| 6. Watch how your teammate solves the problem. | |
| 7. Give specific feedback on how your teammate solved the problem. | "You multiplied the numbers OK, but you have to be careful of the decimal point. If the bill is $24.00, it doesn't make sense that the sales tax is $204.00" |
| 8. Check for understanding. | "Tell me again why you think the sales tax is $2.04 instead of $204.00." |
| 9. Praise your teammate for doing good job. | "Good job!" "Nice work!" "You've got it!" |

From "Helping and Getting Help—Essential Skills for Effective Group Problem Solving" by Sydney Farivar and Noreen M. Webb, 1994, *Arithmetic Teacher,* 41, p. 523. Copyright 1994 by the National Council of Teachers of Mathematics. Reprinted by permission.

and receive feedback on a few skills at a time, and that stages proceed from basic to advanced communications skills so that students can build on skills learned previously.

### The School Site and the Teacher Participants

For the implementation of this cooperative learning program that we studied, we sought a school site that "looked like" many middle schools in California. We selected a school in a district within the greater Los Angeles area with a relatively large Hispanic population (both Spanish and non-Spanish speaking Hispanics), a sizable minority of Anglos, and African-American and Asian-American students as well. The principal expressed interest in the program and identified four teachers—two seventh-grade and two eighth-grade—whom he thought would be interested in participating and who would benefit from the experience. The four teachers were a diverse group. One seventh-grade teacher and one eighth-grade teacher had just completed student teaching; one had graduated from college and the other had just changed careers. The other two teachers each had many years of teaching experience. One had taught mathematics at the middle school level for most of his teaching career. The other experienced teacher was an elementary school teacher by training who had recently moved to the middle school. Although she had taught mathematics before, most of her teaching experience was in language arts and social studies. Only one teacher had any previous experience with cooperative learning. After meeting with us to discuss the program, the teachers agreed to participate, so planning and training sessions began.

## Working With Teachers

### Initial Training Sessions and Staff Development

Prior to each stage of the cooperative learning program, we met with the four teachers on several occasions to discuss the cooperative learning components of the program and the coordination of the curriculum and instruction in the subject matter.

### The Cooperative Learning Program

Half-day training sessions were held in a conference room in the Graduate School of Education at UCLA. Present during the training sessions were the authors, the four middle school teachers, and several doctoral students who served as research assistants. As would be the case in the classroom, we began our training sessions by getting to know one another. We used activities such as finding three things in common and interviewing one another and introducing each other to the group to build what Gibbs (1987) labels "inclusion"—an atmosphere in which everyone feels included. We introduced Gibbs' "Tribes Trail" and shared the key steps along the trail—inclusion, influence, affection: (1) Group work begins with inclusion activities to help all members feel a part of the group, (2) Once people feel included they are comfortable and are able to influence one another, and (3) When people have worked together, they begin to develop affection for one another.

The second part of the training sessions focused on the philosophy of cooperative learning, various notions about what cooperative learning is and is not, and the conceptualization underlying the cooperative learning program to be implemented in their classrooms. The teachers' understanding of cooperative learning ranged from a rudimentary concept best described as "students working in groups" to a somewhat deeper understanding of positive interdependence. So we laid out our conceptualization of small group work and the elements we consider basic to cooperative learning: heterogeneous groups, task interdependence, individual accountability, (limited) reward interdependence, direct instruction of social skills, the teacher as observer and giver of feedback, and processing of the instructional task and social skills.

Everyone actively participated as we discussed the elements of cooperative learning. The teachers raised many questions and concerns, including issues of fairness and grading, the necessity of teaching social skills, the advantages and disadvantages of different ways of forming groups (e.g., random, teacher-assigned, student-selected), and how to make groups heterogeneous. We looked at lessons which used different cooperative learning elements and talked about how each element is a part of the whole program.

Once we felt that the teachers had begun to understand the cooperative learning program to be implemented, the third component of training began: introducing and discussing specific communication and cooperation skills and helping and explaining behaviors that are central to group work. Teachers practiced many of the activities that their students would carry out to build communication and cooperation skills. This helped teachers understand and experience the purpose of the activities as well as gauge the time and special instructions required. Finally, we shared the research on helping, both the kinds of helping behavior that have been found to be related to student achievement (e.g., explanations of how to solve problems vs. only the answer) and the mechanisms by which helping behavior is thought to improve learning (e.g., teaching others helps students reorganize, clarify, and facilitate better understanding of the material).

## Curriculum and Scheduling

After covering the sequence of activities that students would carry out in preparation for group work, we turned our attention to the mathematics curriculum. Because we needed teachers at the same grade level to teach the same curriculum at the same time for research purposes, it was necessary to coordinate the curriculum among the teachers at each grade. Although teachers at the same grade level used the same textbook, they did not necessarily cover topics in the textbook in the same order. The process of selecting the topics to be covered during the cooperative learning program had the unintended beneficial consequence of provoking detailed discussions of curriculum and instruction. As the teachers shared what they taught and in what sequence, questions emerged relating to the underlying reason and rationale for teaching in a specific sequence. This was particularly useful for the first-year teachers who listened carefully as the experienced teachers explained why, for example, teaching a particular chapter before another enabled students to understand the second one better, even though the chapters were not in that sequence in the book. Teachers also shared additional resources and materials they used to enhance the lessons for better understanding. What began as a seemingly simple coordination of teaching units developed into an important dialogue among the teachers about teaching. While close coordination of the curriculum would not be necessary in staff development in non-research contexts, our experience suggests that discussion among teachers (in small groups if the number of teachers is large) about the substance of the curriculum and their planned sequences of topics can have important benefits for teachers.

By the end of this discussion, we identified curriculum units in common that could be taught at each grade level, integrated the preparation for group work with the mathematics curriculum, and blocked it out in a weekly plan book (with daily activities) to ensure that teachers would be doing the same thing at the same time (again, for research purposes). Teachers engaged in important discussions as they negotiated timing of lessons and group work activities and logistical details, such as as taking attendance, handling tardy students, and collecting homework and classwork. With the weekly plan books in hand, the first phase of the study began.

## Continued Staff Development During the Study

The teachers had learned and accomplished a great deal in the initial training sessions. They learned how a cooperative, student-centered classroom is an upside-down version of a traditional teacher-centered classroom. They teased out many of the components that distinguish cooperative from traditional classrooms. They worked together to develop a sequence of lessons that would prepare the students for group work and discussed the "fine points" of each lesson. During the initial training sessions, teachers felt fairly confident about the program they would be implementing in their classrooms. However, when they put the plan into place in their classrooms, it was not as simple as they thought it would be. The experienced teachers found it difficult to let go of old habits. The new teachers, who had relied on their own experiences as students, found the shift from teacher-centered to student-centered to be more difficult than they anticipated. Moreover, for the first time in their teaching careers, the teachers were being asked to coordinate what they did with colleagues, a new and sometimes difficult experience. It became clear immediately that the teachers wanted, and needed, continued staff development during the project.

Fortunately, because we had spent considerable time on inclusion activities and developing a good working relationship with the teachers, the teachers trusted us and each other. The teachers felt comfortable articulating their concerns and asking for help, and were receptive to possible solutions suggested to them. Most of their questions and concerns clustered around issues related to being part of a team and the transition to a student-centered classroom where the focus was on the group, not on individual students.

The first problem that emerged was that teachers had difficulty coordinating the schedules of activities in their classrooms, due to differences between teachers' personalities and teaching styles (e.g., "chatty" teachers took longer to get classes started than more "business-like" teachers), differences in teachers' interpretations of how much time to devote to particular lessons, and differences in handling the cooperative learning activities (e.g., some teachers imposing time limits and others not).

Our solution was to coordinate timing among the teachers by preparing more detailed lesson plans than had been developed during the initial workshops. Rather than just listing the major activities and topics to be covered each day, the revised daily plans stated the cooperative learning and subject matter objectives for the day, outlined the teacher's whole-class introduction (e.g., description of content to be covered, example problems to be demonstrated, cooperative learning principles to be reviewed and/or discussed with the class), listed the exact activities that students would carry out in their groups, and summarized end-of-class procedures (e.g., collection of papers, grading procedures, administration of questionnaires or checklists about small-group functioning, discussions of small-groups' experiences that day). The revised plans also incorporated flexibility to allow teachers to "catch up" when necessary.

The second problem that emerged was the difficulty teachers had in adjusting their teaching styles to give more responsibility to groups

and to students in their groups. The teachers were accustomed to interacting with one student at a time, and to maintaining control over the
interaction, and were slow to adjust to the new dynamics of interacting
with groups and allowing them to develop as effectively functioning
groups. Teachers had particular difficulty calling on groups, rather than
on individual students; using members of the group to handle classroom routines such as getting books for the group and collecting papers
for the group; encouraging students to check for group understanding
of their assignment before they began working; giving the students
enough time to work together; making sure the students' seats were
close enough together for them to be able to work together effectively;
letting the group do their work (without hovering too closely); allowing
students in groups to use one another as resources before giving help;
not helping individual students; reviewing the task and maintenance
skills groups should focus on when carrying out their assigned work;
allowing time for students to talk about ("process") the task/mainte-
nance skills and their assignment at the end of the lesson.

Our solution was to review with teachers how teaching groups is
different from teaching individuals, discuss particular ways of communicating with groups so that they would take charge of their own work
and learning, and set up out-of-class situations where teachers could
practice these skills.

Finally, teachers continued to voice concerns throughout the project about grading and students' completion of their assignments. For
example, teachers were concerned that few students turned in homework regularly. Together, we devised solutions based on the principles
of the cooperative learning program. To take advantage of the interdependence among students, especially to encourage students to motivate
each other to complete their homework, and to increase individual accountability, students received both individual and group scores on
their homework. The group score was the score of one randomly chosen homework paper from each group (a practice which is somewhat
controversial in cooperative learning. See Kagan, chapter five in this
volume). The group homework grade contributed only a tiny portion of
a student's grade because of concerns about the possible detrimental effects of group rewards (such as undermining intrinsic motivation and
interest in the task, Lepper & Green 1978; increasing students' focus on
the reward instead of the task or learning, Damon & Phelps, 1989; blam-
ing each other when the group does poorly, Ames & Murray, 1981; and
negative feelings about one's own contributions, Chang, 1993). Teachers also simplified the logistics by giving students homework on worksheets so that they would not have to carry home the textbook. Teachers

soon reported that many more students were turning in their home-work and that others, who had never turned in homework previously, raced into class and finished the last several problems.

## Effects on Teachers

Participation in this study influenced all four teachers. One effect was increased collegiality: the teachers got to know and like one another. The teachers felt comfortable sharing and discussing problems they were having and seeking suggestions from the group. As a result, they were able to appreciate each other's strengths and began to use each other as resources. In the process they developed new skills and abilities.

The two new teachers learned a lot from the experienced teachers about teaching middle school and interacting with middle school students. Even the experienced teachers became increasingly excited as they began to look at, rethink, and rework their "habits" of teaching. For example, the teachers noted that teaching students in groups was a "more positive" way of teaching. They could see how more of their students were able to understand new concepts when they worked with one another in small groups. The teachers also demonstrated increased awareness of fairness concerning grading practices. Finally, teachers developed an attitude of flexibility and a spirit of innovation about their own teaching, as demonstrated by the following teacher comment:

"This was an experiment so I was trying things. I wasn't being graded and no one was coming in and evaluating me while I was trying things and I didn't know how it was going to work. I had an open door; if it didn't work one day then I would say: what can I do next time to make it work better or is this a good activity to do?"

## Effects on Students

### Teachers' and Students' Observations

The teachers observed that the change to small group work was a positive one for the students: students enjoyed working in groups, and they particularly liked being able to help one another, having help available when they needed it, and not having to wait for the teacher. Finally, teachers observed an increase in completion of homework and classwork.

In written responses regarding the "best and worst things about working in groups," the vast majority of students reported liking working in cooperative groups and felt that they learned more than in their classrooms previously, typically a combination of traditional whole-class instruction and individual seatwork. Students overwhelmingly reported that they most valued the opportunities for cooperation, helping others, and receiving help from others. Some negative factors mentioned pertained to negative communication, such as being teased, being ignored, arguing among students, and other students failing to contribute.

## Empirical Research Findings

### Design of the Study

To investigate the effectiveness of different stages of the cooperative learning program, the empirical study used a staggered design in which some classes of each teacher started the cooperative learning program earlier than other classes of each teacher. While all teachers taught three four-week curriculum units in the same order at the same time (decimals, fractions, and percents for the seventh-grade classes), some classes for each teacher started cooperative learning in the first curriculum unit while other classes for each teacher started cooperative learning in the second curriculum unit. The staggered design made it possible to compare different stages in the cooperative learning program while keeping constant the curriculum that students were studying.

### Student Behavior, Achievement, and Regard for Other Students

Data about students' helping behavior, achievement, and regard for other students were collected at each phase of the study (at the end of each curriculum unit) and have been analyzed in detail for the six seventh-grade classes (see Farivar, 1991, 1992, 1993; Webb & Farivar, 1994, for detailed descriptions of the design, analyses, and results). Positive effects of the program emerged for all three kinds of student outcomes. Students who had more training in building communication skills (who had experienced more of the cooperative learning program) gave and received more elaborated help, showed higher achievement, and showed more positive regard for other students than students who had less training (who had experienced less of the cooperative learning program). The positive effects of the cooperative learning program on helping behavior and achievement were more pronounced for African-American and Latino students than for white students. Importantly, increase in student regard crossed ethnic, gender, and achievement-level boundaries.

## Differences Between Teachers

Although both seventh-grade teachers showed the same patterns of results, the magnitude of effects varied by teacher. First, the program had a greater impact on students' helping behavior and achievement in one teacher's classes than in the other teacher's classes. The difference between teachers seemed to be linked to differences in the teachers' styles of teaching and classroom management. One teacher seemed to model more effective helping behavior than the other teacher, such as asking general leading questions that encouraged students to verbalize the principles and the procedures for solving math problems, rather than describing the numerical procedures and asking the class for the answers (for further details see Webb & Farivar, 1994).

The impact of the program on students' regard for others also varied by teacher, but in the reverse order: the teacher with a smaller impact of the program on students' helping behavior and achievement showed a greater impact of the program on students' regard for others. One reason may be differences between teachers' degree of structure and control over the classroom. The teacher whose students showed dramatic increases in regard for others over the course of the program was very structured and exercised tight control over all classroom activities. Prior to the start of the cooperative learning program, students had no formal opportunities to get to know one another in class and had little opportunity to interact with each other. In this teacher's classes, the cooperative learning program was probably students' first opportunity to work together and, consequently, to increase their regard for one another. The other teacher, in contrast, was very comfortable with students, created an amicable and friendly atmosphere in her classes, encouraged students to get to know each other, and more frequently grouped students' together. Because this teacher had already carried out informal inclusion activities and students knew each other fairly well, there was probably less opportunity for the cooperative learning program to influence students' regard for each other.

The contrasting results between teachers show the potentially strong effects that the teaching and classroom management styles can have on subsequent student behavior and perceptions in small groups, quite apart from the specific activities of the cooperative learning program directed toward students. The teachers in this study received identical preparation in cooperative learning, including specific guidelines in how to work with the students and directions in how to conduct the activities to prepare students for group work. Yet, students had very different experiences depending on which teacher they had. These results clearly show that what teachers take away from staff development, how they implement the instructional methodology in their own classrooms, and subsequent experiences and effects on their students can vary greatly depending on their own styles of teaching and managing the classroom.

### Reflections on Dilemmas

We faced several dilemmas about interacting with teachers during the course of the project. In this section we describe the dilemmas and reflect on how they may be treated in future programs.

Dilemmas

Our first dilemma was where to begin the staff development. Our work with these teachers was different from many staff development situations—although they were willing participants in our study, the teachers did not ask us to come and work with them to learn about cooperative learning. Antithetical to one of the main points of the program, the teachers had not asked for help! Because the cooperative learning program was embedded in a research project, the teachers were teacher/actors who learned a particular role. They did not necessarily need to agree with, or even have opinions on, what we were asking them to do. This does not mean that they were not interested in participating. In fact, they were delighted to learn more about cooperative learning in a personal setting with individual coaching.

Since we had not been invited by the teachers, we did not feel comfortable asking to observe them in their classrooms prior to beginning the training. We spoke briefly with the principal and knew a little about each teacher but did not have firsthand knowledge of their teaching, nor how much they already knew about small group work. Without having visited their classrooms ahead of time, it was impossible for us to be able to pinpoint where to begin the staff development.

As a result, even with careful planning, once the teachers began the implementation of the program we realized that we had spent too little time on some topics and omitted others entirely. For example, we saw that we had not emphasized enough the importance of interacting with groups rather than individuals and giving groups adequate time to do their work. Teachers tended to help individual students or spend most of the class period modeling problems without giving the students enough time to work together. At this point it became necessary for us to coach teachers and revisit what we had taught during the training sessions.

Our second dilemma was how best to deal with teachers' preconceptions about students, teaching, learning, schools, and schooling. Since the group of teachers was small, everyone had an opportunity to share their ideas and to discuss their concerns. In the course of sharing their ideas, teachers sometimes shared feelings and opinions about students that revealed underlying philosophical and/or value differences that were antithetical to cooperative learning. For example, some teachers had preconceived notions about students' potential to learn based on their mathematics placement (general mathematics vs. pre-algebra), believed that students had little to teach each other, and believed that students would learn little without a great deal of teacher guidance and supervision. We knew that teachers' beliefs about students and teaching were powerful and closely held, and that they could impact the decisions they would make about curriculum and instruction. We also knew that this had to be addressed and discussed as part of the change process. In our program, we raised questions and asked teachers to give examples illustrating their opinions. Over time, through discussion with us and each other and by working with the students in new and different ways, their opinions did change.

Reflections

First, we were impressed with the fact that even an imperfect and relatively short period of training and implementation brought about important changes in the students' ability to work together and to help each other. With more time for staff development and implementation, the changes may have been even greater.

Second, we gained new appreciation for how much support teachers need even after "formal" staff development in order to hone their skills and sustain the changes in their teaching. It became clear that teachers needed coaching during the program to be able to implement it as it was designed. They also needed help during the program to plan lessons that made sense. We realized that the lesson plans we prepared together and the scripts we developed during the initial training sessions, as detailed as they were, were not detailed enough. Having continued support throughout the program gave the teachers opportunities to ask questions, clarify misconceptions, and change their plans and behavior in beneficial ways.

Finally, while we were aware that cooperative learning is radically different from the ways most teachers have been accustomed to teaching, it is probably impossible to gauge the extent to which it turns teaching, as most teachers know and practice it, upside down.

## Conclusions

The cooperative program described here and implemented in ten middle school classrooms over the course of a semester had many positive cognitive and social effects on both the students and the teachers. The success of the program did not come "cheaply," however. The positive effects arose from the investment of the teachers, both in time and in effort. Our experience working with the teachers to prepare them for this program, as well as our experience working with teachers in nonresearch contexts, lead to three implications for staff development in cooperative learning. The first is the length of training required to make such a program work (the more, the better). Before teachers began the first step of the program in their classrooms, three full days of training were necessary. And several half-day and full-day workshops were necessary during the program to prepare for subsequent stages. The second is the importance of dividing staff development and implementation into stages. Teachers are less likely to be overwhelmed and more likely to be successful when they have an opportunity to become competent and confident in one stage of a complex program before embarking on the next. The third is the amount of support necessary during the implementation of the program to provide feedback to teachers based on observations of their classrooms, to help teachers solve problems, and to give them encouragement. With extensive training and support provided to teachers throughout the program, it is possible to implement a complex cooperative learning program that can increase students' learning and prosocial behavior and improve their communications skills and attitudes toward others. The program can also improve teachers' attitudes toward their students, increase collegiality among teachers, broaden their teaching repertoires, and give them new perspectives and optimism about what they can accomplish as teachers.

## References

Ames, G. J., & Murray, F. B. (1981). When two wrongs make a right: Promoting cognitive change by social conflict. *Developmental Psychology, 18*, 894–897.

Bargh, J. A., & Schul, Y. (1980). On the cognitive benefit of teaching. *Journal of Educational Psychology, 72,* 593–604.

Chang, S-C. (1993). The effects of group reward on student motivation, interaction, and achievement in cooperative small groups. Unpublished doctoral dissertation, University of California, Los Angeles.

Cohen, E. G. (1986). *Designing group work: Strategies for the heterogeneous classroom.* New York, NY: Teachers College Press.

Cohen, E. G., Lotan, R., & Catanzarite, L. (1990). Treating status problems in the cooperative classroom. In S. Sharan (Ed.), *Cooperative learning: Theory and research* (pp. 203–230). New York, NY: Praeger.

Damon, W., & Phelps, E. (1989). Critical distinctions among three methods of peer education. *International Journal of Educational Research, 13,* 9–19.

DeAvila, E. A. & Duncan, S. E. (1980). *Finding out/descubrimiento.* Corte Madera, CA: Linguametrics Group.

Farivar, S. (1991). *Intergroup relations in cooperative learning groups.* Paper presented at the annual meeting of the American Educational Research Association, Chicago.

Farivar, S. (1992). *Middle school math students' reactions to heterogeneous small group work.* Paper presented at the annual meeting of the American Educational Research Association, San Francisco.

Farivar, S. (1993). *Prosocial attitudes and achievement in middle school mathematics.* Paper presented at the annual meeting of the American Educational Research Association, Atlanta.

Farivar, S., & Webb, N. M. (1991). *Helping behavior activities handbook.* Los Angeles, CA: Graduate School of Education, University of California.

Gibbs, J. (1987). *Tribes: A process for social development and cooperative learning.* Santa Rosa, CA: Center Source Publications.

Johnson, D. W., Johnson, R. T., Holubec, E. J., & Roy, P. (1984). *Circles of learning.* Alexandria, VA: Association for Supervision and Curriculum Development.

Kagan, S. (1992). *Cooperative learning.* San Juan Capistrano, CA: Resources for Teachers.

King, A. (1992). Facilitating elaborative learning through guided student-generated questioning. *Educational Psychologist, 27,* 111–126.

Lepper, M. R., & Green, D. (Eds.) (1978). *The hidden costs of reward.* Hillsdale, NJ: Lawrence Erlbaum Associates.

Mayer, R. E. (1984). Aids to prose comprehension. *Educational Psychologist, 19,* 30–42.

Nelson-Le Gall, S. (1992). Children's instrumental help-seeking: Its role in social acquisition and construction of knowledge. In R. Hertz-Lazarowitz and N. Miller (Eds.), *Interaction in cooperative groups: The theoretical anatomy of group learning* (pp. 49–70). New York, NY: Cambridge University Press.

Peterson, P. L., Janicki, T. C., & Swing, S. R. (1981). Ability x treatment interaction effects on children's learning in large-group and small-group approaches. *American Educational Research Journal, 18*, 453–473.

Sharan, S. & Sharan, Y. (1976). *Small-group teaching.* Englewood Cliffs, NJ: Educational Technology Publications.

Solomon, D, Watson, M., Battistich, V., Schaps, E., Tuck, P., Solomon, J., Cooper, C., & Ritchey, W. (1985). A program to promote interpersonal consideration and cooperation in children. In R. Slavin, S. Sharan, S. Kagan, R. Hertz-Lazarowitz, C. Webb, & R. Schmuck (Eds.), *Learning to cooperate, cooperating to learn* (pp. 371–402). New York: Plenum.

Solomon, D., Watson, M., Schaps, E., Battistich, V., & Solomon, J. (1990). Cooperative learning as part of a comprehensive classroom program designed to promote prosocial development. In S. Sharan (Ed.), *Cooperative learning: Theory and research* (pp. 231–260). New York, NY: Praeger.

Swing, S. R., & Peterson, P. L. (1982). The relationship of student ability and small-group interaction to student achievement. *American Educational Research Journal, 19*, 259–274.

Webb, N. M. (1989). Peer interaction and learning in small groups. *International Journal of Educational Research, 13*, 21–40.

Webb, N. M. (1991). Task-related verbal interaction and mathematics learning in small groups. *Journal for Research in Mathematics Education, 22*, 366–389.

Webb, N. M., & Farivar, S. (1994) Promoting helping behavior in cooperative small groups in middle school mathematics. *American Educational Research Journal, 31*, 369–395.

Webb, N. M., & Palincsar, A. S. (1996). Group processes in the classroom. In D. Berliner & R. Calfee (Eds.), *Handbook of Educational Psychology.*

Wilkinson, L. C. (1985). Communication in all-student mathematics groups. *Theory into Practice, 24*(1), 8–13.

Wilkinson, L. C., & Spinelli, F. (1983). Using requests effectively in peer-directed instructional groups. *American Educational Research Journal, 20*, 479–502.

Wittrock, M. C. (1990). Generative processes of comprehension. *Educational Psychologist, 24*, 345–376.

# 9

## The Cognitive Approach to Cooperative Learning: Mediating the Challenge to Change

### James Bellanca and Robin Fogarty

Cooperative learning appears to be a simple model to introduce into the classroom, but our experiences as facilitators and mediators suggest otherwise, especially when explicit cognitive elements are added. To create a climate in which cooperative learning and cognitive education permeate classroom interactions, a gradual infusion must occur at varying levels. In order to heighten the possibilities of maximum effect (Joyce & Showers, 1983), we designed an approach to cooperative learning that included cognitive strategies as an essential component. The cognitive approach to cooperative learning encourages the teacher to design all lessons, units, projects, problems, and performances in a triple agenda framework that always includes high support, high competence, and high challenge.

High support in classroom interactions focuses on the social structures of cooperative learning and the benefits of team building and learning with others as the primary means for encouraging academic success for all. High competence dictates a relevant, meaningful approach to curriculum content that fosters learning for a lifetime. High challenge demands a cognitive approach to learning in which the teacher mediates the learner's construction of meaning. This occurs as each student works to make sense of new information and concepts in the context of existing schema.

### The Cognitive Approach

The cognitive approach, outlined in *Blueprints for Thinking in a Cooperative Classroom* (Bellanca & Fogarty, 1991), highlights the differences between the act of teaching and the act of learning in a cooperative framework. The teacher may teach in a great variety of skillful and artful ways, all of which are purposefully designed to increase the power of the student to construct meaning. The teacher mediates the student's interactions by developing the student's ability to construct meaning, transfer, assess one's own intellectual and social growth, and develop skills that transcend the immediate situation. As students learn to take conscious command of their cognitive functions in gathering information, understanding information, and transferring information, the locus of learning responsibility shifts. With this shift, students, working alone or in a cooperative group, have the power to direct their own learning.

The cognitive approach draws from two rich research bases: cooperative learning and cognitive education. For cooperative learning, the cognitive approach makes most use of the Schmucks' (1988) research on group processes in the classroom and the conceptual approach developed by Johnson and Johnson (1986). It also relies on Slavin's (1983) studies of team learning, Kagan's (1992) work with the inviting structural approach (see chapter 5 of this volume), Sharan and Sharan's (1992) research on group investigation, Cohen's (1994) meticulous studies of design for group work (see chapter 6 of this volume), and Cummins' (1979) insights on community development.

For cognitive education, this approach starts with Feuerstein's Mediated Learning Theory (1980; Feuerstein & Feuerstein, 1991). We add Beyer's (1987) study of the explicit instruction of thinking skills, Ausubel's (1978) advanced organizers, McTighe and Lyman's (1988) studies of theory embedded tools such as graphic organizers and mindmaps, Fogarty, Perkins, and Barell's (1992) research on learning transfer, Jones' (1987) studies of strategic thinking, and Brown and Palincsar's (1982) important research on metacognition.

The five critical attributes of the cognitive approach, outlined by the acronym BUILD, provide its operational definition:

- *B*uild-in higher-order thinking that challenges students to think deeply and to make relevant transfer.
- *U*nite the students into teams so that they form bonds of trust and respect.
- *I*nvite individual learning in which each student feels responsible for learning.
- *L*ook back and debrief students, not only on the development of social skills but also on the deep understanding of the curricular content and the development of each student's higher-order cognitive functions.

• Develop social skills in students by explicitly targeting behaviors that will enhance the quality of learning for each student.

In addition to cooperative processing, the approach calls upon the teacher to mediate content understanding. The teacher stimulates student processing of content throughout the lesson by checking for understanding (who, what, why, when, where), by mediating for meaning (how, why), and by facilitating the making of relationships (how connected). The teacher guides the students' processing of the content at the end of the lesson by asking questions that probe for knowledge, for understanding, and for the transfer of meaning.

Finally, the teacher mediates students' processing of their thinking. The teacher asks students to "think about their thinking" at the gathering, understanding and transferring information stages. By looking back at the thinking processes they used, by evaluating the hows, the whys, and the wherefores, students reach high degrees of interdependence through deep sharing and individual responsibility. It is in this processing that they form the generalized principles that turn thinking skills into thinking dispositions.

The cognitive approach makes use of four strategies that learners can apply to process their work. The teacher chooses both an agenda (cooperation, cognition, content) on which the students will focus the strategy and how they will make group or individual responses, either within the group or to the entire class.


Teacher Preparation


In the mid-seventies, the Johnsons' broke the accepted, theory-dominant inservice approach by providing multi-level, intense workshops that used cooperative learning methods to teach the model's theory and research (see chapter 11 of this book). Scattered through their work sessions were samples of lessons that modeled classroom application and culminated with each participant designing a lesson that incorporated all that had been learned about cooperative learning. Yet in the past some participants left these inservice training programs asking the questions, "But where do I begin?" and "How do I adapt what I've learned to my students?"

By 1985, Bruce Joyce and Beverly Showers' (1980) landmark studies of peer coaching with a variety of teaching models pointed to the need to facilitate higher degrees of application than normally occurred even after the best of workshops. Their elements included information, modeling, extensive guided practice with feedback, and careful plans for classroom application. Joyce & Showers found that the barrier to implementation was not the workshops or the presenters. More fundamentally, some school systems had values or instructional practices (or both) that ran counter to the values and practices of cooperative learning. These settings either discouraged or provided little support to the reform efforts of all but the bravest of new practice innovators.

Since Joyce and Showers (1980) first pointed out the importance of school-supported peer collaboration and conversation as essential elements for instructional innovation, many others have substantiated and extended the findings. Fullan (1982) described three stages of meaningful educational change: initiation, implementation, and institutionalization. Whether focusing on transfer (Fogarty et al., 1992), the importance of cognition in coaching (Costa & Garmston, 1985), the value of reflective practice (Saphier & Gower, 1985), or the provision of adequate time (Berliner & Casanova, 1996), the researchers have identified a variety of strategies successful in turning even a small innovation into a long-term, well-mediated, systemic effort (Senge, 1990) that achieves academic results. They concluded that the more complex the innovation or the more the model runs contrary to accepted practice, the greater are the demands for protected time, mediation, and systemic support as seamless extensions of the teachers' workshop introduction to the innovative practice (see Brody chapter 1 of this volume).

From the first introductions of the cognitive approach to cooperative learning, it was clear that implementation and institutionalization would require more than workshops. First, very few teachers come with a strong background in cognitive science. In most cases, their prior knowledge about the field of "thinking" was even more limited than their prior experience with "cooperative learning." Second, many discovered that the cognitive approach's emphasis on understanding ran counter to their school's emphasis on curriculum coverage. This conjured the specter of time not merely as a concern to be overcome but as a reality which would stand in the way of the needed changes in curriculum, instruction, and assessment. Where would they find the time to make even the simplest adaptations that would allow for serious implementation? And if they made these changes, how would they know if the changes were appropriate?

The research on the successful implementation of new instructional methods applies directly to cooperative learning implementation. All point out that teachers preparing to teach cooperative learning need support to make the approach a major central model for instruction in their classrooms.

## Initiating the Change:  Awareness Program

Teachers are introduced to the cognitive approach in a brief, three-to-six hour, required awareness program that reviews research, engages them in a few high-energy, cooperative tasks using a simple jigsaw or graphic organizer with relevant content, and concludes with a sample debriefing task that redefines the goals of the cognitive approach.

Teachers may elect to approach their extended study through a graduate course or district-sponsored workshop that provides up to forty-five hours of investigation. Here they explore the strategies and tools that best promote each of the BUILD attributes with lessons designed for their new curricula. When the contact hours are spread over a few months' time, these teachers have the chance to try out their applications, collect artifacts of student performance, share triumphs and failures, and converse with their colleagues about the effects of what they are doing and why. At this point a teacher may change into one of two long-term practices, a field-based master's degree program operated with Saint Xavier University (Chicago) and the Mindful School Network operated with Phi Delta Kappa.

### The Master's Degree Program

The master's degree program holds classes in local school districts. Teachers and teacher teams from schools register on a voluntary basis in a cohort. Cohort members complete all courses as a unit. In the first semester of the thirty-two credit hour degree program, the cognitive approach to cooperative learning is the core element. As with the graduate course and workshop described above, the emphasis is on research, theory, lesson design, implementation, assessment, and reflection on classroom results from the cognitive approach. In this initiation course, the participants also begin compiling a professional portfolio, join the first of two long-term base groups, and maintain a reflective journal. The portfolio, the journal, and base groups are used in all aspects of the program.

In addition to the introductory cooperative learning course, participants investigate cognitive instruction, assessment, multiple intelligence theory and practice, advanced cooperative learning, curriculum integration, classroom management, teacher leadership, and action research. After completing classroom application tasks for each course, participants must assemble a portfolio of their best practices, complete an action research project based on a major classroom application derived from course work, demonstrate the ability to collaborate in a team, and present the results of their research project in a public exhibition.

The Mindful School Network

The Mindful School Network was formed with the same purpose as the master's degree program. However, it serves a different constituency with different needs. Only a school team may join the Network. After the entire faculty, including the principal, have completed a three-to-six hour introduction to the approach and to the Network, they decide together whether to enter into the three-year membership. In the first year of membership, the faculty spends two days developing an action plan for the first year's initiation of the cognitive approach. This plan must include: scheduled time for investigating the approach; scheduled time for base group meetings in which grade-level or interdisciplinary teams will plan and assess implementations; team meetings with a Network consultant six days per year; and the school's leadership team interacting with other schools via email and at the annual Network conference.

Implementing the Cognitive Approach

When the cognitive approach is introduced in a graduate course or in a multi-day workshop, its implementation in the classroom, more often than not, is left to the wits and courage of the teachers, unless the workshop or course schedules allow for between-session applications, the gathering of classroom artifacts, peer observations, and conversations. Only if the school site is willing to schedule weekly or monthly follow-up sessions—to encourage teachers to continue the process of planning and assessing what they learned, revising curriculum, maintaining journals, and talking about the implementation process—does the actual application percentage match what the research highlights as optimal. If the formal support is lacking, most teachers drop back to using an occasional strategy.

The Network of Mindful Schools, the Field-Based Master's Program, and single district strategies that encourage high degrees of follow-up and district support of implementation all rely on structured conversations scheduled over a prolonged time. Scheduled conversation allows implementors of the cognitive approach to move through the implementation stage and into the institutionalization stage. The strategies (e.g., reflective journals, base groups,) introduced during the initiation stage are extended throughout each of the programs.

In the degree program, participants meet weekly over a two year period. There are three interlocking course tracks. All build on the basic content of the first course, which introduces the cognitive approach to cooperative learning. In the first track, the cohort groups extend their study of cognitive education by investigating the theory of mediated learning experiences, metacognition, cognitive interactions, and cognitive functions in the classroom. This work is followed by studies of authentic assessment, multiple intelligences theory and practice, and advanced cooperative learning. In the second track, entitled "team seminar," the cohorts participate in base groups for planning, observing, and assessing the classroom applications designed in Track I. Base groups interact with each other to share common successes and concerns and to give support to each other. In the third track, action research groups form to investigate how action research differs from classic research and to devise a project that will use ideas from Track I courses to solve a classroom or school site problem. Reflective journals, data analysis, and a final exhibition of the action research results conclude the project.

In the Network, the implementation processes are similar. In the Network school team, grade-level base groups are scheduled to meet at least twice monthly. While individuals maintain their own reflective journals, base groups plan, observe, and assess the applications made by team members. After the basic introduction to the cognitive approach, the school team plans what new information is needed to deepen and extend the approach's application. Typically, site teams examine authentic assessment, multiple intelligences, problem-based learning, and curriculum integration as they extend the change journey into years two and three. In addition to charting how each base group progresses with its applications, the leadership team maintains a focus on the change process for the school site.

Base groups of grade-level teachers (elementary) or subject-area teachers (secondary) are the structure that support application and transfer. Participants practice with each other what they expect of students in a cooperative and thoughtful classroom; members examine student artifacts, review instructional strategies, and exchange ideas. As the teachers feel more comfortable taking risks with each other and with new ways of facilitating student learning, they grow more confident with the results of their work and more comfortable as guides and coaches.

When so structured for success, the early stages of implementation melt resistance and concerns. As the teachers begin to sense the positive changes they have initiated in their classrooms, they examine their belief systems and their long-used practices. Moving from a teacher-centered classroom to a student-centered classroom, facilitating interactions, and mediating understanding call for a major shift. Without base groups to provide support and to mediate the challenge, the cognitive approach has little chance for survival in all but a few classrooms.

Weaving the Cognitive Approach Into the Institutional Fabric

As teachers advance through the implementation stage, they notice a new look and a new role in their classrooms. These changes can feel awkward and even alarming for the teachers, the students, and even the parents. To move through this stage, all levels of the school organization must begin to provide visible, accessible, and genuine support. When that support becomes public, the institutionalizing stage is starting.

To foster success at the district level, administration and staff must understand and support the innovation. Although the provision of follow-up and support for the implementors is a necessary start, it is insufficient. Parents unaccustomed to the cooperative approach or fearful about critical thinking will raise questions and voice concerns. Initially, some parents may wonder why their gifted children are being asked to teach slower children or why their child has to do all the work in a group or why their child has to suffer with a low group grade. Other parents will want to know why time is taken from the basics in order to socialize students or to teach ways to think that may lead children to critique their parents. Unless the district is prepared to address these concerns and to support the innovators in their risk-taking, initial parental concerns can quickly overwhelm the innovation and drive it out. It is essential that the district not only provide the time and the funds for integrated development programs but also adopt a board policy recognizing the approach's legitimacy, publish background information explaining the approach's benefits to students, and provide backup for teachers whose use of the approach may be questioned (see Munger, chapter 14 of this volume, for an example).

Both the Network and the master's degree programs encourage administrative involvement. In the Network, a condition of membership is the participation of the principal as a coach and supportive leader. In the master's degree program, the principal of each enrolled teacher is drawn into the program at the initiation stage. The cohort group's facilitator meets each year with all principals who have faculty members enrolled in the group. The facilitator, the principal, and the teachers discuss the applications each is making, ideas for action research projects, and the ways the principal can assist. All principals are encouraged to visit classrooms and see what the teachers are doing with what they have learned about the cognitive approach.

At the school site, it is important that the principal devote time to understand the philosophy and practices of the approach. More importantly, the principal will help institutionalization by scheduling time for base groups, facilitating cross-grade teams in the modification of curriculum and assessment to include the approach, recognizing the risks the implementors are experiencing, and communicating with parents about the benefits to children. Finally, the principal may coach individual teachers who may experience difficulty in making the transfer from theory to classroom use.

The principal as coach reinforces the expectation that, as each teacher learns the cognitive approach, he or she is expected to use it in the classroom immediately. The principal encourages each adult learner to track progress through the levels of transfer described next (Fogarty and Bellanca, 1989). Preparation for the innovation should deal with the concerns of those at level one who either intentionally or unintentionally find "nothing useful" in the introductory material.

More likely, a number of participants will duplicate strategies exactly as modeled. "I did the cooperative jigsaw with science vocabulary, just as we did in class." Often, at this second level, the learner fails to generalize the idea as a generic strategy that may have many variations. As a duplicator, the learner copies the strategy.

In the third level of application, a person can repeat a learned strategy in a similar context. For instance, she may have learned to use think-pair-share to introduce a new lesson. Every new lesson then starts the same way, but little consideration is given to using this strategy in the middle of a lesson or at its end. At this level the idea is replicated, keeping some of the original application, but fit into a single groove.

At the fourth level, the participants are able to integrate the newly-learned strategies with prior knowledge, adjust the strategy to specific situations, and look for a variety of ways to adapt it across the curriculum. In the past, these integrators may have used a strategy such as cooperative roles but never given it a label or formalized its value. Now, seeing the potential of the strategy, the teacher forges new ways to improve instruction with the strategy.

At the fifth level, the participants make conscious plans for the adaptation and adoption of a new strategy within deliberate lesson designs. They see a variety of contexts in which the use of the strategy is appropriate. "I used the idea of Venn diagrams embedded within a study of two continents. I also see how I can use that same organizer to teach comparing and contrasting with two short story characters or to use other organizers such as right angles and 'fishbones' with other literature."

By the sixth level, the participants are ready to create new ideas. They enhance the original strategy with personal touches, inventive elaborations, and unusual connections within a cooperative lesson. This level of transfer is marked by the divergent modifications of the strategy.

The Case of Hinton High School

In 1991, the West Virginia State Board of Education placed Hinton High School in the small city of Hinton, on probation. Its continued low performance on state standardized tests, faculty dissension, and high dropout rate marked the school for an immediate notice to improve or be closed down. Two individuals, Jim Irwin and a colleague, identified five high school faculty members and asked them to explore what might be done. These explorations lead the team to study Arthur Costa's (1991) *The school as a Home for the Mind*. Subsequently, they attended the annual Network of Mindful Schools conference sponsored by Phi Delta Kappa. After this conference, the team made a decision—bring Hinton High School into the Network. The Network, built on Costa's principles for intelligent behavior, gave the team access to a mediated change process. This meant Network consultants would visit Hinton six times in the year to help the team implement Costa's principles into their own classrooms and at the same time develop and mediate changes that would solve the school's problems using the cognitive approach to co-operative learning. Within five years, Hinton High School became a different place. The probation ended, test scores rose, and faculty dissension waned. Classroom instructional practices changed, and faculty committees worked to align assessment and curriculum with the intelligent behaviors framework. The effort has now spread beyond the high school into the middle school and elementary schools.

A critical element in the success of changing Hinton High School was the willingness of a small cadre of administrators and teachers to use the cognitive approach to change how they taught. Others noticed the cadre members' willingness to confront myths about students' low ability and prior motivation, parental apathy, insufficient funds, and local anti-education traditions, and teachers responded to the invitation to participate. As the cadre expanded its membership to include a critical mass of teachers, parents, and administrators, the mediation role of the Network consultants changed. As cadre members learned how to set annual action goals, assess results, and regulate their school change work, the consultants became facilitators and coaches of the two-fold task of professional development for individual change and organizational development for systemic school and district change.

In several ways, the Hinton High School transformation defies some conventional beliefs about the importance of the principal and the need for extra funding: at Hinton, the principal supported the change but was neither the leader nor the facilitator of the effort. Neither was there an abundance of money to fund the effort. These limits (not uncommon in many schools) were overcome by the cadre's persistence, risk taking, and commitment.

The Hinton leadership team applied the action planning skills introduced by the Network consultant. The principal arranged teaching schedules to include base group and team planning time, peer coaching time, and his own classroom visits. These strategies helped the faculty create a community for change and resulted in high application ratios. After the first year, teacher and staff time focused on the integration of cognition and cooperation across the content areas exceeded time with the network consultant by a ratio of 10:1. Over three years the school expended a grand total of $4,000 to integrate the cognitive approach into daily lessons.

One of the strongest elements of this school's approach to instruction through the cognitive approach is the development of alternative assessment and parent communication tools. These were used in addition to the traditional assessments of basic skills via teacher-made tests.

## Summary

The cognitive approach to cooperative learning, incorporated into classrooms with careful nurturing by strategies that respect the process of change for individuals and organizations has resulted in successful learning for many children. Long-term, focused teacher support produces significant collaboration among key players in the change process. It is this purposeful collaboration that makes the changes work.

## References

Ausubel, D. (1978). *Educational psychology: A cognitive view* (2nd ed.). New York: Rinehart & Winston.

Bellanca, J., & Fogarty, R. (1991). *Blueprints for thinking in the cooperative classroom.* Palatine, IL: IRI/Skylight Training and Publishing.

Berliner, D., & Casanova, U. (1996). *Putting research to work in your school* (2nd ed.). Palatine, IL: IRI/Skylight Training and Publishing.

Beyer, B. K. (1987). *Practical strategies for the teaching of thinking.* Boston: Allyn and Bacon.

Brown, A., & Palincsar, A. (1982). Inducing strategic learning from texts by means of informed, self-control training. *Technical Report No. 262.* Cambridge, MA: Bolt, Baranek, and Newman.

Cohen, E. G. (1986). *Designing groupwork: Strategies for the heterogeneous class-room.* New York: Teachers College Press.

Costa, A. L. (1991). *The school as a home for the mind.* Palatine, IL: IRI/Skylight Training and Publishing.

Costa, A. L., & Garmston, R. (1985, March). *The art of cognitive coaching: Supervision for intelligent teaching.* Paper presented at the Annual Conference of the Association for Supervision and Curriculum Development, Chicago, IL.

Cummins, J. (1979). Linguistic interdependence and the educational development of bilingual children. *Review of Educational Research, 49,* 222–251.

Feuerstein, R. (1980). *Instrumental enrichment.* Baltimore: University Park Press.

Feuerstein, R., & Feuerstein, S.(1991). Mediated learning experience: A theoretical review. In R. Feuerstein, P. S. Klein, and A. J. Tannenbaum, (Eds.), *Mediated learning experience (MLE): Theoretical, psychological and learning implication.* London: Freund Publishing House.

Fogarty, R., & Bellanca, J. (1989). *Patterns for thinking: Patterns for transfer.* Palatine, IL: IRI/Skylight Training and Publishing.

Fogarty, R., Perkins, D., & Barell, J. (1992). *The mindful school: How to teach for transfer.* Palatine, IL: IRI/Skylight Training and Publishing.

Fullan, M. (1982). *The meaning of educational change.* New York: Teachers College Press.

Johnson, D. W., & Johnson, R. (1986). *Circles of learning: Cooperating in the classroom.* Alexandria, VA: Association for Supervision and Curriculum Development.

Jones, B. (1987). *Teaching thinking skills.* Washington, DC: NEA Professional Library.

Joyce, B. R., & Showers, B. (1980). Improving inservice training: The message of research. *Educational Leadership, 37*(5), 379–385.

Joyce, B. R., & Showers, B. (1983). *Power in staff development through research and training.* Alexandria, VA: Association for Supervision and Curriculum Development.

Kagan, S. (1992). *Cooperative learning.* San Juan Capistrano, CA: Resources for Teachers, Inc.

McTighe, J., & Lyman, F. (1988). Cueing thinking in the classroom: The promise of theory Embedded Tools. *Educational Leadership, 45*(7), 18–24.

Saphier, J., & Gower, R. (1985). *The skillful teacher: Building your teaching skills.* Carlisle, MA: Research for Better Teaching, Inc.

Schmuck, R., & Schmuck, P. (1988). *Group processes in the classroom.* Dubuque, IA: Wm. C. Brown.

Senge, P. (1990). *The fifth discipline.* New York: Doubleday.

Sharan, S., & Sharan, Y. (1992). *Expanding cooperative learning through group investigation.* New York: Teachers College Press.

Slavin, R. E. (1983). *Cooperative learning.* New York: Longman.

# 10

## Professional Development for Socially-Conscious Cooperative Learning

### Nancy Schniedewind and Mara Sapon-Shevin

Cooperative learning has been promoted as a strategy that can be used to "teach anything." While this is true in many ways, we are interested in cooperative learning as a process and a commitment to teaching—not just anything—but something very important. We share an approach to cooperative learning and teacher development that teaches about cooperation as an idea and value and links cooperative learning in the classroom to the broader goal of building a more cooperative and just society.

### Socially-Conscious Cooperative Learning

We call our approach "Socially-Conscious Cooperative Learning" and this means two things:

1.  Teachers and students become aware of how competition and cooperation in our schools, culture, and institutions affect their lives and examine how their own behavior in classrooms maintains or challenges these practices. This helps teachers become more conscious of the relationship between competition and social inequality, and cooperation and social justice. We support cooperative learning that is designed to help students and teachers engage in such consciousness raising.
2.  Teachers and students become responsible for acting powerfully and positively to make a difference in their world. People who feel empowered and confident about their potential and their opportunities can change existing, inequitable social structures, in other words, develop a greater "social conscience."

This approach emerges from values inherent in cooperation and in cooperative learning: democracy; shared power and participatory decision-making; respect for diversity; and working for the common good. Once we make these values explicit, educators can reflect upon the degree to which they are part of their teaching practice. In doing so, forms of inequality such as racism and sexism and other types of discrimination that thwart these values become important to address. Through Socially-Conscious Cooperative Learning, teachers and students explore cooperative strategies for transforming social inequality to social justice.

Within our approach, cooperative learning is both pedagogy and content, and the strategies used are compatible with the broader goals of social justice and equity within a democratic society. It includes thoughtful reflection and practice at three levels: (1) the implementation of cooperatively-structured learning activities; (2) a commitment to the creation of fully cooperative classrooms and schools; and, (3) a goal of a transformed society that mirrors the values of cooperation, democracy, and social responsibility. Socially-Conscious Cooperative Learning asks teachers to question three major areas—content, process, and vision—each of which has direct implications for practice.

*Content.* Are we using cooperative learning strategies to teach something that matters, content that has potential to move students forward in their understanding of the world and in their ability to foster cooperation and social change within and outside of school? Are we teaching students to become more conscious of the effects of competition and cooperation on their own learning, their schools, and their society through the content of what we teach?

*Process.* Is the process of cooperative learning being implemented in a way that is consonant with the overall goals of creating an inclusive, cooperative classroom community? Are tasks structured so that the skills and talents of all students are used and valued? Is collaboration valued throughout, or is there an explicit or implied competition within and between groups? Are students explicitly helped to gain an understanding of how cooperative learning works and why they are learning that way?

*Vision.* Does the cooperative learning that is implemented help move students and teachers towards seeing connections between school and society? Does it articulate a vision of more democratic, cooperative, and equitable classrooms, schools, and society? Does it help them become more powerful learners, teachers, and change agents, and move out into the broader community with these insights and skills?

This chapter discusses Socially-Conscious Cooperative Learning, and provides examples of ways in which teachers have carried it into the classroom. We share thoughts about the complexities involved in helping teachers embrace a more holistic, inclusive vision of cooperative learning and cooperative classrooms.

## Not Just How We Teach, But What We Teach:
## A Reconsideration of Content

Some cooperative learning enthusiasts emphasize that cooperative learning can be used successfully to teach whatever content a teacher would typically teach. While this is true, it is essential that teachers ask themselves about the value (and the values) of what students are to learn. Simply because a lesson is implemented cooperatively does not assure its value. A "business as usual" curriculum taught cooperatively loses the potential to maximize students' understanding of their world and of the idea of cooperation itself.

Content should be thoughtful, inclusive of diversity, and support cooperation as an idea and a value. We recently watched a teacher implement a cooperative learning lesson on Christopher Columbus' expedition to the New World. Students worked cooperatively to represent the Nina, the Pinta, and the Santa Maria, and to draw Columbus' first encounter with Native Americans. While the lesson's structure and the students' interactions were thoughtfully designed, there was no attention to unpacking the concept of "discovery" of the new world. Can someone discover things that are already there? What's the difference between a discovery and an invasion? An inclusive curriculum should present the perspective of the Native people about Columbus' arrival and its subsequent events, as well as Native Americans' response today to the celebration of Columbus Day. It should broaden students' understanding of the Columbus controversy or even acquaint them with the inadequacy of modern-day recountings of past events.

Had the teacher introduced the Native American perspective in this lesson, young people could have learned more about cooperatively-structured societies as well. The Taino, living on the island of Hispanola where Columbus landed, were a cooperative people. They lived in peace and harmony, did not have weapons, and shared all they had. Students studying Taino culture as part of the curriculum, could consider issues about the effects of a cooperatively-structured social order on peoples' lives; they would have the basis for comparing that to a competitively-structured society, such as Spain and other European countries. This teacher's training in cooperative learning might have focused only on structures and process and not encouraged her to explore the significance of the content as well.

Many teachers use cooperative learning to teach the standard curriculum, much of which assumes that competitive ideas, institutions, and relationships are normative and desirable. A questioning stance toward the standard curriculum can, on the other hand, help students become conscious of those competitive assumptions and develop cooperative strategies that foster systemic change. We begin by asking, "Is cooperative learning merely a structure we, as teachers, impose on our students or are students exposed to the principles of cooperation and the ways in which examples of cooperation exist all around them?" We want students and teachers to teach about cooperation, and not just "do" cooperative learning.

Teachers can help raise student consciousness about cooperation and competition as ideas and values in the content not only of the curriculum, but in the "content" of school practices, norms, and activities. We recently heard a dedicated, thoughtful teacher explain how she tried to shape her classroom around principles of democracy and consensus decision-making. Her goal was to turn over to the students many of the decisions she was asked to make and to provide them with opportunities to develop their decision-making skills. When her administrators asked her to select a "citizen of the week" to receive an award at the next assembly, she invited the students to make that decision cooperatively and supported their process. We invited her to consider promoting another kind of discussion by encouraging students to explore the underlying assumptions of the task itself: Should only one student be selected as "citizen of the week"? What would be the effects on other students of the selection process? Why do schools have awards' assemblies? Are there other ways to build school spirit and encourage excellence without placing students in competition with each other? Teachers may not be conscious of the underlying values implicit in such a task. They can, however, help students become conscious about possible alternatives to competition.

There are many opportunities to help students explore principles of cooperation and competition and their historical and current applications. When cooperative groups might be used to study the traditional content about World War II, students could also explore the role of competition in causing wars and, alternately, cooperative methods of conflict resolution. A cooperative learning lesson on advertising principles could include a segment on the role of organized cooperative movements, such as boycotts or consumer organizations, in working for the removal or modification of dangerous or damaging products.

Students might read stories or novels that highlight the effects of competition or cooperation on characters, and then discuss the results of those dynamics. A unit on South Africa would include the study of the anti-apartheid movement as an example of cooperation and solidarity in order to promote social justice and equality. An ecology unit could culminate in a booklet or legislative proposals about cooperative ecological projects for the community.

What kinds of support do teachers need in order to actively encourage their students to learn about cooperation and competition as ideas and values? What professional development would expand teachers' imaginations and perspectives beyond cooperative learning as a "method"?

### A Focus on Process That Is Collaborative and Inclusive

Many of the key components of cooperative learning focus on process: how groups are assembled, how children are taught to work together and discuss their own process, how tasks and assessment are structured and so on. Each aspect of the cooperative learning process provides opportunities to teach students about inclusion, respect, and collaboration. We can explicitly shape our process and share our thinking about process with our students so we not only teach cooperative skills but also an awareness about larger issues. Socially-Conscious Cooperative Learning invites teachers to consider the following topics and questions:

*Diversity.* How can we use the composition of the groups and group selection to promote appreciation and valuing of all people and the elimination of limited or stereotypical labeling? Having "boy groups" and "girl groups" in cooperative learning, letting students choose their own groups, or allowing certain students to either exclude themselves or be excluded from cooperative learning groups, does not lead to one of cooperative learning's major goals, that students learn repertoires of appropriate social skills and that they come to see their classmates in deeper and more appreciative ways.

Teachers can develop and model inclusive practices related to classroom diversity. Many have found it helpful to share explicitly their own goals relative to inclusion and acceptance: the importance of learning to work with others, why different students do different work in the classroom, and supporting group members whose behavior is difficult or bothersome. Students themselves can be active participants in discussions and strategizing relative to how all students can be included and supported. This kind of problem-solving has a direct relationship to the kinds of problems that students will face outside of school, in their homes and work places.

*Teaching Social Skills and Processing.* Teachers must actively teach (and not assume) that students have the necessary group skills and processing repertoires. Focusing on group skills has direct connections with students' abilities to act powerfully for themselves and on behalf of others beyond the classroom. Rather than seeing group/social skills "training" as a method of "managing" student behavior or insuring compliance, emphasizing social skills teaching and processing is critical to sharing responsibility for learning with students, and involving them in decisions that affect their lives. Citizens in a democracy need to listen well, to ask questions, to negotiate conflict, and to support others— behaviors fostered by teaching social skills. Socially-Conscious Cooperative Learning provides teachers with opportunities to process their own group/social skills and social learning as well.

*Positive Interdependence/Individual Accountability.* Effective cooperative learning activities are structured so that students need one another and help one another and are also personally responsible for their own learning. Thoughtful attention to issues of diversity and inclusion must be part of both task design and models of accountability. Cooperative learning tasks should support the efforts of a diverse range of students, and groups' tasks can be individualized so that a student with limited reading skills, for example, is a valued and needed member of the group (see Lotan & Cohen Chapter 6 of this book). Individual accountability does not mean all students need to be accountable for the same learning or achievements. Students' individual goals can be accomplished within the context of the group's activity, even when those goals are significantly different.

Operationalizing a commitment to diversity and inclusion within cooperative learning tasks and evaluation also requires the elimination of competition from our implementation. Prizes for the "first cooperative learning groups finished," and other forms of group ranking and competition are not compatible with teaching students that learning and interpersonal relationships are the primary goals of schooling.

## Students and Teachers Developing a Vision

Developing a new vision draws from the two previous challenges around content and process. Cooperative classrooms can be microcosms of a transformed larger society. Teachers can help students make connections between their efforts to create more democratic, cooperative, and equitable classrooms and schools with the process of creating a similar society. Students can think about how the values of democracy, shared power and participatory decision-making, respect for diversity, and working for the common good are visible (or invisible) in their classroom and school. Students can consider how these values are visible or invisible in the broader society.

Caring for one another is an underlying value in a socially-conscious cooperative classroom. Students can explore how care, or to the contrary, mean-spiritedness, is reflected in the policies and practices of our society's institutions and its leaders. Students analyze current political issues, cultural mores, and community practices for the extent to which care for others is an underlying value. To the extent that it is missing, they discuss alternative policies, mores, and practices that would evidence such care. They pinpoint people and organizations working toward those ends, learn more about them, and become involved in a change effort they believe in.

Teachers can encourage students to make connections, for example, between the ways they have learned to make decisions within cooperative learning groups and the ways in which workers could manage their work life, making collective decisions about work schedules, health and safety issues, and distribution of profit. In a competitive classroom, as in a competitive economic system, winners are rewarded. Students can investigate the implications of applying principles from a cooperative classroom where "we sink or swim together" to our economic system. In a more cooperative economic system, would we have a society in which 1 percent of the population possessed more wealth than the bottom 90 percent? What economic policies would bring us closer to a society in which there was less disparity between rich and poor? What would happen if "the common good", rather than profit, was the bottom line in economic decision-making?

Since respect for diversity is an underlying value in the cooperative classroom, students can investigate the ways in which such respect is evident in our society and the changes needed to foster greater appreciation of difference. Students may discuss the relationship between sexism and sexual harassment in the school and their visions of how women and men should treat one another in work settings and in the community. How are students with disabilities or who are different in other ways treated within the school, and how does that relate to issues of inclusion and discrimination in the larger community? What organizations are working to change racism, sexism, homophobia, anti-Semitism, and other forms of discrimination in our society? What can students learn from these groups and how can they act for change where they are?

Valuing the common good in the cooperative classroom means encouraging students to see problems as common problems and solve them in ways that meet the needs of all. Students can investigate to what extent our communities and society look out for the collective good in policy-making. In the cooperative classroom, teacher and students attempt to include, not exclude, to see that no one is left out or left behind. What are the implications of such a process and value system for dealing with homelessness, inadequate health care, and poverty in our society? What kind of social responsibility is called for? Students can investigate national budgetary priorities: how much is spent on health care, housing, and education as compared to military spending, and discuss what changes could be made. They might investigate the current system of taxation and compare it to a progressive tax structure as a means of thinking about the "hows" of meeting the common good. Students can use their experience in a cooperative classroom as the basis of a vision for a more cooperative society, and consider ways they would want to begin to work towards that vision in their school and community.

Students need to see themselves as active producers of knowledge and not just consumers, as agents and not victims of societal change; we want to encourage students to build bridges between the known and the unknown, the comfortable and the uncomfortable, the familiar and the unfamiliar.

For teachers to engage students in a process of critical reflection, they themselves must be supported in a similar exploration. Such reflection requires dedicated time; it cannot be accomplished instantly or without contextual support. Alfie Kohn (1992) has said that asking people to think about competition is like asking a fish about the water—its pervasiveness and on-going presence makes it invisible and often difficult to discern or describe. Given the challenges of developing a critical vision and putting it into practice in the classroom, how can we support teachers in their efforts?

The Practice of Socially-Responsible Professional Development

Our program, Socially-Conscious Cooperative Learning, ideally requires a minimum of 30 hours with teachers. While this perspective can be integrated into shorter teacher development plans, this amount of time is needed for most teachers to be able to effectively put theory into practice. We have taught this approach in a variety of formats. We focus here on the ways in which we integrate a socially conscious perspective.

The goals of our teacher development program are:

1. To enable teachers to structure cooperative lessons that include positive interdependence, individual accountability, teaching social skills, and processing.
2. To have teachers experience pedagogical skills, processes, values, and critical/reflective thinking they can transfer to their own classrooms.
3. To provide teachers an opportunity to reflect on competition and cooperation as ideas and values; consider cooperative alternatives to competitive practices in classrooms and schools; examine curricular approaches to teaching about cooperation and competition as ideas and values.
4. To enable teachers to articulate their visions of democratic, cooperative, and equitable classrooms, schools, and society and consider how their teaching practice contributes to making that vision a reality.
5. To improve the effectiveness of cooperative group work for diverse students, particularly for those of different racial and gender backgrounds and for those with different learning styles and strengths.

Between meetings, teachers implement cooperatively-structured learning activities in their classroom based on what they learned in the session. We begin with simple formats, such as partners, and work toward more complex ones like interdisciplinary, thematic learning centers. Similarly the essential elements of cooperative learning are built in sequentially, first introducing positive interdependence and individual accountability, followed by teaching social skills and processing. When teachers return to each session, they report what they tried and provide each other with feedback in small grade-level groups. In the large group teachers share particularly wonderful successes and discuss solutions to especially difficult problems. All activities and group sharing sessions are structured cooperatively.

Classroom-based support is also built into this model. The course facilitator meets with each participant at least once in her/his classroom or school. Individually this takes the form of planning or observing a cooperatively structured lesson followed by feedback. As a group this can take the form of a school-based meeting of course participants for sharing successes and problems. Most effective are peer visitations. In this situation one teacher in a school volunteers to teach a cooperatively-structured lesson. The course facilitator and the teacher's colleagues observe the lesson. Together they meet afterward to offer encouragement and constructive feedback.

The heterogeneity of a K–12 group of teachers serves our approach. Teachers learn to appreciate the ideas and perspectives of the educators who teach different grades and subject areas. After the completion of the first 30 hours, teachers are urged to form school-based support groups as a long-term support system. Some teachers return to take the advanced 30 hour course in which they are also provided training in peer coaching and support group facilitation to enable them to be leaders in cooperative learning in their schools.

### An Approach to Socially-Conscious Teacher Development

Building a cooperative community among teachers in our program is an essential first step. Only when teachers feel they are in a safe, non-threatening environment will they be ready to grapple with the often difficult value-related issues raised by a socially-conscious approach to cooperative learning. By using base groups, peer buddies, personal sharing, and providing refreshments, teachers get personal experience learning in a warm and nurturing environment.

Cooperation as an idea and value is a theme in the content of many of the cooperative-learning activities that we use to teach the basic elements of a well-structured cooperative learning activity. This value is reflected in our terminology. We consciously chose not to use the word "team," but instead use "group." The word "team" connotes working together in order ultimately to win over someone else, whether on the athletic field or in a business venture. We want teachers and students to experience and value cooperation as an ultimate goal. The examples below are suggestive of ways to foster social consciousness in cooperative learning.

An initial activity, the peer interview, enables teachers to get to know each other. At the same time, the questions on the interview form focus on the participants' experiences with cooperation. (see Table 10.1.) The pair interview allows people to reflect on their life experience with cooperation. Processing questions for this activity encourage teachers to think about the value of their cooperative experiences. Many teachers articulate surprise at the experiences shared, most of which they had never thought about before as examples of cooperation. Thus this activity serves the purpose of introducing teachers to each other, model-

TABLE 10.1

Coooperative Interview

1. Share something you've recently done cooperatively in your personal life.
2. What is something you've done cooperatively in your professional life—with students, colleagues, or other classes/schools—that you feel positively about?
3. What memory of learning cooperatively stands out from your school experience as a youth?
4. As you think back over your life, what stands out for you as an exhilarating or rewarding experience that reflected the cooperation of many people?
5. Make up a question yourself that helps your partner reflect on her/his experience with cooperation.

ing a cooperative structure, and raising teacher awareness about cooperation as an idea and value.

Throughout the program the majority of cooperatively-structured activities that teachers engage in are multicultural and gender-fair, and have cooperation as a content theme. This models what we hope teachers will replicate in their classrooms. To present the jigsaw format of cooperative learning teachers participate in an activity about the multi-faceted life of Harriet Tubman, remembered as a former slave who freed people via the underground railroad.

Teachers reflect on this activity relative to the cooperation built into both process and content. They talk about their experience with the jigsaw format and its implications for their classrooms. When focusing on the content, teachers are asked to think about how the underground railroad was an example of cooperation and ways in which cooperation was necessary to its success. They consider similar contemporary experiences, pointing to cases such as the Sanctuary Movement.[1] While teachers are learning cooperative pedagogy they are becoming more familiar with examples of cooperation in our history and culture that foster social justice.

When learning to use cooperatively-structured learning centers, teachers participate in an interdisciplinary activity, "The United Farm Workers' Boycott" (Schniedewind and Davidson, 1987). Teachers use geography, math, social studies, language arts, and drama to understand how the Chicano-led, U.F.W. boycott in the late 1960s was built on the cooperation of different groups of people across the country. Debriefing the activity not only involves discussion of the cooperative pedagogy, but focuses on the boycott as an example of nationwide cooperation and the boycott as a strategy for economic and social justice.

Cooperation is not inherently a positive value; cooperation was necessary to build the Nazi regime and cooperation unites a group of young people ganging up on someone less powerful than themselves. We continually encourage teachers to ask the question, "Cooperation for what?" Earlier, we argued that the values implicit in cooperative learning include democracy, shared power and participatory decision-making, respect for diversity, and working for the common good. We encourage teachers to use these values as criteria for assessing classroom practice, school policies, and their broader efforts to shape community, state, and national educational policy.

Teachers either read articles by Alfie Kohn or his book, *No Contest: The Case Against Competition* (1992). We discuss what Kohn argues are the myths about the positive value of competition in our lives, schools, and society. Challenging many central assumptions teachers have grown up believing, discussions about this book are usually heartfelt and difficult. In the end, however, this reading, reflection, and discussion often profoundly affects both teachers' professional practice and personal lives.

Concurrently teachers read *Cooperative Learning, Cooperative Lives: A Sourcebook of Learning Activities for Building a Peaceful World* (Schniedewind and Davidson, 1987). This book provides both a framework and wide range of interdisciplinary, cooperatively-structured activities for classroom use that enable students to think about the effects of competition, and the possibilities for cooperation, in their own lives, the school, our nation, and the world.

Because we view teachers and students as socially conscious and socially active, *Cooperative Learning, Cooperative Lives* provides ideas and activities for teachers to use with students for taking action to foster change to bring the values of cooperation—democracy, respect for diversity, and responsibility to self and others—to their school, community, and broader society. A special issue of the *Cooperative Learning Magazine*, "Cooperative Learning and the Challenge of the 90's" is an excellent resource for practical examples of socially-conscious cooperative learning in action.

Activities and discussions about approaches that help assure serving diverse student populations are integrated into our approach. Teachers experience cooperatively-structured activities that are designed to challenge learners at many skill levels. Teachers also plan for the inclusion of a student with a disability into a cooperatively-structured activity they plan. Teachers observe the gender and racial interaction patterns within cooperative groups in their classrooms. Often what emerges are common patterns of behavior and values such as "the male prerogative" playing themselves out in patterns of interruption, or patterns of female tentativeness and deference to the ideas or roles of boys. Teachers discuss ways to stucture activities to mitigate against this, and how to talk about these with young people to help them become conscious of the patterns and change them.

How do racism, class bias, sexism, and ableism contribute to inequality in our relationships with others and in the dynamics of cooperative groups? By helping students understand how these factors contribute to inequities in both society and cooperative groups, they can embrace the notion that "fair is not always equal" and be more accepting of young people whose abilities and contributions are different from theirs. Teachers devise plans to help students take what they have learned about racial and gender bias and other oppressive practices within their own classrooms and apply them to broader societal situations (see Schniedewind and Davidson, 1998, for more activities.)

Toward the end of the program, teachers are ready to look closely at their own teaching practice and consider the extent to which it either contributes to the potential of cooperative learning to transform classrooms, schools, and society or maintains the status quo (Sapon-Shevin & Schniedewind, 1989/90). We have developed a variety of practical case studies that teachers work with to both examine these issues and to consider cooperative alternatives to traditionally competitive practices in schools (see Table 10.2).

After discussing the case study on extrinsic rewards, for example, one teacher eliminated her practice of promising pizza parties for meeting behavioral goals. Instead the class planned a celebration when they collectively decided that they had been working particularly cooperatively. Each child contributed a food, song, or poem to this celebration.[2] Through these various methods our approach broadens teachers' perspective of cooperative learning to one that is both pedagogically effective and socially conscious.

We discuss the constraints teachers face in many schools. Some issues are general ones that many teachers face in implementing cooperative learning: dealing with concerns of parents, grading issues, and finding time to use cooperative learning and "cover" the curriculum.

Some constraints teachers face arise directly from a socially-conscious approach to teacher development in cooperative learning. For example as teachers discuss the effects of competition on their schools, they come face to face not only with their practices but the practices of their colleagues and school policies. While doing the case study

TABLE 10.2

School Scenarios

---

*Competition and Extrinsic Rewards*

Ms. Garcia has assigned students in her class to cooperative learning groups to work on projects on whales. She has set criteria for evaluation and the group with the best project will get to display their winning project in the entrance of the school. Members of the winning group will also be rewarded with a pizza.

a. How could Ms. Garcia restructure this situation so as to make it cooperative so that all students felt pride in their work?

b. What examples of the use of competition and extrinsic rewards with cooperative learning are prevalent in your school/school district? What is the effect on students? How could they be changed?

*Cooperative Learning and Competition in Schools*

Mr. Lee has developed a very cooperative classroom during the year. All students have been doing very well. His school is participating in the country's science fair. His students will contribute science projects to the school's science fair. The three best projects from the school will get to compete in the district fair.

a. What suggestions could Mr. Lee and his class make to the science fair committee for a revised science fair that was cooperatively structured?

b. What examples of competition in school-wide and district-wide events are prevalent? What are the effects on students? How could they be changed?

---

about the science fair, for example, a group of teachers realized that in their own school a teacher who at that very time was organizing the science fair had, for the first time since the fair began, announced that there would be a "winning project," complete with a prize. These teachers decided to speak with him about the change in structure and share their rationale for keeping the science fair noncompetitive.

## Teacher Change and Continuing Challenges

Teachers who have participated in Socially-Conscious Cooperative Learning develop both expertise in implementing cooperatively-structured learning activities and a raised consciousness about the transformative potential of a cooperative approach to their teaching and lives. Initially, participants are surprised by all the examples of competition they see around them that they had never consciously identified as competition before.

These teachers bring a new critical perspective to their own teaching and to their schools and seek to create more cooperative practices in place of traditionally competitive ones. For example, a high school English teacher who had run the poetry contest for years, changed it to an open poetry reading where all those contributing read their poetry and celebrated their work, followed by a reception to which everyone also donated a favorite food. This cooperative context resulted not only in many more students participating, but provided the structure for them to appreciate each other's work and experience the energy of their collective accomplishment.

Teachers have revised their standard curriculum in simple ways to help students become more conscious of cooperation and competition as ideas and values. An elementary teacher had her students make a competition collage and a cooperation collage, discussed the feelings and experiences associated with both, and applied those frameworks to various aspects of the curriculum throughout the year. A high school English teacher asked her students to analyze how competition affected the characters in Authur Miller's play, *Death of a Salesman* and think about how their lives would be different had they lived in a cooperative society.

Students in classrooms of teachers who experienced socially-conscious staff development initiated social change projects. For example, fourth graders catalyzed a sister city project with a community in El Salvador, providing powerful multicultural lessons as well. Teachers also initiated school-wide plans for change. Following a discussion of the competitive and classist underpinnings of the annual book fair, teachers brainstormed a cooperative alternative whereby, rather than having some students parade into the class with 15 new books and others none, money would be raised for each child to buy one book and additional funds from parents would be used to buy books for the classroom that all children could share.

The biggest barrier to a socially-conscious approach to teacher development is insufficient time to engage in critical reflection. Teachers need time to read, reflect, and discuss ideas, attend to the pedagogical skill-building, as well as reflect on the bigger questions, like "Cooperation for What?" In order for critical reflection to form a cornerstone of professional development for cooperative learning, the following five criteria are important.

1.  Opportunities for reflection must be on-going and take place over time (typically 30 hours). While shorter lengths can be valuable, establishing reflection as a priority means investing in teachers and their work over an extended period of time.

2.  Asking teachers to think about and critique their own beliefs about cooperation and competition is challenging work. Conditions of trust and safety must be established in order for teachers to share openly and honestly on this topic. Creating those conditions of support and safety is certainly related to the opportunity to meet over time with a consistent, supportive group of peers.

3.  Reflection should be emergent and not impositional. Teachers should not be presented with a fait accompli political or philo- sophical approach that they are asked to implement. Rather, they need to engage in a process of discussion and exploration.

4.  The approach is most effective when teachers are engaged in ac- tively supporting each others' efforts in the classroom. Through processes of peer coaching, peer support and peer feedback, they can improve their own practice and become important members of a collaborative effort to strengthen cooperative-learning practices within- and across- schools.

5.  Lastly, this approach affords teachers multiple opportunities to practice what they have learned and receive formative feedback. Socially-conscious cooperative learning bridges theory and practice and requires that teachers engage in the processes they are learning.

Many teachers have embraced Socially-Conscious Cooperative Learning because it is intellectually stimulating, personally meaningful, and socially relevant, as well as educationally sound. All teachers should have opportunities to envision the kinds of classrooms, schools, and society they desire and to examine the relationship between their teaching practices and the creation of such a vision. Without such op- portunities and emphasis, cooperative learning loses its potential as transformative pedagogy and its capacity to build connections between schools and society.

## Notes

1. The Sanctuary Movement has been called the contemporary under- ground railroad. US church people helped Salvadorans and Guatemalans and others from Latin America who were fleeing political repression in their home- lands find sanctuary in churches and homes as they moved north through the US.

2. A reward system is structured as "If you do X, you will receive Y." Peo- ple are often motivated to learn or take particular action so as to get the reward. A celebration is entirely different in that it comes after an accomplishment as an affirmation of hard, collective work for those involved.

## References

*Cooperative Learning Magazine,* Special Issue "Cooperative Learning and the Challenges of the 90's", Vol. 14, No. 2, International Association for the Study of Cooperation in Education, Box 1582, Santa Cruz, CA.

Kohn, A. (1992). *No contest: The case against competition.* Boston: Houghton Mifflin.

Sapon-Shevin, M. and Schniedewind, N. (1989/90). Selling cooperative learning without selling it short. *Educational Leadership,* Vol. 47 (4), 63–65.

Schniedewind, N. and Davidson, E. (1987). *Cooperative learning, cooperative lives: Learning activities for building a peaceful world.* DuBuque, IA: W. C. Brown. (Available from Circle Books, 30 Walnut St. Somerville, MA 02143).

Schniedewind, N. and Davidson, E. (1998). *Open minds to equality: Learning activities to affirm diversity and promote equality.* Needham, MA: Allyn and Bacon.

# PART III

# THE LEARNING COMMUNITY: COOPERATIVE LEARNING AND ORGANIZATIONAL CHANGE

❧

# 11

## EFFECTIVE STAFF DEVELOPMENT IN COOPERATIVE LEARNING: TRAINING, TRANSFER, AND LONG-TERM USE

### DAVID JOHNSON AND ROGER JOHNSON

Staff development in cooperative learning is aimed at improving teachers' expertise in using cooperative learning in a way that maximizes the likelihood teachers will still be using cooperative learning ten, twenty, or even thirty years later. To do so, staff development has to focus on the three stages of staff development to achieve at least five purposes:

1. *Pre-Training:* Preparing for the training by creating the conditions for successful staff development in cooperative learning.
2. *Training:* Conducting the staff development sessions in ways that ensure participants master the conceptual framework and actual procedures for using cooperative learning.
3. *Post-Training:*
   a. Providing support for transfer of what is learned about cooperative learning in the sessions to the actual use of cooperative learning in the classroom.
   b. Providing support for long-term maintenance of the use of cooperative learning with fidelity and appropriate flexibility.
   c. Institutionalizing cooperative learning as a standard instructional practice supported by the district.

Frequently, staff developers act as if what is good for one purpose is good for all. Unfortunately, some of the practices that increase the level of mastery of cooperative learning during a staff development session (and affect teachers' positive reactions to the session) reduce the likelihood of transfer and long-term maintenance of the use of cooperative learning. Staff developers may have to choose between short-term popularity and long-term effectiveness. This chapter discusses the factors influencing the long-term effectiveness of staff development in cooperative learning. Six principles of effective staff development are presented:

1. Establish long-term goals as well as immediate goals.
2. Deal with assumptions that interfere with effective staff development.
3. Create collegial teaching teams as the heart of staff development efforts. To change teachers' instructional behavior, focus on teams, not individuals.
4. Plan multi-year staff development programs.
5. Coach post-training-session efforts. What happens between and after staff development sessions is more important than what happens during staff development sessions.
6. Change the school's organizational structure from a mass-production structure to a team-based, high-performance structure. Behavior follows structure. Teachers' behavior is largely determined by the organizational structure of the school.

Principle One: Establish Long-Term Goals

I (David) had the privilege of studying with Matthew Miles while he was writing his landmark book, *Innovation in Education* (Miles, 1964). What was so clear from the research on innovation is that changing instructional practices takes decades, not days. It does little good to plan a series of inservice sessions to be given only during the next academic year. Serious staff development is based on long-term goals that point the direction for the implementation of cooperative learning for years to come.

The long-term staff development goals for cooperative learning are (a) for teachers to increase continually their expertise in using cooperative learning throughout the rest of their careers with a combination of durable fidelity and appropriate flexibility in adapting to changing conditions, and (b) for cooperative learning to be institutionalized in the school and district (e.g., majority of teachers using cooperative learning the majority of the time, administrators creating cooperative schools, and staff developers providing ongoing support and assistance for teachers using cooperative learning). The immediate staff development goals are to ensure that participating faculty:

1. Can take any lesson in any subject area and structure it cooperatively.
2. Use cooperative learning the majority of the time. At least 60 to 80 percent of learning situations should be structured cooperatively.

To reach this level of use, teachers need to practice and practice the use of cooperative learning until it is an automatic habit pattern.

3.  Can describe precisely what they are doing and why they are doing it in order to (a) communicate to others the nature of cooperative learning and (b) teach colleagues how to implement cooperative learning in their classrooms and settings.

4.  Apply the principles of cooperation to other settings, such as collegial relationships, parent conferences, and faculty meetings.

### Principle Two: Deal With Assumptions That Interfere With the Effectiveness of Staff Development

High-quality staff development may be blocked by a number of interfering assumptions or may be enhanced by a number of facilitating assumptions. Staff developers need to confront and deal with the assumptions that interfere with the effectiveness of staff development. One barrier to effective staff development is the view that cooperative learning can be divided into small component parts and taught to teachers in ways that eliminate their need to understand what cooperation is and how it works. The assumption is that the most effective way to train is to instruct teachers in prepackaged strategies, activities, and lessons that are simple to use and may be mastered quickly. Teachers are viewed as technicians who add new cooperative learning techniques to their bag of tricks. This assumption tends to trivialize cooperative learning. At the other end of the continuum is the view that teachers are engineers who constructive cooperative lessons tailored to their specific circumstances from a thorough knowledge of the five basic elements that make cooperation work (Johnson & Johnson, 1989):

1.  *Positive interdependence:* Members believe that they are linked with others in a way that one cannot succeed unless the other members of the group succeed (and vice versa), that is, they "sink or swim together." Positive interdependence may be structured through mutual goals, joint rewards, shared resources, complementary roles, and a common identity. All cooperative learning starts with a mutually-shared group goal.

2.  *Individual accountability:* Members know that the performance of each team member will be assessed and the results given to the group and the individual. It is important that group members know who needs more assistance and that they cannot "hitch-hike" on the work of others.

3.  *Promotive, face-to-face, interaction:* Members help, share, assist, encourage, and support each other's efforts to achieve and produce.

4. *Interpersonal and small group skills:* Members use leadership, decision-making, trust-building, communication, and conflict-management skills appropriately. Procedures and strategies for learning social skills may be found in Johnson (1991, 1996), Johnson and F. Johnson (1996), and Johnson, Johnson, and Holubec (1993).
5. *Group processing:* Members reflect on how well the group is functioning and how its effectiveness may be improved. Two common processing questions are (a) "What is something each member did that was helpful for the group?" and (b) "What is something each member could do to make the group even better tomorrow?"

Approaches to using cooperative learning may be ordered on a continuum from direct/prescriptive approaches to conceptual/adaptive approaches (Johnson & Johnson, 1994b). Direct approaches train teachers to be technicians who use prepackaged curricula, lessons, strategies, and activities in a lock-step prescribed manner. Conceptual approaches train teachers to be engineers who use the five basic elements (positive interdependence, individual accountability, promotive interaction, social skills, and group processing) to (a) plan and tailor cooperative learning lessons specifically for their circumstances, students, and needs and (b) solve any problems their students have in working together cooperatively. Virtually all technological arts and crafts use the conceptual approach.

A second barrier to effective staff development in cooperative learning is the individualistic perspective. Staff development may be aimed at changing individual faculty members due to the individualistic myth that individuals (a) work more efficiently when they work alone, by themselves, without contact or interaction with others and (b) are motivated by the opportunity to maximize their own success and rewards (Johnson & Johnson, 1994a). As long as staff development is aimed at training individual teachers, its effectiveness is limited. Changing instructional practices is not done in isolation from colleagues, it is done with the ongoing help and support from colleagues who are sincerely committed to one's success. Effective staff development programs require that the individualistic perspective needs to be changed to a team perspective (Johnson & Johnson, 1994a).

The third barrier to effective staff development in cooperative learning is the focus on changing teachers' heads, not hearts. Most staff development programs are based on the assumptions that (a) the commitment to improve one's teaching is intellectually based and (b) when teachers are told about an instructional strategy, they will in fact implement it. While intellectual understanding is important, most teachers who persist in the arduous work of continuously improving their expertise in using cooperative learning do so because of what is in their heart (Johnson & Johnson, 1994a). Staff developers reach teachers' hearts and build their commitment to implement cooperative learning primarily through their relationships with colleagues. By using cooperative procedures during staff development sessions and building and supporting collegial teaching teams in the school, staff developers build positive relationships among participating teachers and increase their commitment to using cooperative learning.

In summary, to achieve the long-term and immediate goals of staff development in cooperative learning, staff developers must cultivate the assumptions that facilitate goal accomplishment. Continuous inservice training on cooperative learning is needed throughout each teacher's entire career because teachers need to understand cooperation conceptually, not just have a number of structures and activities to use. Successful staff development focuses on teams not individuals, and teachers' true commitment to use cooperative learning through their career comes from their hearts, not just their heads.

Principle Three:  Collegial Teaching Teams
Are at the Center of Staff Development

The adage, "Never use one where two will do," is based on the assumption that staff developers need to create for teachers the same cooperative culture that teachers are expected to create for students (Johnson & Johnson, 1994a, 1994b). Educating modern students often imposes greater mental and physical demands than one person can perform in isolation. Collegial teaching teams and instructional excellence go hand-in-hand. Collegial teaching teams are small cooperative groups (from two to five faculty members) whose purpose is to improve continuously teachers' expertise and success in using cooperative learning and other instructional procedures (Johnson & Johnson, 1994a; Johnson, Johnson, & Holubec, 1993). Collegial teaching teams are safe places where:

1. Members like to be;
2. There is support, caring, camaraderie, laughter, and celebration;
3. The primary goal of improving each other's competence in using cooperative learning is always central.

Collegial teams meet regularly, at least once a week and (a) engage in professional discussions about implementing cooperative learning,

(b) co-plan cooperative lessons, (c) co-teach cooperative lessons, and (d) solve implementation problems in order to continuously improve the quality of their use of cooperative learning (Johnson & Johnson, 1994a; Johnson, Johnson, & Holubec, 1993). Collegial teaching teams provide the setting in which the quality of the use of cooperative learning may be continuously assessed and improved. By planning a lesson together, conducting it, and processing it afterwards, team members help each other progress through the initial awkward and mechanical stages to a routine-use, automatic level of mastery of cooperative learning. The cycle of co-planning, parallel teaching, and co-processing is followed by one of co-planning, co-teaching, and co-processing.

There are a number of reasons for making collegial teaching teams the heart of staff development efforts. McLaughlin (1989), in her review of the research on innovation in schools, concludes that high-quality teaching depends on productive collegial relationships and organizational structures that promote open communication and feedback among teachers. In another review, Fullan, Bennett, and Rolheiser (1989) conclude that collegial interaction is the key to effective teaching. Cooperation among teachers breaks the grip of psychological isolation from other adults that presently characterizes the teacher's workplace (Sarason, 1971) and creates a forum for teachers to publicly test their ideas about teaching (Lortie, 1975). Participating in collegial teaching teams expands teachers' expertise by supplying a source of intellectual provocation and new ideas (Little, 1987; Shulman & Carey, 1984). In addition, there is evidence that for the most part, the teachers participating in a staff development program are the ones who teach each other how to use cooperative learning and sustain each other's interest in doing so, not the trainers conducting the sessions, and teachers need to have "on call" help and support when they need it (Berman & McLaughlin, 1978; Johnson, 1970; Lawrence, 1974; McLaughlin & Marsh, 1978).

Isler, Johnson, and Johnson (1995) surveyed 174 educators who had participated in a state-wide cooperative learning staff development program in South Carolina. Three years following training:

1. Age, gender, ethnicity were not related to level of use of cooperative learning.
2. Technical support and a positive view of staff development were only slightly related.
3. The factors most highly related to a high level of long-term use of cooperative learning were (a) involvement in a collegial teaching team, (b) personal encouragement and support from colleagues,

administrators, and students for using cooperative learning, and (c) personal commitment to cooperative learning.

In addition to the staff development literature, there are numerous studies comparing team and individual performance on a wide variety of outcomes. We conducted a meta-analysis on the effectiveness of teams compared to individuals working competitively or individualistically, for adults—individuals 18 years and older (Johnson & Johnson, 1993). The studies were divided into those using individual productivity as the measure of success and those using team productivity as the measure of success. The results for the over 120 studies that compared teams and individuals on individual productivity indicated that working in teams resulted in higher individual productivity than did working competitively or individualistically (effect sizes of 0.54 and 0.51 respectively). These results held true for verbal, mathematical, and procedural tasks. Over 57 studies were found that compared team and individual work on team productivity. Overall, working in teams resulted in higher team productivity than did having team members working competitively or individualistically (effect sizes of 0.63 and 0.94 respectively). These results also held true for verbal, mathematical, and procedural tasks. Working in teams was also found to promote more positive relationships and social support among members as well as greater psychological health, self-esteem, and social competencies.

Principle Four: Plan Multi-Year Staff Development Programs

I (David) had the privilege of working with Max Goodson as part of a national project known as the Cooperative Project for Educational Development (COPED) in the 1960s. Its intent was to systematically implement school-based decision making throughout schools in the United States. The results of COPED made it very clear that changing schools requires a multi-year effort. Staff developers need to plan long-term programs that go on for years, not days.

There are numerous reasons why staff developers should plan a multi-year, long-term staff development program rather than a number of short-term, varied staff development sessions. First, in order for teachers to implement cooperative learning procedures to a routine-use level, teachers need time to gain experience in an incremental step-by-step manner. Second, adopting a new teaching practice requires substantial shifts in habits and routines. These shifts take time. With only a moderately difficult teaching strategy, for example, teachers may require (a) 20 to 30 hours of instruction in its theory, (b) experience in using the teaching strategy 15 to 20 times in actual lessons, and (c) an additional 10 to 15 coaching sessions to attain higher-level skills (Joyce, Weil, & Showers, 1992). For a more difficult teaching strategy like cooperative learning, teachers need considerably more time, experience, and support. Third, role overload and feelings of helplessness may result when teachers are expected to gain expertise in cooperative learning in too short a period of time with too little staff development. When given limited training, teachers can feel overwhelmed and unable to cope. Two to three years may be the average amount of time required to become a skilled user of cooperative learning procedures.

## Our Staff Development Plan

We prefer three years to train teachers. During the past thirty years we have worked with hundreds of school districts to implement cooperative learning. Our cooperative learning network extends throughout North, Central, and South America, Europe, Africa, the Middle East, and Asia. An overview of our teacher staff development program in cooperative learning is as follows. The staff development begins with an awareness session for all teachers and staff members so that everyone shares a common understanding of cooperative learning. The awareness session gives faculty and staff a common understanding of what cooperative learning is, how to use it, and why they need it. As a result of the awareness session, interested teachers are asked to volunteer to participate in a multi-year, long-term staff development program. There are three rules of organizational change that are relevant here. The first is, "Start with your strength." Only the best teachers who volunteer to be part of cooperative learning staff development are included in the initial staff development program. The second rule is, "Load all your resources for the success of initial efforts." The initial teachers trained should be given whatever it takes to implement cooperative learning successfully. Staff developers cannot afford to have the initial implementation efforts fail, because if they do, the entire faculty is inoculated against using cooperative learning in the future. The third rule is, "Build an in-house demonstration project." The initial teachers trained become demonstration sites for other faculty who wish to see cooperative learning in action.

The first year, teachers who volunteered receive six days of training in the fundamentals of cooperative learning and meet weekly in collegial teaching teams to help each other implement what they have learned (Johnson, Johnson, & Holubec, 1993). The staff development sessions are distributed throughout the year. The staff development focuses on the nature of cooperative learning, the teacher's role in using cooperative learning, the basic elements that make cooperation work, and the research supporting the use of cooperative learning. Weekly collegial teaching team meetings help each group member to implement cooperative learning. The participating teachers become an in-house demonstration project for other teachers to view and then emulate by also taking the training and using cooperative learning in the classroom.

The second year, the same group of teachers receive six days of training in the advanced use of cooperative learning and meet weekly in their collegial teaching teams to help each other implement what they have learned (Johnson, Johnson, & Holubec, 1992). The staff development sessions are distributed throughout the year. The staff development focuses on (a) using all three types of cooperative learning (formal, informal, and base groups) in an integrated way, (b) using cooperative, competitive, and individualistic learning in an integrated way in the same curriculum unit, (c) teaching small group skills, and (d) using cooperative learning procedures to teach generic lessons such as writing a theme or learning vocabulary words. Weekly collegial teaching team meetings help each group member to continue to implement cooperative learning. The participating teachers continue as an in-house demonstration project. A new cadre of teachers may begin the training in the fundamentals of cooperative learning.

Also in the second year, administrators and leaders receive six days of training in how to lead the cooperative school (Johnson & Johnson, 1994a). The staff development sessions are distributed throughout the year. The administrators and other leaders learn to (a) organize faculty and staff into cooperative teams, (b) use cooperative procedures effectively in meetings, (c) encourage and supervise teacher use of cooperative learning, and (d) be part of an administrator collegial support group focused on helping each other implement cooperative procedures in their schools and district. Teachers need support and advocacy from building and district administrators.

The third year the same teachers receive six days of training in using conflict creatively to enhance learning and meet weekly in their collegial teaching teams (Johnson & Johnson, 1991, 1992b). In staff development sessions distributed throughout the year the training focuses on how to (a) use structured controversies within the cooperative learning groups to increase critical thinking, higher-level reasoning, perspective-taking ability, motivation, and achievement, and (b) train students to be peer mediators and help each other negotiate constructive resolutions to their conflicts. Cooperation and conflict go hand-in-hand. The more committed individuals are to achieving the group's goals and the more committed individuals are to each other, the more frequently conflicts will occur. Resolving conflicts constructively becomes the central issue of managing long-term cooperative efforts. Students, teachers, and administrators, therefore, need to learn how to make creative and high-quality team decisions, how to negotiate constructive resolutions to conflicts, and how to mediate conflicts among other team members (Johnson & Johnson, 1995a, 1995b). Weekly collegial teaching team meetings help each group member to implement cooperative learning and conflict resolution. The participating teachers continue as an in-house demonstration project. The second cadre of teachers takes the advanced cooperative learning training and a new cadre of teachers can begin on the fundamentals of cooperative learning.

Expert teachers and other interested district personnel enter a leadership training program and receive six days of staff development in how to conduct the cooperative learning staff development sessions and facilitate the implementation of cooperative learning. Eventually, each school district has an ongoing, in-house staff development program in cooperative learning operated by teachers and staff development personnel within the district. The teachers who develop the most expertise in using cooperative learning and who wish to train other teachers enter a leadership training program that teaches them how to (a) conduct the staff development courses, (b) give in-classroom help and support to the teachers being trained, and (c) organize and facilitate the functioning of collegial teaching teams. What results is continuous staff development in cooperative learning throughout the district from in-house personnel.

In order to conduct this three years of staff development, there are pre-training, training, and post-training factors that need to be attended to if teachers are going to learn how to use cooperative learning effectively.

Principle Five: What Happens Between and After Training Sessions Is More Important Than What Happens During Training Sessions

Teachers need to be supported over a long period of time to make changes in their instructional practices. Gusky (1994) notes that teachers implementing a new instructional practice almost always achieve better results the second year than the first. The first year, he notes, is a time of experimentation while in the second year teachers' efforts are typically more refined and efficient. If continued support is not offered during the second and third years, teachers may not get the kind of results that are really possible. The impact of cooperative learning, in other words, may be underestimated until the second or third year the teacher uses it.

The most effective practice is to focus on team implementation of cooperative learning. As has been discussed earlier, post-training activities are best carried out in collegial teaching teams. Collegial teaching teams facilitate the implementation of cooperative learning in a number of ways. First, in collegial teaching team meetings, implementation goals get highlighted. Dean Tjosvold has conducted a series of studies (Tjosvold, 1990; Tjosvold & McNeely, 1988) indicating that the more a team is focused on cooperative goals of implementing new practices, the greater the innovation and restructuring of work that takes place, even when team members have quite diverse perspectives.

Second, collegial team members encourage each other's use of cooperative learning. Teams can ensure that opportunities to use what is learned are available and the learned cooperative learning procedures and skills are immediately practiced. Pentland (1989) conducted a study involving IRS managers and found that attempts to practice trained computer skills immediately on returning to the job had a major impact on long-term retention of the skills. Ford, Quinones, Sego, and Speer (1991), in a study of Air Force technical trainees, noted that there were significant differences in opportunity to apply the training and wide variations in the length of time before trainees first performed the tasks for which they had been trained. Supervisor and peer support were found to be related to the extent to which airmen had opportunities to perform the trained tasks.

Third, collegial team members hold each other accountable for using cooperative learning. Teams create an expectation that each trainee will be held accountable for using what he or she has been trained in. Baldwin and Magjurka (1991) found that trainees who expected to be held accountable for what they learned left training with stronger intentions to transfer their learning. Marx and Karren (1990) found that trainees were more likely to apply time management skills when follow-up occurred three weeks after a time management course. Being a member of a collegial teaching team, furthermore, ensures that faculty members "go public" with their efforts to implement cooperative learning and makes their implementation efforts visible and observable. Testimonials in Weight Watchers, for example, make a person's level of commitment quite visible to others. Visibility makes it nearly impossible for faculty members to deny their choice to use cooperative learning with fidelity for the rest of their careers.

Fourth, collegial team members can coteach cooperative lessons together. Frequently coteaching cooperative lessons enables teachers to provide each other with useful, continual feedback as to the accuracy of their implementation and encourage each other to persevere in implementation attempts long enough to integrate cooperative learning into their ongoing instructional practice. The co-teaching experience and the resulting feedback and encouragement enable faculty to progress through the initial awkward and mechanical stages to a routine-use, automatic level of use of cooperative learning. The more colleagues are involved in each other's teaching, the more valuable the help and assistance they can provide each other.

Fifth, collegial team members can provide each other with the support needed to improve continuously their use of cooperative learning. To persist in preparing and delivering high-quality cooperative lessons day after day, teachers need support, encouragement, and assistance. Collegial teaching teams provide faculty with both professional and personal support for implementing cooperative learning regularly, appropriately, and with fidelity, and for solving any implementation problems.

In their review of the literature, Baldwin and Ford (1988) found seven studies that examined the influence of the work environment on the transfer of training. In these seven studies, social support was the most important influence on transfer. Social support is required for:

a.  Increasing members' self-efficacy (when working as part of a team, "I can't" is typically changed to "We can!"—what seems impossible for an individual usually seems quite obtainable by a team);
b.  Motivating members to create great lessons daily (intrinsic motivation to achieve is encouraged and enhanced when individuals work as part of a team);
c.  Reducing members' stress (the greater the professional and personal support teachers receive from colleagues, the less stress the teachers experience);
d.  Reducing members' apprehension about the possibility of being negatively evaluated by peers and superiors; and
e.  Increasing teacher instructional success (the amount of social support a person receives is directly related to the person's productivity). The supportive interaction leads to the development of caring and committed relationships among team members.

Sixth, collegial team members provide each other with a positive transfer-climate. Transfer-climate consists of goal, social, task, and structural reminders for trainees to use their training. Rouillier and Goldstein (1991) studied assistant managers who completed a week-long training program. The managers were randomly assigned to one of 102 organization units. Trainees demonstrated significantly more trained behaviors in units with a more positive transfer-climate, even after controlling for learning and for unit performance. Teams are an ideal structure for providing members with goal, task, and social reminders to use cooperative learning.

Finally, in collegial teaching team meetings, members provide each other with feedback about their implementation efforts and celebrate the success they are having in using cooperative learning. Teams can provide both feedback about and reinforcement for transferring what was learned to the job situation. Fleming and Sulzer-Azaroff (1990) studied paraprofessionals at a facility for the handicapped. They found that implementation and maintenance of the procedures and skills learned during training was increased when paraprofessionals were assigned to pairs and provided their partners with feedback and reinforcement. They concluded that stable and enduring performance of newly learned skills in application settings is very much impacted by the social support and rewards provided by other implementers.

Teams can, therefore, influence the transfer and maintenance of what is taught in the staff development program by highlighting implementation goals, encouraging immediate use of cooperative learning, holding teachers accountable for using what they have learned, providing social support for using cooperative learning, providing a climate for transfer, and giving feedback and social rewards for transfer efforts.

It is essential to provide participating teachers with the resources they need to implement cooperative learning effectively. One teacher, one classroom, and one set of students is the curse of modern schools. The most important resources are colleagues with whom they can frequently plan, design, prepare, and evaluate lesson plans together. Integrated curriculum and thematic teaching depend on such co-planning and co-designing. Transfer, furthermore, is facilitated when teachers are given such resources as:

a.  Time during the work day to meet in their collegial teaching teams;
b.  Procedures that make it easy to co-teach and visit each other's classrooms;
c.  Multiple copies of materials they wish to jigsaw or otherwise use in a cooperative lesson;
d.  Direct encouragement from the principal.
e.  Even providing some food for team meetings may make a difference in teachers' efforts to implement cooperative learning.

There is evidence that if the organization has clear goals, incentives, and job aids for using what was learned, transfer is encouraged (Tjosvold, 1990a, 1990b, 1990c; Tjosvold & McNeely, 1988). Transfer is discouraged if peers who did not take the training ridicule the use of the new skills, if job responsibilities have not been modified to require the use of the new competencies, or if the equipment or materials necessary to do so is lacking. The resources provided influence whether the initial implementation of cooperative learning succeeds or fails. If initial implementation efforts fail, the entire faculty may be inoculated against the use of cooperative learning.

Considerable clarification of what cooperative learning is and how it may be used has to take place over a period of months after the training sessions have ended. Clarification takes place in professional discussions in collegial teaching teams. Professional discussions among colleagues are essential for building collaborative cultures in schools (Fullan & Hargreaves, 1991; Little, 1990), supplying a source of intellectual provocation and new ideas (Little, 1982), creating a forum for teachers to publicly tests their ideas about teaching (Lortie, 1975), and providing the social support that is critical for the ongoing professional development of teachers (Nias, 1984). We require each teaching team to gather concrete data on the frequency and fidelity of members' implementation of cooperative learning. Concrete data about the quantity and quality of the implementation of cooperative learning motivates teachers to continuously improve. The concrete data promote self-assessment and reflection on one's use of cooperative learning and problem-solving discussions with colleagues on how to improve. In Japan, the mutual dedication to continuous improvement is called *kaizen,* a society-wide covenant of mutual help in the process of getting better and better, day by day.

Have teams celebrate members' success in implementing cooperative learning. Team celebration involves having others knowledgeable about one's implementation efforts and thereby able to communicate respect and admiration for the results of one's work. One aspect of team celebrations involves walk-throughs (Johnson & Johnson, 1994a). A walk-through is a visit to a colleague's classroom for less than fifteen minutes with the intent of observing something good about the use of cooperative learning and giving the teacher positive feedback. There are three parts to a walk-through: (1) visiting a classroom, (2) focusing on a concrete and specific teacher action, and (3) giving honest, specific, and positive feedback about its effectiveness (either in oral or written form). The positive feedback teachers receive increases the teacher's self-efficacy ("I can use cooperative learning!"), commitment ("I want to use cooperative learning!"), and enthusiasm ("I like using cooperative learning!"). It also increases trust in the relationship.

Refining and increasing one's expertise in using cooperative learning is a life-long process. Like all complex aspects of teaching, teachers will continuously improve their skills in using cooperative learning throughout their careers (Johnson & Johnson, 1994a). After the staff development sessions in cooperative learning have ended, the focus is placed on team, not individual, implementation of cooperative learning. Collegial teaching teams are more effective than isolated individuals in transferring what was learned in the training sessions to the classroom and maintaining the use of cooperative learning throughout teachers' careers. The resources needed to succeed in implementing cooperative learning need to be provided. Continued clarification of the nature of cooperative learning and how it may be implemented continues long after the training sessions have ended. The continuous improvement of expertise in using cooperative learning has to become a way of life for teachers; it is facilitated by frequent team celebrations. Refining and improving one's use of cooperative learning is a life-long process. Cooperative learning is far more than an instructional procedure; it is at heart a change in organizational structure that should occur at all levels of the school district.

### Principle Six: Teachers' Behavior is Largely Determined by the Organizational Structure of the School

Staff development programs may be facilitated or demolished by the organizational structure of the school. W. Edwards Deming and others have argued that more than 85 percent of an individual's actions in an organization are directly attributable to the organization's structure, not to the nature of the individual (cited in Johnson & Johnson, 1994a). For nearly a century, schools have functioned as mass-manufacturing organizations. The mass-manufacturing organizational structure divides work into small component parts performed by individuals who work separately from and, in many cases, in competition with peers. Teachers have worked alone, in their own room, with their own set of students, and with their own set of curriculum materials. In this view, students can be assigned to any teacher because teachers are all equivalent, interchangeable parts and, conversely, teachers can be given any student to teach because all students are considered to be

238        *David Johnson and Roger Johnson*

interchangeable. This organizational structure promotes competitive and individualistic learning and obstructs the long-term implementation of cooperative learning.

In order for schools to focus on improving instruction, they need to adopt the team-based, high-performance organizational structure, generally known as the cooperative school (see Johnson & Johnson, 1994a). The team-based, high-performance organizational structure organizes members into teams (often self-managing) that are responsible for continuously improving work processes. The assumption is that if the quality of the process through which work is done is continuously improved, the final outcome will take care of itself. Thus, in a cooperative school students work primarily in cooperative learning groups, teachers and building staff work in collegial teaching teams, and district administrators work in collegial teams (Johnson & Johnson, 1994a). Each team is responsible for clarifying the learning, teaching, or administrating processes they are responsible for and working to continuously improve the quality of their efforts. Students work together to improve the quality of their own and each other's efforts to learn. Teachers work together to improve the quality of their own and each other's teaching. Administrators work together to improve the quality of their own and each other's efforts to facilitate instruction and manage the school and school district. Such a cooperative organizational structure influences greatly the pattern of day-to-day behavior of individuals within the school and significantly increases their productivity. It also requires continuous staff development and increases the effectiveness of staff development programs.

## Summary

Staff development in cooperative learning is a process aimed at improving teachers' expertise in using cooperative learning effectively. To be effective, staff development has to focus on (a) creating the conditions for successful staff development prior to training, (b) conducting high-quality training sessions that result in mastery of the conceptual framework and procedures for using cooperative learning, (c) providing support for the transfer of what is learned in the sessions to the classroom, (d) providing support for long-term maintenance of the learned procedures for years afterwards, and (e) institutionalization of cooperative learning as a standard instructional practice supported by the district. To accomplish these purposes staff developers need to follow all six principles of effective implementation.

## References

Baldwin, T., & Ford, J. (1988). Transfer of training: A review and directions for future research. *Personality Psychology*, 41, 63–105.

Baldwin, T., & Magjurka, R. (1991). Organizational training and signals of importance: Effects of pre-training perceptions on intentions to transfer. *Human Resources Development*, 2(1), 25–36.

Battig, W. (1979). The flexibility of human memory. In L. Cermark & F. Craik (Eds.), *Levels of processing in human memory*. Hillsdale, NJ: Erlbaum.

Berman, P., & McLaughlin, M. (1978). Federal programs supporting educational change, Vol. VIII: *Implementing and sustaining innovations*. Santa Monica, CA: Rand Corporation.

Bjork, R., Dansereau, Druckman, D., Eich, E., Feltz, D., Jacoby, L., Johnson, D. W., Kihlstrom, J., Klatzky, R., Reder, L., Wegner, D., & Zajonc, R. (1994). *Learning, remembering, believing: Enhancing human performance*. Washington, D.C.: National Academy Press.

Cohen, D. (1990). What motivates trainees. *Training Development Journal*, November, 91–93.

Dempster, F. (1990). The spacing effect: A case study in the failure to apply the results of psychological research. *American Psychologist*, 43, 627–634.

Farr, M. (1987). *The long-term retention of knowledge and skills: A cognitive and instructional perspective*. NY: Springer-Verlag.

Fleming, R., & Sulzer-Azaroff, B. (1990). Peer management: Effects on staff teaching performance. Paper presented at the 15th Annual Convention for the Association of Behavior Analysis, Nashville.

Ford, J., Quinones, M., Sego, D., & Speer, J. (1991). Factors affecting the opportunity to use trained skills on the job. Presented at the 6th Annual Conference of Social Industrial Organizational Psychology, St. Louis.

Fullan, M. (1993). *Change forces: Probing the depths of educational reform*. NY: Falmer Press.

Fullan, M., Bennett, B., & Rolheiser, C. (1989). Linking classroom and school improvement. Paper presented at the Annual Meeting of the American Educational Research Association, San Francisco, March 27–30.

Fullan, M., & Hargreaves, A. (1991). *What's worth fighting for? Working together for your school*. Toronto, Ontario: Ontario Institute for Studies in Education.

Fullan, M., & Stiegelbauer, S. (1991). *The new meaning of educational change*. NY: Teachers College Press.

Guskey, T. (1994). Quoted in, G. Todnem & M. Warner, An interview with Thomas R. Guskey. *Journal of Staff Development*, 15(3), 63–64.

Hicks, W., & Klimoski, R. (1987). Entry into training programs and its effects on training outcomes: A field experiment. *Academy of Management Journal*, 30, 542–552.

Horton, D., & Mills, C. (1984). Human learning and memory. *Annual Review of Psychology*, 35, 361–394.

Huberman, M. (1983). Recipes for busy kitchens. *Knowledge: Creation, Diffusion, Utilization*, 4, 478–510.

Isler, A., Johnson, D. W., & Johnson, R. (1995). Long-term effectiveness of a statewide staff development program in cooperative learning. Research report, University of Minnesota, submitted for publication.

Johnson, D. W. (1970). *Social psychology of education*. NY: Holt, Rinehart, & Winston.

Johnson, D. W. (1979). *Educational psychology*. Englewood Cliffs, NJ: Prentice-Hall.

Johnson, D. W. (1991). *Human relations and your career*. Englewood Cliffs, NJ: Prentice-Hall.

Johnson, D. W. (1996). *Reaching out: Interpersonal effectiveness and self-actualization* (6th Ed.). Boston: Allyn & Bacon.

Johnson, D. W., & Johnson F. (1996). *Joining together: Group theory and group skills* (6th Ed.). Boston: Allyn & Bacon.

Johnson, D. W., & Johnson, R. (1993). Team versus individual training for adults. Mimeographed report.

Johnson, D. W., & Johnson, R. (1994a). *Leading the cooperative school* (2nd ed.). Edina, MN: Interaction Book Company.

Johnson, D. W., & Johnson, R. (1994b). *Learning together and alone: Cooperative, competitive, and individualistic learning* (4th Ed.). Boston: Allyn & Bacon.

Johnson, D. W., & Johnson, R. (1995a). *Teaching students to be peacemakers* (3rd Edition). Edina, MN: Interaction Book Company.

Johnson, D. W., & Johnson, R. (1995b). *Constructive controversy: Intellectual challenge in the classroom* (3rd Edition). Edina, MN: Interaction Book Company.

Johnson, D. W., Johnson, R., & Holubec, E. (1992). *Advanced cooperative learning* (2nd Edition). Edina, MN: Interaction Book Company.

Johnson, D. W., Johnson, R., & Holubec, E. (1993). *Cooperation in the classroom* (6th Edition). Edina, MN: Interaction Book Company.

Johnson, D. W., Johnson, R., & Smith, K. (1991). *Active learning: Cooperation in the college classroom.* Edina, MN: Interaction Book Company.

Joyce, B., Weil, M., & Showers, B. (1992). *Models of teaching.* Boston: Allyn & Bacon.

Lawrence, G. (1974). *Patterns of effective inservice education: A state of the art summary of research on materials and procedures for changing teacher behaviors in inservice education.* Tallahassee: Florida State Department of Education.

Lee, T., & Genovese, E. (1988). Distribution of practice in motor skill acquisition: Learning and performance effects reconsidered. *Research Quarterly for Exercise and Sport, 59,* 277–287.

Little, J. (1981). School success and staff development in urban desegregated schools. Paper presented at the American Educational Research Association Convention, Los Angeles, CA: April, 1981.

Little, J. (1982). Norms of collegiality and experimentation: Workplace conditions of school success. *American Educational Research Journal, 19,* 325–340.

Little, J. (1987). Teachers as Colleagues. In V. Koehler (Ed.), *Educator's handbook: A research perspective* (pp. 491–518). New York: Longman.

Little, J. (1990). The persistence of privacy: Autonomy and initiative in teachers' professional relations. *Teacher's College Record, 9,* 509–536.

Lortie, D. (1975). *School teacher: A sociological study.* Chicago: University of Chicago Press.

Louis, K., & Miles, M. (1990). *Improving the urban high school: What works and why.* New York: Teachers College Press.

Magill, R., & Hall, K. (1990). A review of the contextual interference effect in motor skill acquisition. *Human Movement Science, 9,* 241–289.

Marx, R., & Karren, R. (1990). The effects of relapse prevention and post-training followup on time management behavior. Presented at the Annual Meeting of Academic Management, San Francisco.

Mathieu, J., Tannenbaum, S., & Salas, E. (1990). A causal model of individual and situational influences on training effectiveness measures. Presented at the 5th Annual Conference on Social, Industrial, and Organizational Psychology, Miami.

McLaughlin, M. (1989). The RAND change agent study ten years later: Macro perspectives and micro realities. Paper presented at the Annual Meeting of the American Educational Research Association, San Francisco, March 27–30.

McLaughlin, M., & Marsh, D. (1978). Staff development and school change. *Teachers College Record, 80,* 69–94.

Miles, M. (1964). *Innovation in education.* New York: Teachers College Press.

Nias, J. (1984). Learning and acting the role: Inschool support for primary teachers. *Educational Review, 33,* 181–190.

Pentland, B. (1989). The learning curve and the forgetting curve: The importance of time and timing in the implementation of technological innovations. Presented at the 49th Annual Meeting of Academic Management, Washington, DC.

Rosenholtz, S. (1989). *Teachers' workplace: The social organization of schools.* New York: Longman.

Rouillier, J., & Goldstein, I. (1991). Determinants of the climate for transfer of training. Paper presented at the meeting for Social, Industrial, and Organizational Psychology.

Sarason, S. (1971). *The culture of the school and the problem of change.* Boston: Allyn & Bacon.

Schendel, J., & Hagman, J. (1982). On sustaining procedural skills over a prolonged retention interval. *Journal of Applied Psychology, 67,* 605–610.

Schneider, W. (1985). Training high-performance skills: Fallacies and guidelines. *Human Factors, 27,* 285–300.

Slamecka, M., & McElree, B. (1983). Normal forgetting of verbal lists as a function of their degree of learning. *Journal of Experimental Psychology: Learning, Memory, and Cognition, 9,* 384–397.

Tjosvold, D. (1990a). Cooperation and competition in restructuring an organization. *Canadian Journal of Administrative Sciences, 7,* 48–54.

Tjosvold, D. (1990b). Making a technological innovation work: Collaboration to solve problems. *Human Relations, 43,* 1117–1131.

Tjosvold, D. (1990c). Cooperation and competition theory: Antecedents, interactions, and consequences in 1,000 incidents. Burnaby, B.C.: Simon Fraser University, Research Report.

Tjosvold, D., & McNeely, L. (1988). Innovation through communication in an educational bureaucracy. *Communication Research, 15,* 568–581.

# 12

## MUTUALLY-SUSTAINING RELATIONSHIPS BETWEEN ORGANIZATION DEVELOPMENT AND COOPERATIVE LEARNING

### RICHARD SCHMUCK

This chapter explores how collegial relationships among the staff members of a school and teacher-student relationships in that school's classes can reciprocally affect one another. I present an analysis of school culture, describing how the staff development strategy of Organization Development (OD) can evoke a culture of collegial collaboration, and portray school cultures and classrooms in which OD and Cooperative Learning (CL) become mutually enhancing and sustaining.

A school culture is composed of norms, roles, structures, and procedures. A norm exists when most everyone implicitly concurs that some behaviors are approved, while others are disapproved. Roles are norms about how people in particular organizational positions should perform. Structures are norms about roles assigned to several interrelated jobs, about performance in those jobs, and about responsibilities among the jobs. They have vertical dimensions of authority and hierarchy, and horizontal dimensions of a division of labor and specialization of work. Procedures are actions taken through the structures for accomplishing specific tasks. Formal and informal norms, roles, structures, and procedures combine to make up the unique culture of a school. Organization development (OD) is a staff-development strategy for helping school participants move toward a more collaborative school culture.

### Organization-Development Strategy

OD, as delineated by Schmuck and Runkel (1994), aims at helping school participants to manage their school collaboratively and effectively.

It focuses on improving the participants' communication and meeting skills and on their learning together to carry out cooperative goal setting, problem solving, action planning, decision making, and assessment of outcomes. It strives to help school participants develop the shared norms, roles, structures, and procedures that will enable them to cooperate in order to enhance student learning.

There are four guiding principles in an OD strategy. First, the OD is effective only when it is carried out with all members of a team, cabinet, department, committee, or school. It should not be carried out with individual educators who do not work together closely in the same school. When all members of an actual subsystem participate in OD workshops together, all can see that their colleagues are accepting new group norms, roles, structures, and procedures and are truly ready and willing to act accordingly.

Second, OD should generate valid data for the members of the school about how their culture works. The data should deal realistically with the staff's own norms, roles, structures, and procedures, thus offering staff members a figurative mirror for viewing themselves clearly as a living culture.

Third, discrepancies between current outcomes of the school and the school's ideal performance goals are used as leverage points for problem solving and proposed change. Goals for the school come from state statutes, board policy, and the school participants themselves. Typically, the core goals have to do with student learning, student attitudes and behavior, and teacher morale. By comparing ideal goals to data on how things actually are transpiring in the school, dissonance is created which can motivate the participants to work together to change their norms, roles, structures, and procedures.

Fourth, OD makes use of the available resources within the school or in the proximal environment to solve problems and develop plans for change. The OD strategy is a process that does not in itself offer solutions. Rather, the OD strategy offers problem-solving and cooperative procedures for helping participants to think of a number of creative alternatives for their culture of the present, and it helps school participants develop viable plans of action to implement those creative alternatives. For detailed information about the theory and technology of OD in schools and colleges, see Schmuck and Runkel (1994).

## Staff Development and OD

Staff developers strive to facilitate changes either in individual educators (personal change) or in the social systems in which the educators work together (cultural change). Typical targets of personal change are knowledge, attitudes, values, and skills. Targets of cultural change are norms, roles, structures, and procedures.

Until about a decade ago, staff development was synonymous with in-service workshops for individual educators. The workshop presenters aimed to upgrade each participant's knowledge about curriculum and student psychology, or his or her skills of teaching, advising, and counseling. Individual teachers chose the workshops they wished to attend and they went to them as free agents in search of professional development rather than as representatives of their school.

During the last decade, perhaps because of the influence of OD, more and more in-service workshops were carried out with teachers who worked together in the same school. Those staff-development interventions were variously labeled site-based in-service, school-based professional development, school development, and organization restructuring. Particularly in school districts with more than 2,000 students, a district-office administrator, charged with the job of staff developer, would assess each staff's needs for improvement and then arrange for appropriate instructors to offer tailored workshops to satisfy some of those needs. Although some district-office-based staff developers believed they were doing OD, most of those presenters focused on changing individuals' knowledge and skills. They did not focus on the school's norms, roles, structures, and procedures. Instead of OD, they were doing individual development, focusing on personal change in colleagues who happened to be working in the same school.

Today, under the leadership of both the National Staff Development Council and the International Association for the Study of Cooperation in Education, staff developers, school administrators, and school consultants are attempting to integrate the professional development of educators with organization development for schools and districts.

### School Culture and Student Behavior

During the last 25 years, theory and research on the association between school culture and student behavior have been accumulating. We review a few of the more classical studies here.

In a creative field study, Menuchin and colleagues (1969) showed that school culture can affect classroom group processes and student behavior. The researchers studied all fourth-grade classes in pairs of schools with contrasting cultures. Two school cultures had norms in support of strict student discipline, administrators with authoritarian roles, hierarchical staff structures and many bureaucratic procedures; the other pair of school cultures had norms in support of student empowerment about school rules, administrators with democratic roles, equalitarian staff structures, and few bureaucratic procedures. The researchers found that students in the second pair of schools had higher self-esteem and more favorable attitudes toward school, and more higher-order thinking skills. Those same schools had more settings in which girls and boys participated in similar activities and were not separated by sex, and more instances and time in cooperative group projects.

Research by Bigelow (1971) on 20 junior high classrooms, ten each in two schools with contrasting cultures, demonstrated that teachers who collaborate often with colleagues to set instructional goals and to solve teaching problems also initiate more cooperation and give more emotional support to students in the classroom. Using a modified Flanders' Interaction Analysis, Bigelow found that classrooms within the more collaborative school culture, in contrast to those in the less collaborative school culture, were characterized more by teachers initiating broad questions, accepting more student ideas, and accepting more student feelings. Students were initiating talk with teachers much more in the collaborative school than they were in the less collaborative school. Finally, the research also showed that teachers in the more collaborative school culture initiated more cooperative group projects in their classes in comparison to their counterparts in the less collaborative school culture.

Seeman and Seeman (1976) did research on 35 classes in 12 schools, all taking part in Goodlad's League of Cooperating Schools. The Seemans observed that in some schools, the teachers were engaged in "dialogue, decision making, and action planning to improve the curriculum." In those schools, the level of staff collaboration was much higher than it was in the other schools. The Seemans showed that teachers engaged in the collaborative dialogue, decision-making, and action planning had students with more favorable attitudes toward school and were initiating more cooperative group projects in their classes than the teachers in school cultures with low levels of staff collaboration.

Rutter et. al. (1979) studied associations between school culture and student behavior in 12 senior highs in London, England. The longitudinal data showed that in schools where staffs planned collaboratively and where the norms were in support of teachers encouraging and helping one another, the students were in attendance more often and committed delinquent acts less frequently. Also, examination successes were more frequent in schools where discipline rules were agreed upon consensually by teachers working in teams, rather than left to individual teachers to work out for themselves.

Finally, research by Johnson and Johnson (1989) has demonstrated how a collaborative school culture can be set up to support cooperative learning in classrooms. The ideal school culture is restructured to include three types of collaborative adult teams: (1) teacher support teams of three or four to learn about and to implement cooperative learning in their classes; (2) school-wide task forces to develop and evaluate solutions to school-wide problems; and (3) ad hoc problem-solving teams at faculty meetings. The OD strategy offers designs and activities for introducing and nurturing such adult teams in collaborative school cultures.

## From OD to Cooperative Learning

The following case studies offer data on the bi-directional relationship between OD for school staffs and CL in the classroom. The cases in this section demonstrate how OD can increase teachers' readiness to risk trying cooperative learning strategies in their classrooms. Via participation in an OD project, staffs establish norms in support of collaboration and teamwork, more interdependent social structures, and more cooperative group procedures during their meetings; these in turn, improve the social-emotional climate and the spirit of innovativeness of the adult group. The collaborative norms, structures, and procedures also present real models of social interaction which teachers can transfer to their classrooms. As a consequence, clusters of teachers come to work together to implement cooperative learning methods.

### Smallwood Middle School

The Smallwood staff received a grant from the State Department of Education to improve its methods of communication, group problem solving, and staff decision-making. The OD intervention began with a six day workshop in late August with virtually the whole site staff present. The 54 participants included all the administrators, all but two of the teachers, plus the head secretary, the head cook, and the head custodian. The six days were devoted to communication skills and exercises in effectively setting goals, running meetings, group problem solving, and staff decision-making.

The summer workshop was followed by three OD events of one day each spread over the fall, winter, and spring of the school year. OD facilitators collected questionnaire and interview data from staff members about how the new group procedures were going. Through survey-data-feedback methods, staff members pinpointed their process problems and set out actively to solve the problems. The last of the three follow-up workshops aimed to evaluate staff progress in solving its problems, to increase clarity about new staff roles and group structures, and to invigorate any lagging communication and meeting skills.

Since the primary focus of the Smallwood project was OD for the adult staff, the facilitators learned only inadvertently about the teachers making use of OD experiences in their classrooms. Even though no question was asked about classroom applications in the evaluation questionnaires, seven teachers wrote about plans to make use of OD activities in their classrooms. Six months later, 21 teachers from Smallwood volunteered to write essays on how the OD workshops had affected the school. While all 21 believed that the staff was communicating more effectively because of the OD, 15 also wrote about how they were trying to use OD procedures in their classrooms. After that, follow-up interviews were carried out with a random sample of 20 teachers at Smallwood, and 19 of them mentioned trying out group projects in their classes. The change was extraordinary; indeed, 11 of those 19 commented on specific cooperative learning strategies that they were implementing.

## Benton Elementary School

With 44 teachers and specialists, Benton is large for an elementary school in Oregon. After studying about OD at the University, the principal of Benton decided to collect questionnaire data from the staff about its views of the effectiveness of their staff meetings once-a-week. As she suspected, the data revealed a high amount of discontent with the large-group meetings. After considerable staff discussion, the principal asked me to consult with the whole staff about alternative ways of structuring the school for effective communication, problem solving, and decision-making.

After 3 days of intensive discussion the Benton staff agreed to try restructuring into a matrix organization. (The matrix organizational structure has small face-to-face teams that are linked both vertically and horizontally). The principal, an assistant principal, and eight faculty members constitute "the Benton Leadership Team." The eight faculty members on that team come one each from kindergarten, grades 1–6, and the specialists. Thus, Benton is linked vertically with one staff member from each of the instructional teams being represented on the leadership team.

Benton also has four school wide committees, each made up of from 9 to 12 members with representatives from each grade level and the specialists. The School Climate Committee is to boost school pride and spirit by developing and implementing programs focused on positive reinforcement of student accomplishments, student self-esteem, and a unique Benton identity. The Care Team is to generate programs to increase feelings of success for students with special needs, to act as a clearinghouse for ideas about how best to serve "at-risk" students, and to give support to colleagues who are facing the challenge of working closely with troubled students. The school-wide Procedures Committee is to keep Benton running smoothly by dealing with concerns about school procedures such as discipline cases, fire drills, scheduling, and school rules. Finally, the Curriculum and Instruction Task Force is to select, organize, and present new curriculum goals and materials to the staff and to give support to teachers who are trying new curriculum or instructional techniques. The committees help link Benton staff horizontally.

When I visited the school a few months later, I discovered that the Curriculum and Instructional Task Force was sponsoring a series of workshops on cooperative learning. Twenty two Benton teachers were taking part. I interviewed six of them, each of whom was planning to use either some form of quality circle or of jigsaw. They commented on how they saw a natural fit between the OD procedures that I had used with the staff and the new cooperative learning practices that they were trying out in their classes. For example, two teachers were using quality circles to elicit ideas from students about how to improve the classroom climate for learning. Those teachers had used sociometric data to form student steering committees for climate improvement. One teacher asked several highly influential students to serve as classroom leaders for one month with an understanding that eventually all students in the class would get an opportunity to spend one month on the steering committee. The teacher told the students that a steering committee—like the driver of a bus—helps "steer the class" in the right direction. To facilitate the quality circle discussions, the teachers divided their classes into small groups and asked each steering committee member to record (and later to report on) the ideas that came out of the small groups.

Four teachers decided to use the jigsaw-puzzle technique in their classes. They organized their classes into four-member learning groups. Each individual in a learning group was assigned either number 1, 2, 3, or 4. Next, the teachers divided text materials into four parts and asked the 1's, 2's, 3's, and 4's each to become experts in one of the four parts. Next the teacher formed ad-hoc expert trios, i.e., three 1's, three 2's, etc., to plan how best to teach the content of their part of the text to others in their learning groups. Then the experts returned to their learning groups, each to teach his or her part and to learn about the other three parts from their peers in the learning group.

## From Cooperative Learning to OD

Schools in which a critical mass of teachers are employing cooperative learning in their classrooms can be ripe contexts for OD projects with the adult staff. Teachers who see the power of cooperative learning come to recognize that several heads frequently are more effective than one. Their consciousness about the strengths of interdependence and synergy is raised, and they become frustrated over the lack of cohesiveness, teamwork, and social support on the staff. They think, "let's practice what we preach" or "let's walk the talk." The stage is set for becoming engaged in an OD effort at the staff level.

### Agate Senior High School

Three English teachers and three social studies teachers from Agate attended a large two day conference on cooperative learning at which they were introduced to jigsaw and the group investigation methods. At the conference, they agreed to try out some cooperative learning strategies in a few of their classes. Back home they formed into three pairs, with an English teacher and a social studies teacher in each pair. The two members of each pair taught the same-age students during the same 90 minute period of the day. One pair taught sophomores during first period, another taught juniors during second period, and the third taught seniors during third period. The pairs co-taught their students during their period in common using cooperative learning methods. The pair with sophomores put together a jigsaw design, while the other two pairs adapted the group-investigation method to their curriculum.

After the six teachers had been implementing cooperative learning with enthusiasm for six weeks, the principal asked them to describe their teaching strategies to their colleagues at a faculty meeting. Two science teachers, a math teacher, and an art teacher asked if during their prep periods they could observe one of the pairs using cooperative learning. All three pairs agreed to be observed. A few weeks later those four teachers began to try out jigsaw and group investigation in their classes. In a few months several more teachers had also decided to experiment with both cooperative learning methods in a few of their classes. At the end of the school year 18 out of the 75 teachers on the Agate faculty were using some form of cooperative learning in their classes.

During the summer, seven of those eighteen teachers met with the principal to complain about the lack of collaboration and cooperation on the faculty. They wondered if some of the techniques of cooperative learning could be applied to faculty meetings. For example, they said, why not divide the faculty into cross-departmental groups and use group-investigation methods to help solve some of the school's discipline and morale problems? With regard to student discipline, many teachers were frustrated over their colleagues' lack of consistency in intervening when students lost control; in turn, those frustrations were undermining the trust and support that teachers felt for one another. The principal was interested, but felt that his site council should agree to become involved in cooperative learning if it were to be legitimate with the larger faculty. He decided to have the site council go off on a team-building retreat to decide on the issue before school started up again in September. I was asked to facilitate the site-council retreat, and Agate High was off and running with an OD project. The goals of that OD effort focused on preparing a handbook on student life in the school, with emphasis on celebration and discipline, as well as increasing trust and supportiveness on the faculty.

## Farmington Middle School

Four Farmington teachers attended a summer school course at a nearby university on action research for teachers. They learned how to design practical action research, how to create questionnaires, interview guides, and observation systems, and how to use data for problem solving and action planning. A course requirement called for them to design and implement an actual action research project in their school. The instructor of the course encouraged the four Farmington teachers to collaborate on a single action research project at their school.

Since cooperative learning had only recently been introduced into their school and because two of the four were deeply involved in using cooperative learning methods, the team decided to collect data from students, teachers, administrators, and parents about what those stakeholders thought and felt about it. In the course of responding to the questionnaires and interviews a number of teachers and parents became aware of cooperative learning for the first time. Indeed, the data tended to show that those students, teachers, and parents who did know about cooperative learning held favorable attitudes about it, while those who had not heard of it or knew very little about it were either neutral or negative toward it. The data also showed that the teachers at Farmington knew very little about one another's classroom practices. In general, most respondents felt that staff communication and collaboration was at a very low level, and that it should be higher.

When the action research team told the principal and two assistant principals about the results, all present decided to show the same data to the whole faculty. I was asked to help facilitate that feedback session and Farmington became engaged in an OD project. The goals of that OD effort were to increase understanding of how staff members with diferent jobs think and feel about the school, to develop clear communication channels up, down, and across, and to enhance the involvement of more staff members in decision-making about important matters at Farmington.

## Toward a Cooperative School Culture

The relationship between cooperative learning and organization development is two way and reciprocal. The starting point for moving toward a cooperative school culture can be either through OD or through CL but, I believe, for either OD or CL to be sustained effectively over the long run, both OD and CL must be going on. In the cases cited above, for example, OD and CL became interdependent and mutually reinforcing. OD and CL are like two sides of the same coin. Indeed, when concern about OD begins to waver in a school, we may expect that the teachers' interest in CL will also diminish, and that as teachers give up on CL, they will also lose interest in OD. Just as we may posit an iso-

TABLE 12.1

Goals of OD and CL

| OD | CL |
|---|---|
| 1. To increase understanding of how staff members with different jobs interrelate and effect one and other. | To increase empathy and understanding among students with different personal characteristics. |
| 2. To develop clear communication networks up, down, and laterally. | To establish clear communication among all classroom members. |
| 3. To increase understanding of different educational goals in different parts of the educational system. | To help students understand the different values and attitudes that exist in their own peer group. |
| 4. To uncover organizational conflicts for constructive problem-solving. | To assist students in dealing with conflicts and in converting frustration into problem solving. |

morphic relationship between the hierarchical school and the teacher-controlled classroom, I posit an isomorphic relationship between OD and CL. In effect the school culture is more of an integrated psychological bundle than the image of a loosely-coupled organization would imply. Table 12.1 shows how the goals of OD and CL compare.

Those who argue for school restructuring implicitly assume that there is a causal and reciprocal relationship between the humanistic quality of interpersonal relations among staff members and the humane ways teachers behave toward students in the classroom. A typical scenario might go as follows:

When teachers collaborate with their principal and colleagues in setting school goals and in planning new instructional patterns, they begin to feel empowered as teachers, and their professional self-concepts and commitments to humane practices become increasingly stronger. Because they feel supported and respected, they can more easily give their support and respect to students. Moreover, when teachers become more interdependent with one another, they can more readily use the skill of constructive openness, thereby improving their teaching strategies through the giving and receiving of feedback. The prototype of such an exchange of feedback, nowadays, occurs in peer coaching and peer mentoring. As teachers feel more self-worth and freedom to experiment with new, more responsive classroom teaching strategies, they have the self confidence to express more emotional support, understanding, and compassion for students. The students recognize the teacher's trust and confidence in them, feel better about themselves, and put increased effort into learning.

Some norms, roles, structures, and procedures, already common in cooperative learning, must become part of the school culture if cooperation is to be sustained as a system of values in education. The cooperative school culture has norms in support of respecting every one's ideas and feelings, of equalitarian teamwork and collaborative effort, of openness, candor, and honesty, of warmth and friendliness, of caring for people of all ages, and of seeking self-esteem for everyone. The cooperative school culture has administrators, teacher leaders, and student leaders who know how to act democratically in their roles. It has structures of small groups within the large organization that are linked together both vertically and horizontally. It has procedures for continual evaluation and debriefing, reaching out for knowledge and resources both outside and inside, and problem solving and decision-making methods that are understood by all participants.

Cooperative school cultures can be developed. We have the concepts, strategies, designs, and techniques to achieve that. The theory and technology of OD and CL are mature enough now to achieve that. But achieving cooperative school cultures will require all key actors—administrators, teachers, specialists, students, parents, and citizens-at-large—to take their part in making them work for everyone.

## References

Bigelow, Ronald. (1971). Changing classroom interaction through organization development, in Schmuck, R. A., and M. B. Miles (eds.) *Organization development in schools*. Palo Alto, CA: National Press Books.

Johnson, David and Roger Johnson. (1989). *Leading the cooperative school*. Edina, MN: Interaction Book Co.

Menuchin, Patricia (1969). *The psychological impact of school experience: A comparative study of nine-year-old children in contrasting schools*. New York: Basic Books.

Rutter, Michael et. al. (1979). *Fifteen thousand hours*. Cambridge, MA: Harvard University Press.

Schmuck, Richard and Philip Runkel. (1994). *The handbook of organization development in schools and colleges*. 4th edition. Prospect Heights, IL: Waveland Press.

Seeman, Alice and Seeman, Melvin. (1976). Staff processes and pupil attitudes: A study of teacher participation in educational change. *Human relations* 21 (1), 24–40

# 13

## FACULTY DEVELOPMENT USING COOPERATIVE LEARNING

### SUSAN ELLIS

There are at least two practical reasons for encouraging the use of cooperative groups in school faculty meetings:[1]

1.  Cooperative groups can be effective arrangements for engaging people in problem-solving and coming to consensus; and
2.  Regular participation in cooperative problem-solving groups can enhance teachers' ability to use cooperative learning in their classrooms with students.

In addition, an important long-term reason for encouraging the use of cooperative groups in faculty meetings is their potential for changing the entire culture of a school from one of competition and isolation to one of professional collegiality.[2] As teachers develop trust in their colleagues and experience the value of sharing ideas and points of view to solve school-wide problems, they become more open to giving and receiving feedback on classroom issues, including their delivery of curriculum and their instructional practices. This "norm of collegiality" is essential if a school is going to engage successfully in continuous improvement (Little, 1982).

### Creating Interest

What makes a principal and a faculty interested in restructuring their usual decision-making process? How can a staff developer stimulate consideration of this dramatic change in business-as-usual? Two ingredients are essential. One is a principal willing to share leadership and power with teachers. If the principal is not genuinely in favor of a change to cooperative decision-making, she or he is likely to sabotage the process by vetoing faculty decisions or by agreeing with the decisions but interfering with their being carried out. The second ingredient is equally important: a "critical mass" of faculty members who have had at least some training in cooperative learning. While practice in problem-solving using cooperative groups can reinforce a teacher's understanding and use of cooperative learning strategies, it can't take the place of direct training in those strategies and in the research that informs their use.

If your school system has been training teachers in cooperative learning, undoubtedly you also have been training principals in strategies that will enable them to support their teachers' progress. You can promote interest in cooperative faculty meetings among principals by using at least one of these training sessions to focus on the value of using cooperative learning structures in school-wide decision-making. An "outside expert" may be helpful for this phase of principals' training: such a person may have more credibility and therefore more influence on administrators than does a staff member from their own district.

However you introduce the idea of cooperative faculty meetings to principals, be prepared to offer at least two kinds of support to those who embark on the change: literature and facilitation. Readings designed especially for principals can give further legitimacy to their undertaking this radical restructuring of school governance as well as provide practical suggestions for getting started and maintaining enthusiasm for the process.[3]

While some principals may feel sufficiently skilled in teaching and using cooperative structures to take on the role of facilitator of this change themselves, many will wish to have the services of a facilitator from outside the school. Not only does the use of a facilitator relieve the principal of the burden of leading the faculty meetings at which the new behaviors are learned and practiced, but it also frees the principal to be a participant in the meetings—a role consistent with the cooperative culture being established.

If two or more principals in the school district decide to change to cooperative faculty meetings—particularly if they are facilitating this change themselves—you can offer a third kind of support: organizing and facilitating regular meetings of a collegial support group for those principals. Just like support groups for teachers, such meetings provide a forum for principals to share their successes, help each other solve problems that they encounter, and give each other encouragement to continue experimenting.

## The "Basics" for a Cooperative Faculty

As a school faculty moves toward cooperative decision-making, most staff members will need instruction in four topics: the role and importance of team-building; team structures that are appropriate for solving different kinds of problems; actual cooperative structures that can be used for problem-solving; and consensus-building strategies. The amount of practice needed for each will depend on the background knowledge and experience a faculty brings to the process as well as the level of their commitment to changing to cooperative decision-making. Another important topic not discussed here is the extent of a school's authority to make decisions independent of any central office review, as well as the limits—if any—on the decisions the principal is willing to delegate to the faculty. These will need to be spelled out by the principal before any training begins.

### Team-building

Team-building is the process of helping group members feel sufficiently comfortable with the other members of their group so that they are able to contribute their own ideas to the group's discussions, accept the group's evaluation of those ideas, listen to and evaluate the ideas of their colleagues, and come to a consensus. Since teachers rarely have opportunities to interact personally or professionally with most of the other teachers in their school, never assume that such a comfort level already exists within a faculty. Just as teachers who use cooperative groups need to provide activities that enable students to develop comfort with and trust in each other, facilitators of cooperative faculty meetings should devote time to a team-building activity at the start of each session. The investment of time in regular team building is quickly repaid by the group's increased level of trust and enhanced willingness to work together cooperatively.

The kind of team-building activities you choose will depend on the level of collegiality and comfort that already exists in a group. Don't be put off by some people's expressed distaste for anything they perceive as "touchy-feely." I have successfully facilitated team-building activities with a group of 60 administrators from a school system, with several high school faculties (who are notoriously "difficult"), and with mixed groups of participants in workshops at national conferences. In each case I carefully explained the purpose for the team-building before we began the activity and later asked participants to process the activity in light of that purpose. While in two different instances one person maintained his[4] certainty that the activity was a "waste of time," all the other participants expressed their appreciation for the experience, and many described their intention to use similar activities with their faculties or students.

Team Structures

*Ad hoc groups.* The most common team structure for decision-making is the ad hoc group. These are small (4–6 members), heterogeneous groups that are formed from the larger faculty during a meeting to discuss an issue or proposal and come to a consensus which they share with the whole group. Ad hoc groups can also be used to brainstorm ideas at the start of a discussion. Ad hoc groups need the elements of any cooperative learning group: positive interdependence, individual accountability, attention to social skills, and regular processing of group interactions.

*Task Forces.* Ad hoc groups are not appropriate for all decision-making, however. Many topics which school faculties wish to address require study and/or planning before any appropriate action can be taken. Whenever such a topic is identified, the team structure needed is the task force. As its name implies, a task force is charged with a task by the faculty. Generally it will be asked to research a topic and come back with a recommendation for the faculty to consider. Or—if the topic is not a "serious" one—the task force may be empowered to come back with a decision. Task forces can also be used to develop implementation plans after the faculty has come to a decision about an issue.

Like ad hoc groups, task forces are small (4–6 members), and their construction is usually heterogeneous, although the make-up of the group should be determined by the problem to be solved or issue to be addressed. For example, a task force that is investigating interdisciplinary curriculum should have members who can represent most or all the disciplines, while a task force that is planning an orientation for ninth graders in a high school might consist of a couple of ninth grade teachers, a social worker or guidance counselor, and two or three other faculty members who have had experiences with different kinds of orientation programs. Task forces may invite parents, other members of the community, and/or outside consultants to help them in their deliberations.

*Collegial Support Teams.* The third team structure is not used in cooperative faculty meetings, but it is an important component of a cooperative school: the collegial support team. Collegial support teams bring together people who have a common interest and would like to participate in ongoing dialogue around that interest. Unlike the two previous structures, these teams may be of any size and may be homogeneous or heterogeneous, depending on their focus. For example, they might be grade-level teams, interdisciplinary teams, or study groups. While organizing such teams will not be your responsibility as a facilitator of faculty meetings,[5] you will certainly wish to encourage teachers to think about their possibilities (see Johnson & Johnson, Chapter 11 of this book for further discussion). Not only do collegial support teams serve as an important vehicle for breaking down isolation among teachers and contributing to their members' professional growth, but also—as their name implies—they provide ongoing support to teachers as they struggle with challenges from implementing new curricula to dealing with difficult students.

Ad hoc decision-making groups can use the same format every time: group discussion, with a recorder to take notes, a monitor to keep the group on-task and within the stipulated time limit, and a leader or facilitator who makes sure everyone has a chance to participate. However, just as cooperative learning groups can be set up with a variety of structures, so can ad hoc decision-making groups. The use of different structures not only fights monotony and resulting boredom (the "here-we-go-into-small-groups-again" syndrome), but it also provides teachers with exposure to effective structures they can use with their students. Spencer Kagan (1992) has created a compilation of such structures and organized them into chapters according to their most appropriate use. The following sections on how to help a faculty move to cooperative decision-making include descriptions of several such structures.

Consensus-building

Consensus is an appropriate strategy for decision-making in a cooperative school, since it requires all participants to be actively engaged in decision-making by stating their beliefs and opinions and by coming to agreement. If a faculty has not had instruction in consensus—both what it means and how to reach it, include such instruction in your work with them. (Straight voting in a cooperative school should be used in the way that competition is used in a cooperative classroom: occasionally, for a change of pace, when the subject is not too serious, and when those who "lose" will not feel excluded or less-valued by the group.)

Getting Ready: Meet with a Representative Faculty
Group for Planning

The following step-by-step plan for facilitating a school's change to cooperative decision-making assumes a faculty that has had a range of experience with cooperative learning—from neophytes with only a general notion of what cooperative learning looks like, to several experienced users.

If you have been asked to facilitate a school's change to cooperative faculty meetings, your first step is to meet with a group representing that faculty, such as a staff development committee or an agenda committee for faculty meetings. If no such planning body exists, you will need to create an ad hoc one with the assistance of the principal. Since the focus of the faculty meetings you facilitate will be on identifying and addressing school-wide issues and problems, the planning group needs to be sufficiently diverse so that it can represent the interests and concerns of all the faculty.

The first meeting with the planning group has two purposes: (1) stating clearly the process for the faculty meetings, and (2) finding out from the group the issues and problems that should serve as the content of those meetings, at least initially. It is not necessary to obtain a comprehensive list of issues and problems. Your function is to teach the faculty how to solve problems cooperatively so that they are able to proceed without you after a few meetings, not to facilitate the solving of every problem existing in the school. Any list of school-wide issues that the planning group generates can be used as a starting point.

As you talk with the planning group about the processes you will use to help the faculty learn to solve problems cooperatively, describe the importance of including team-building exercises at the start of each meeting you facilitate. Explain that you will be helping the faculty to understand several kinds of teams they can use to solve problems, as well as several different cooperative learning structures to use within those teams. The first faculty meeting will focus on the various problem-solving teams; the second (and any additional sessions) on cooperative structures. Lastly, as part of each meeting, you will be teaching the faculty several consensus-building strategies they can use as part of their cooperative decision-making. The planning team can inform you of the amount of experience the faculty has had in consensus-building, so you will know how much training to include in each meeting.

Ask the planning group to name the problems that are likely to be generated in the first meeting. Explain that you would like to use one of these problems to model cooperative decision-making, and the problem needs to be of sufficient importance to the faculty so that resolving it will enable them to leave the meeting feeling satisfied. Select one that can be solved by ad hoc decision-making teams, and ask if that problem is important enough to address first.

If a member of the faculty is particularly skilled at using cooperative learning, ask the planning group if she would like to co-facilitate.

This practice is good for two reasons: it gives recognition and increased credibility to a person who can serve as an in-school resource for cooperative learning, and it makes your job as facilitator much easier. In my own work with one school in our district I have co-facilitated each meeting with a teacher from that school who is a certified Johnson and Johnson trainer in cooperative learning. We have co-planned the agenda and time line for each meeting and have alternated responsibility for facilitating the various segments of the meetings. We have also modeled collegiality by welcoming comments and suggestions from each other as the sessions progress.

## Getting Started:  First Meeting

During your first meeting with the whole faculty, it is important for you (and your co-facilitator, if you have one) to state clearly what you will and will not do during that session, so that faculty members know what to expect.

1. Give them an experience in one kind of team-building.
2. Describe several kinds of cooperative teams and give them guidelines for when and how to use each to solve problems.
3. Give them practice in using one kind of cooperative team to actually solve a problem of their choosing.
4. Make it clear that you won't address all the problems and issues they identify.

Their first activity will be whatever team-building activity you have chosen. Once that is completed and processed, including a discussion of how the activity might be used with students, your next step is to engage the faculty in identifying all the issues/concerns that currently face them. Although the planning committee will have given you a preliminary list from which you have already selected a topic for the final problem-solving activity, it is important that everyone on the faculty have a chance to contribute to the list. If your team-building activity results in groups of four, ask the faculty to generate this list in their small groups. If the activity results in pairs, ask the pairs to join a pair near them and then generate the list. The instructions (which should be on an overhead for people to refer to) are the following:

1. The person whose birthday is closest to today is the recorder. S/He writes a list of issues as they are raised.

2.  Each person in turn identifies a school-wide issue/problem and says why it is an issue or problem that needs to be addressed. This process continues until no one in the group has any more issues to raise.
3.  The group picks the two issues/problems that they would most like to see addressed by the whole faculty.

It helps to model step two as follows: "Be sure to give a reason or example for the issue or problem you identify. For example, if I say that school safety is an issue, I might explain that by saying I've seen children running down the halls and bumping into others, or I've noticed children pushing others off the swings." While the groups are working, circulate among them and ask clarifying questions if any groups or individuals forget to elaborate on the issue they name.

Give the groups eight minutes to work, with a two-minute warning signal that it is time to choose the two most important topics if they have not yet done so. When the time is up, ask the recorder of each group to give you one of the topics selected by his/her group. As the topics are stated, write them on newsprint in large enough letters so that all can see, and ask for the group's reasons for thinking each was important to address. If more than one small group identifies the same issue, as is likely to happen, add a hash mark (/) next to an issue each time it is named.

Overview of Teams

Some of the items listed are likely to be ones that can be addressed by the faculty immediately, while others will need additional information from data-gathering, readings, visits to other schools, etc. Inform the group that you are going to describe several kinds of cooperative teams that they can use to solve problems, and that while you are doing that, you would like them to be thinking about which kind of team would be appropriate for each of the problems they have listed.

"Walk" participants through a handout of team descriptions, not by reading it, but by describing the three kinds of teams, giving examples of when each might be appropriate, including the variations on the task force. Emphasize the importance of creating a task force to investigate and design a solution to any issue or problem that requires more information than exists within a faculty, such as the choice of a school-wide reading program. Note that ad hoc decision-making teams are appropriate for addressing those issues for which sufficient knowledge resides in the faculty without any further study, such as how to organize an Open House for parents. Of course, ad hoc decision-making groups are also appropriate for receiving and deciding whether to accept the recommendations of a task force.

At this point ask the faculty to look at the list of issues/problems they have generated and decide which kind of cooperative team is most appropriate for addressing each item. Once the list has been categorized, state that the only problems that can be solved by the faculty that day are the ones they have identified as calling for ad hoc decision-making teams. Read those, noting any which were identified by more than one group. Identify the one you have agreed upon with the planning group and say that you will show them how to use ad hoc decision-making teams to solve that problem—for example, developing rules for using playground equipment.

## Using Ad Hoc Decision-Making Groups

To give the teachers an opportunity to work with other individuals, have everyone count off by the number that will result in groups of five, and tell the new groups where to gather. Assign a recorder. (This time the recorder could be the tallest person in the group.) Tell the groups that they have five minutes to generate ideas for addressing the identified problem. All ideas should be accepted without comment, but clarifying questions can be asked. After five minutes of brainstorming, they will have ten minutes to come to agreement about the ideas they will propose to the whole faculty. During this period they should weigh the pros and cons of each idea and determine which they can support. Be sure to give them a signal when the five minutes for brainstorming are up and a warning signal a minute before the ten minutes for coming to agreement are up.

After you bring the groups back together, ask for one contribution in turn from each group and write these on newsprint. As you are writing, ask for clarification if needed. Once all contributions have been written and posted so that everyone can see them, invite questions and reactions to the suggestions. During this period, some groups may decide to withdraw one or more of their suggestions as they hear their colleagues' reactions. In your role as facilitator you do not advocate for or against any suggestion, but you should prevent too-easy capitulation by asking groups to explain their reasons for making a suggestion and encouraging them to value their own ideas. On the other hand, if a group wishes to withdraw a suggestion and no other group urges them to leave it on the list, you can remove it.

## Coming to Consensus

Since you are promoting cooperative decision-making, you will want to use some kind of consensus-building to make a final decision, rather than straight voting. I often use variations on "finger-voting." You can make the fingers stand for whatever seems appropriate. In the case of a faculty deciding on playground rules, I distributed a sheet with the following:

- 5 fingers = "I'm all for it and I can provide leadership."
- 4 fingers = "I'm all for it and I will provide support."
- 3 fingers = "I'll support it."
- 2 fingers = "I'm not sure. Can we talk?" (People choosing this option must be prepared to specify their objections, concerns.)
- 1 finger = "I have reservations; I cannot go along with this suggestion as is." (People choosing this option must be prepared to say what would enable them to move to at least a '3.')
- fist = "I'm opposed." (People choosing this option must be prepared with an alternative.)

Assure the group that people who have any reservations should indicate that by raising just one or two fingers. Those who do are helping the group by making their reservations or objections public. It is the hidden reservations or objections that sabotage a group's work. I find that if I am sufficiently convincing in stating the need for people to make their reservations known, one or two brave individuals will raise just one or two fingers for some of the suggestions, and the group will quickly see how valuable these individuals' insights are. (In each case that this has happened in groups I have facilitated, the group agreed with the reservations expressed and eliminated the suggestion under discussion from their list.)

After the voting is complete, it is time to bring the meeting to closure and prepare for the next one. Remind the group that they have engaged in three cooperative activities—in addition to the team-building exercise—in order to come to a solution they can all support: brainstorming lists of issues, generating solutions to an identified problem, and engaging in finger-voting. Ask them to think about one positive reaction they have to using these activities for decision-making in faculty meetings. Ask them also to reflect on ways they could—or already do—use these activities with their students.

After a few people have contributed their reactions, remind the group that they have identified issues that should be addressed by task forces, and that they will need to decide which issues to attend to first, and therefore which task forces to establish. (Determining when these decisions will be made can be the responsibility of the principal and planning group. The school I worked with chose to set up task forces at their next faculty meeting—one which I did not facilitate.) It is helpful to distribute an outline of task force operation.

Inform the faculty that during your next meeting with them you will take them through another problem-solving exercise using ad hoc decision-making groups and a variety of different cooperative structures, so that they can expand their repertoire of cooperative structures for both problem-solving in faculty meetings and classroom instruction. They will have an opportunity to help the planning committee decide which topic should be the focus for the next meeting.

## Introducing Structures:  Meeting Two

In preparation for the second training meeting, meet with the planning committee to find out what progress the faculty has made in establishing task forces, as well as to learn what issue the faculty would like to focus on next using ad hoc groups. Be sure that the topic is one that lends itself to ad hoc decision-making groups. You may also need to help the planning group define the topic. The school I worked with identified dissatisfaction with students' behavior and performance in a variety of areas. After much discussion, we narrowed the topic for our second meeting to "Raising Students' Expectations for the Quality of Their Work."

At the beginning of the faculty meeting, distribute an outline of the afternoon's agenda that includes the actual instructions for each activity you will be using. As the meeting progresses and the faculty experiences a variety of cooperative structures, they can refer to their outline for instructions in each of those structures. They can also take the handout with them for their own planning if they decide to try various structures with students.

## Team-building

My recommendation for team-building for this second meeting is a series of three of Kagan's structures: Similarity Pairs to bring people together around a common interest such as a sport, followed by Paraphrase Passport for preparing the partners to introduce each other to another pair, followed by Round Robin for the actual introductions. Similarity Pairs often brings people together who would not otherwise know they had anything in common. Teachers like to learn Paraphrase Passport, because it is useful for teaching listening skills to students. Round Robin is an all-purpose structure that can be used for a variety of teaching situations. Whatever structures you chose, be sure to process them by reviewing the structures, talking about their various uses, and asking the faculty how and when they might employ each with students.

Problem-Solving

For this second meeting with the faculty, now that they have had an introduction to using ad hoc groups for decision-making, engage in a more sophisticated kind of problem-solving with three parts: defining the problem, generating solutions to the problem, and coming to consensus about solutions. Defining the problem itself has two steps: first deciding what the problem is and then determining what has caused or contributed to its existence. For agreement on what the problem is, I asked for volunteers who would identify examples of students' not having high expectations for the quality of their work and wrote these on an overhead, asking each time if others had observed the same behavior. This whole group discussion led to clarification of the actual student behavior that the faculty would like to change.

For the second part of problem-definition, I used Kagan's Three-Step Interview. The quartets from the Round Robin activity reformed into two different pairs, and each person in each pair had two minutes to describe her/his understanding of what had caused or contributed to the problem—not in terms of "who is to blame" but in terms of "what I have observed." I asked the faculty to focus particularly on things under their own control or influence, such as teacher and student behavior, school rules and procedures, etc. The quartets then reformed, and each person described one thing s/he remembered from listening to her/his partner and wrote that idea on the group's newsprint. Newsprints were posted around the room, and—after processing the Three-Step Interview strategy and its uses with students—the whole group examined the various sources of the problem that had been generated.

Whatever structure(s) you use for this part of the process, you will need to allow time for clarification of and agreement with the ideas generated, before moving on to solutions.

For the solution-generating phase in the problem-solving process I introduced the faculty to Talking Chips. It is important for everyone to be part of the process of looking for solutions, and this structure guarantees that every person will make a contribution to a group's discussion. (Each person in the quartets was given two strips of paper. Whenever one spoke, s/he put one strip into the middle of the group. Once a person's strips were gone, s/he couldn't speak again until everyone's strips had been used and were redistributed.) Participants were told that they could build on another's suggestion, but that no one was to evaluate any suggestions at this point. After two rounds of Talking Chips, participants were to agree on at least one solution they could all accept, with the group's recorder writing that idea on a newsprint.

Again, we processed the Talking Chips structure, both by reflecting on the faculty's experience and by discussing its usefulness with students.

## Coming to Consensus

Finally we posted the newsprints around the room and discussed each solution as a whole group, asking for clarification when necessary. Because the faculty had liked the finger voting process from our previous meeting, we again used this process for coming to consensus, with the added stipulation that the faculty would revisit each of the solutions they accepted after six months to see if they were working. We also agreed that anyone could bring up a concern at an earlier faculty meeting if one arose.

You can choose different structures and a different consensus-building technique for this second meeting. The point is to have the faculty actually experience a variety of structures in team-building and solving problems that are important to them, so that they gain skill in solving problems cooperatively and learn structures they can use with their students.

## Building Independence

Since a good consultant builds him/herself out of a job, your next task will be to help the faculty develop its own capacity to design cooperative faculty meetings without you. One way to do this is to co-plan the next meeting with the planning group. So that they will not be limited to the structures you have used, ask each member of the group to read a section of Kagan's book or other source and learn at least three structures that could be used in team-building, cooperative decision-making, and/or consensus-building.

If no one in the planning group feels ready to take on the job of facilitating the faculty meeting alone, you can offer to co-facilitate, or to prepare a group of facilitators, each with responsibility for a portion of the meeting. You can also offer to be present as an on-the-spot consultant. Be sure to remind people of the need to reflect on both the process and the structures used, so that the dual purpose of learning to solve problems cooperatively and learning cooperative structures to use with students can continue to be achieved.

## Conclusion

The above step-by-step process is meant to be illustrative, not prescriptive. It is a framework for facilitating a school-based change to faculty meetings in which problems are identified and addressed cooperatively. The amount of time needed for each step will vary according to the readiness of the faculty and the complexity of the problems to be solved.

## Notes

1. This chapter appeared in a slightly different version in *Cooperative Learning*, a publication of the International Association for the Study of Cooperation in Education, 18, (2), 1996. Copyright 1996, IASCE. Adapted by permission.

2. For a thorough description of the values of a cooperative school culture, and step-by-step suggestions for how to develop one, see Johnson, D. W. and Johnson, R. T. 1989.

3. *Leading the Cooperative School* (Johnson and Johnson, 1989) is a particularly helpful book for principals; many of the ideas suggested in this chapter are derived from it. Also Spencer Kagan's Cooperative Learning (Kagan, 1992) contains descriptions of cooperative structures that can be used in faculty meetings.

4. Both happened to be men, but there are also women who do not like team-building activities.

5. Because they exist over a peiod of time, collegial support groups usually go through the normal processes of team growth, including "forming," "storming," "norming," "performing," and perhaps "reforming." You might offer a training session on these processes in order to increase team members' understanding of how to make their groups successful.

## References

Johnson, D. W. and Johnson, R. T. (1989) *Leading the cooperative school.* Minnesota: Interaction Book Company.

Kagan, S. (1992) *Cooperative learning.* San Juan Capistrano, CA: Kagan Cooperative Learning.

Little, J. W. (Fall, 1982) "Norms of collegiality and experimentation." *American Educational Research Journal.* 19, 3: 325–340.

# 14

## Developing a Collaborative Environment through Job-Embedded Staff Development: One District's Journey

### Linda Munger

In the summer of 1990, a new superintendent was hired with a vision of developing a collaborative environment. At the same time six elementary teachers were enrolled in the foundation course of cooperative learning. Their vision was developing collaborative classrooms. At the end of that school year 1990–91, the superintendent and six elementary teachers met with an outside consultant for a top-down, bottom-up proposal of a job-embedded staff development program. The end result of that meeting was a journey[1] the district took implementing cooperative learning through the use of a professional development paradigm (see Figure 14.1).

What is job embedded staff development and how is that different than what we have usually done? Job embedded staff development means that leaders (e.g., superintendent, curriculum director, principals, and teacher leaders) within a district teach others and view their role as staff developers as an important responsibility. Teachers and administrators within the district offer training and ongoing support in acquiring new knowledge and skills (Sparks, 1994).

This article focuses on one district's journey over four school years (1990–91, 1992–93, 1993–94, 1994–95) in a job embedded staff development program that provided training and ongoing support in the implementation of cooperative learning and other teaching strategies plus methods of sharing teaching and learning in a collaborative environment (e.g., study teams and peer coaching) in order to meet the district's goal of increasing student performance.

FIGURE 14.1

Professional Development Plan

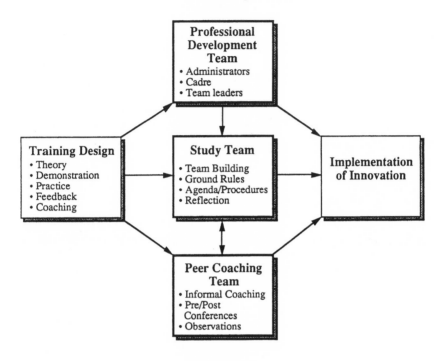

Background

Norwalk is a suburban school district with approximately 1900 students, K–12, five miles south of Des Moines, Iowa. It has one high school, one middle school, and two elementary schools. One of the district's goals has been to improve overall student performance. Because of the research base on cooperative learning increasing student achievement, the district chose cooperative learning as the instructional strategy for the long-term staff development program.

In the spring of 1991 due to a top-down, bottom-up suggestion for a focus on the implementation of cooperative learning as a district initiative, I met with a core group of teachers and administrators to propose a professional development plan to implement cooperative learning (Munger, 1990).

The professional development plan has served as a model for increasing effective training and promoting ongoing support as teachers have implemented cooperative learning.

## Profile of 1990–91 School Year

As a new administration began the 1990–91 school year, the focus became change. Based on research and prior experience as a high school principal, the superintendent wanted the district to focus on change by teaching administrators, teachers, and students how to work together. Teachers and administrators were assigned to study groups to read articles and discuss the change process.

At the same time, six elementary teachers (three from each elementary building), who had participated voluntarily in the first level of training in the Johnsons' Learning Together model of cooperative learning during the summer at the local educational agency (Heartland AEA 11 located in Johnston, IA), began to implement cooperative learning in their own classrooms.

## Profile of 1991–92 School Year

As a result of the research-base on cooperative learning increasing student achievement, the positive results of implementation of cooperative learning in the elementary classrooms, and the recommendations of the six elementary teachers, the district began a mandated, long-term district initiative on implementation of cooperative learning.

The first phase of the professional development plan was with the professional development team (see Figure 14.1) prior to the school year starting. Teachers were one part of the professional development team. The original six elementary teachers became team leaders for training and ongoing support for colleagues in implementation of cooperative learning. In order to be district trainers, the teachers obtained additional training in advanced cooperative learning using the Johnsons' Learning Together model. Consultants provided the training at the local educational agency during the summer. Another part of the professional development team was the administrators. I trained the administrators (i.e., superintendent, curriculum director, and principals) in the elements of cooperative learning designed specially for administrators (i.e., *Leading the Cooperative School*, David and Roger Johnson, 1990).

Using the research on effective staff development (Joyce, 1988), the professional development team (i.e., administrators and team leaders) developed the long-term staff development program for implementing cooperative learning. The professional development plan during this school year was to follow an effective training design and have all teachers and administrators involved in study teams. This was accomplished by first involving all staff (i.e., administrators and teachers) in the basic training I conducted, in the foundation course of the Johnsons' Learning

Together model. The first part of the training was a two-day session during the August in-service days.

The ongoing support and training continued throughout the school year. Each elementary building had their three elementary teachers that were trained and experienced in cooperative learning become a cooperative learning training cadre. Their role was to continue training in cooperative learning during the monthly early dismissal session for staff development and to provide support for the teachers involved in the study teams (e.g., meeting twice a month for a minimum of 30 minutes before or after school on Tuesdays). Since there were no trained cooperative learning cadre members at the high school or middle school at this time, I continued with the training and support at these two building sites during the early dismissal staff development days. The goal was to have a total of at least thirty hours of training completed by the end of the school year plus practice in the classroom, feedback, and coaching.

We provided feedback and coaching to the teachers in two ways. First, the teachers were given feedback regularly by either the building administrator and/or cooperative learning cadre on what was happening during study team meetings, by monitoring the study team logs, and on cooperative learning lesson plans that were turned in on a weekly basis by the teachers. Second, I made classroom observations by invitation only. The teachers opted for feedback from classroom observations.

We monitored the change process by having all teachers complete the Stages of Concern Questionnaire and by identifying interventions necessary to address the concerns of the teachers about implementation of cooperative learning. I met with the superintendent and each building principal to look at individual, study team, and school profiles. We gave teachers copies of their individual and study team profiles. Using the data about concerns, suggestions were made by the consultant to guide interventions to respond to the concerns of the teachers. (e.g., Interventions for Management Concerns addressed specific "how-to" issues, provided practical solutions to some logistic problems, and set timelines for accomplishments) (Hord, 1987).

Profile of 1992–93 School Year

The professional development team (i.e., administrators and cadre) increased by having four new teams of teachers and administrators (i.e., approximately three teachers and one administrator) from each building attend further training in advanced cooperative learning in the Johnsons' Learning Together model. The purpose was to have a well-trained cadre (i.e., classroom experience and two levels of cooperative learning training) at each building site to provide further training and ongoing support.

I provided additional support once a month. I met with the cooperative learning cadre and administrator at each building site for approximately 1½ hours once a month to solve problems and provide assistance in planning for the monthly early dismissal training sessions conducted by the cadre leaders at each building site throughout the school year.

We continued on-going support through the monitoring of study team logs. Classroom observations were made by cadre members upon request by individual teachers, and involvement in study teams continued twice a month either before or after school on Tuesdays.

All teachers completed the Stages of Concern Questionnaire for the second year to continue to monitor the stages of concern and the changes over time that had occurred during implementation. As teachers' concerns were being met, there was evidence of movement through the different stages of concern. Administrators and cadre members received feedback in order to identify the appropriate interventions needed to address the concerns of the teachers as they continued to implement cooperative learning (e.g., collaborative interventions were addressed by providing more time and professional growth opportunities for teachers to develop skills necessary for working collaboratively) (Hord, 1987).

Profile of 1993–94 School Year

All three support components of the professional development plan were now in place. First, to increase the critical mass trained in more advanced strategies of cooperative learning, more new teams of teachers (i.e., approximately 15 teachers from the district) went in the summer to the educational agency for advanced training of cooperative learning. At the same time, four teachers, one from each building, went in the summer to the Cooperative Learning Institute for leadership training by the Johnsons in Minneapolis, MN. The purpose was to prepare a team of trainers to train any new teachers hired to the district.

Although the study team meetings continued with the same meeting schedule, a new study team log was introduced to increase the use of the cooperative components in study team meetings. This was one intervention that addressed the concerns identified in the Stages of Concern Questionnaire.

The third component of the professional development plan was now to be implemented for all teachers. All teachers and administrators were trained during the in-service days on peer coaching using a collaborative approach (e.g., pre-conference, classroom observation, and post-conference or co-planning a lesson) (Costa & Garmston, 1988).

To provide incentive and recognition for involvement in the support structures of the professional development plan, we made available staff development credit from Heartland AEA and college credit from Drake University to teachers and administrators for work in study teams, peer coaching, and action research.

The professional development team continued to provide training and ongoing support. A leadership team (i.e., the four teachers who were now certified trainers) taught a cooperative learning training session to the twelve new teachers hired in the district for the 1993–94 school year. This leadership team developed a form for peer coaching to encourage and monitor different types of peer coaching: pre/post conference with observation, walk throughs, video analysis, sharing within study teams, and co-planning of lessons.

Two specific expectations were required of all teachers. In order to link accountability for the staff development initiative to the implementation of cooperative learning in the classroom, each teacher on the evaluation cycle was required as part of his/her formative evaluation to have the building administrator observe one formal cooperative learning lesson. The district required one pre-conference, classroom observation and post-conference each semester with teacher's choice of peer coaching partner. One of the two observations needed to be a cooperative learning lesson. The district provided ongoing support by funding a substitute at each building for one full day each month to allow release time for peer coaching.

As the professional development team within the district gained more knowledge and skill, the need for my support continued to diminish. During this school year, I worked one day every other month in the district. Half the day was spent with the four teachers of the leadership team (i.e., teachers that were now certified trainers) and the other half of the day was spent with the administrators. The purpose of the meetings was to problem-solve and monitor the district initiative of cooperative learning with study teams and peer coaching in place.

At the end of that day, I met with an action research team of teachers and an administrator from each building. The building teams first shared questions, concerns, and successes from their own buildings. The purpose of this sharing was to increase communication across the district and promote networking of ideas. Each building team also established several areas to monitor for continuous improvement in cooperative learning to share at the large group meeting. For example, the middle school analyzed study team logs and identified that reflection was the component that was most frequently neglected at the end of a team meeting. The high school identified the number of cooperative learning lessons done per week in order to focus more on appropriateness of use and frequency of lessons each day. The elementary teachers identified areas of focus for growth and comfort level in peer coaching.

Profile of 1994–95 School Year

The ultimate goal of having so many teachers trained in cooperative learning was to have a team of two certified trainers at each building site. This would provide the opportunity to empower the teachers at each building site to focus on their own building initiatives. The certified, trained teachers would use their cooperative knowledge and skills to facilitate teachers working together as they learned other teaching strategies and became more involved in decision-making.

As a result of this goal, another team of four teachers (i.e., one teacher from each building) was sent during the summer to the Cooperative Learning Institute for leadership training, to take what is called the Brown Book. This team would be expected to do the first level of training during the school year in the district for any new teachers hired. The original four teachers (i.e., one from each building previously certified in leadership training of the Brown Book) were sent during the summer for the next level of leadership training on advanced cooperative learning. This team would be expected now to continue training teachers in the district on advanced cooperative learning rather than sending teams of teachers each summer to the educational agency. The district expectations were that all future levels of cooperative learning training would be done in-house; other neighboring districts would be invited to be a part of future training sessions, and skills learned in the cooperative learning training would be applied by staff developers in training teachers in other teaching strategies (e.g., concept attainment, inductive thinking, Dimensions of Learning).

To empower the teachers in making decisions based on research, a cadre of teachers and an administrator from each building met before the school year began to develop an action plan for designing a cooperative school. The action plans focused on developing a collaborative environment for both students and teachers. Plans included further learning of other cooperative learning models, making connections with other models of teaching, doing mini-sessions on components of cooperative learning during early dismissals, training in Dimensions of Learning, greater focus on teaching and monitoring of social skills, further work in peer coaching, and continuous improvement through action research.

Many components of the professional development plan remained constant. First, district expectations were again set to have cooperative learning observation as part of the evaluation cycle, continue peer coaching with a substitute hired at each building to allow for release time, have study teams meet a minimum of 30 minutes before or after school every Tuesday, and have two monthly early dismissals (i.e., half the time focused on staff development and the other half focused on curriculum issues). Second, staff development and college credit were available for teachers taking either the first or second level of cooperative learning provided by the in-district trainers, involvement in peer coaching mini-sessions and classroom observations, and involvement in study teams.

As the staff development program became more job embedded, there was less need for the outside consultant. During the last year, I was hired to be in the district once every nine weeks, meeting 1½ hours with cadre and building administrators at each building site and then meeting at the end of the day with cadre/administrator representative, superintendent, and curriculum director to problem-solve and monitor for continuous improvement.

The teacher leaders and administrators assumed more responsibility for facilitating meetings. All in-district meetings (e.g., middle school teams, study teams, curriculum meetings, grade level or department meetings, and administrative meetings) used the study team log to focus on four components for conducting effective meetings (e.g., beginning a meeting with a focus activity, reviewing established ground rules, agenda with processes and role assignments that encourage participation by all, and reflection of content and process).

The teachers and administrators assumed new responsibilities for other training and ongoing support. First, another outside consultant, who was trained in Dimensions of Learning and had done previous training in the district on models of teaching, was hired to do an in-service before school on "Dimension One: Positive Attitudes and Perceptions about Learning" (Marzano, Pickering, Arrendondo, Blackburn, Brandt, & Moffett, 1992) to make the connections between cooperative learning and new training in Dimensions of Learning. Then the cadre members (previously known as two separate cadres—cooperative learning and models of teaching) from each building were involved in building level training of "Dimension Two: Thinking Involved in Acquiring and Integrating Knowledge." This dimension would make connections between cooperative learning and concept attainment training that teachers had previously implemented in their own classrooms. The purpose of the choice of Dimensions of Learning at this time was to empower the cadre with the responsibility of designing future training and making connections with all the previous work in the district with other models of teaching (e.g., concept attainment and inductive thinking).

Many of these same teachers and administrators have been involved in another long-term project (i.e., AMOEBA project) at the educational agency focusing on group process skills that were utilized this past year (1993–94) in group investigation of designated topics for the district (e.g., assessment and tech prep). The purpose of this study was to continuously have a core group of teachers and administrators acquiring new knowledge and skills in order to assume the responsibility within the district as staff developers.

## Outcomes

Three years (1991–92, 92–93, 93–94) of implementation of cooperative learning have resulted in significant changes at Norwalk Community School District. Stages of Concern Questionnaires, peer coaching logs, study team logs, classroom observations, research data collected by each building action team, and information verbally shared by teachers about their teaching and learning have provided extensive data on how the job embedded staff development program, as well as the amount of time and energy spent by the teachers in continuous improvement in cooperative learning, have made a difference in the Norwalk Schools for teachers, administrators, and students. Five main questions (Fullan, 1991) served as guidelines in reflecting on the outcomes based on the data collected of how the teachers have thrown their energies into a change effort.

*Does Training Address an Important Need?* As the district first looked at the staff development program for training district-wide in cooperative learning, the purpose was to increase collaboration among teachers, administrators, and students to meet one of the district's goals, to improve overall student performance. Standardized test results indicate student performance is improving. The district now provides full inclusion for students with special needs, and the application of appropriate social skills and acceptance of all students is evident in the classrooms. A "shadow study" of middle level learners conducted by a local university, demonstrates that students are more engaged. The middle school associate principal used classroom observations and concluded that "students are becoming problem solvers. They tend to turn to team members and address conflict within the group rather than relying on adult intervention."

*Is the Administration Endorsing the Change and Will Resources Be Available for the Innovation to Succeed?* The superintendent remains committed to long term involvement and success of the implementation of cooperative learning. The district has provided an outside consultant for four years, funds for continuous training for cadre members, and funds for substitutes to allow for released time for peer coaching. Most of the funding has occurred through Iowa's Phase III fund for school transformation. Teachers have received a stipend from Phase III funds each year for their involvement in classroom implementation of cooperative learning and an additional stipend for cadre members for the extra time spent outside of the school day for meetings.

*Do Other Teachers Show an Interest in the Change?* The original interest in cooperative learning was from the grass roots—elementary teachers that had been trained in cooperative learning and tried it in their own classrooms for a year. The time spent in study teams has allowed teachers to build trust and share their teaching and learning over time. The middle school teachers have developed effective interdisciplinary teams that meet daily and are involved in block scheduling. Early dismissals give teachers additional time to learn new instructional strategies, share successes and problems, and learn from each other. The district supports time for teachers to be members of a cadre to learn other new strategies (e.g., concept attainment, inductive thinking), practice in their own classrooms, and then teach and coach their colleagues. Many of the teachers have investigated other educational issues (e.g., tech prep, assessment, early childhood developmentally appropriate practices) and now make presentations at state, regional, and national conferences.

*Do the Teachers Assume Responsibility for Making a Contribution to the Development of a Collaborative Work Culture?* Numerous visitors (e.g., teachers and administrators from other districts, university professors, parents, and other community members) to the schools make positive comments about how the administrators, teachers, and students are engaged learners in a collaborative environment. The superintendent recently received a letter from the Iowa Department of Education noting evidence of collaboration in the different buildings. Teachers have learned to work so effectively in study teams that the format has become the norm throughout the district no matter what type of meeting one attends. One middle school teacher commented at another meeting outside the district, "The district has high expectations and we work hard together to make a difference for the students." As the district has moved toward full inclusion of children with special needs, there is more team teaching which is increasing collaboration among teachers and students. The middle school teachers are working extensively together to identify the most critical concepts in their curriculum and then match appropriate teaching strategies with teachers in different discipline areas to deliver that curriculum in the most effective way to increase student performance.

*Do Teachers That Wish to Play a Larger Leadership Role Have the Opportunity for Coaching and Mentoring?* There are at least three teachers at each building site that are members of the leadership cadre. For several years there were two cadres—one cooperative learning cadre and one models of teaching cadre. Their job was to be ahead of the rest of the teachers in learning and practicing new strategies in order to eventually teach their colleagues. In 1995 there was only one cadre per building made up of teachers with expertise in various teaching strategies. The cadre members developed an action plan for their building and monitored for continuous improvement throughout the year. They were also involved in doing some training at the building level on Dimension 2 of Dimensions of Learning. Teachers in the district have continuously been encouraged by both the superintendent and building administrator to learn and take a leadership role in their building as well as in the district. Several teachers have left the district and have become administrators (e.g., elementary principal, curriculum director) in other districts.

## Lessons Learned

Based on Norwalk's experiences with this job embedded staff development program, the following insights have been drawn in reference to the change process. These insights may serve as useful guidelines for other staff developers trying to enact change.

### Change Requires a Balance of Top-down and Bottom-up Processes

The beginning initiative to implement cooperative learning came both from the top-down (i.e., superintendent making a decision based on research) and the bottom-up (i.e., a core group of enthusiastic elementary teachers who had tried and experienced success in their own classrooms). There was a definite need to keep the line of communication open so that everyone knew the district, building, and individual expectations for the implementation of cooperative learning. The avenue for this communication was a view by an outside consultant on a regular basis, ongoing meetings at building sites, and combined meetings with a roundtable sharing by representation of teachers and administrators from all buildings. The role of the outside consultant was to listen and see through a different set of eyes what was happening within the district and guide any problem solving for continuous improvement.

Change Requires Altering the Culture of the Schools

Accountability by teachers for implementing a staff development initiative (i.e., cooperative learning) was new. The accountability factor was built in several ways. Although not always seen as positive, the means of holding the teachers accountable also provided immediate feedback and often coaching opportunities. These means were through monitoring study team logs, cooperative learning lesson plans, and peer coaching logs. The monitoring of study team logs provided the administrator with knowledge of what instructional improvements the teachers were focusing on during these meetings that would affect student outcomes in the classroom. The monitoring of the cooperative learning lesson plans provided the cadre members with specific data for decision-making of future staff development training sessions. The peer coaching logs provided the administrator with knowledge of how much cooperative learning was being done and how teachers were working together to improve their teaching repertoire.

Effective Approaches are Needed to Change, Combine and Balance Contradictory Factors (e.g., Simplicity and Complexity, Looseness and Tightness, Strong Leadership, and Participation)

Although the school system still maintains some of its loosely-coupled organization (e.g., teachers teaching in self-contained classrooms, some of the actions of one teacher do not affect the actions of another), they have become a more tightly-coupled organization by emphasis on social skills (e.g., one elementary building focuses on a social skill per month for the building), emphasis on positive interdependence (e.g., goal interdependence established in the action plan for the school year), emphasis on individual accountability (e.g., peer coaching logs), and emphasis on systematic processing of group and organizational effectiveness (e.g., action research via surveys, interviews, observation forms). There have been two changes in administration since the process began. The middle school principal left at the end of the 1992–93 school year and the high school principal left at the end of the 1993–94 school year. Both left for reasons of professional advancement but their buildings continued to professionally grow and continually improve in cooperative learning and other teaching strategies. According to Fullan (1991), participation, initiative-taking, and empowerment are key factors from the beginning. The district constantly has focused on getting everyone involved by empowering the teachers in the decision-making process: what they want to focus on for their building action plan and how they will participate in increasing their teaching repertoire in order to increase student performance.

Change Is a Long-term Continuous Process

The teachers have entered their fourth year with implementation of cooperative learning in their classrooms. The goals have been to develop a cooperative school so that teachers, administrators, and students are working collaboratively together, for teachers to reach routine level of use in cooperative learning, and the strategy is institutionalized within the district. As some administrators and teachers leave the district or leave their place as a member of the leadership cadre, the building and district focus remains constant—continuous improvement toward developing a collaborative environment for all students, teachers, and administrators with the ultimate goal of increasing student performance.

The district has realized that in order for any change effort to become embedded in the structure there had to be changes in policy, budget, and time allocation. It has adopted the policy that focuses on staff development initiatives as part of the evaluation cycle. The Phase III funds continue to allow moneys for staff development. It has been helpful in designing the change effort and creating a great "buy-in" by teachers and administrators that Iowa has required a three year staff development plan and Phase III has required part of the plan to include a training design that focuses on theory, demonstration, practice, feedback, and coaching plus the involvement of teachers in study teams. The Board of Education has allowed the teachers to increase their number of early dismissal days to twice a month.

According to Fullan, Rolheiser-Bennett, and Bennett (1990), when the teacher is learner, there is collaboration, inquiry, reflective practice, and technical skills development. Maeroff (1993) states that teachers will not create the setting that fosters cooperative learning or any other innovation in their classroom unless they are persuaded of its merits, taught how to implement it, and then nurtured through the early stages of implementation. The Norwalk Community School District has provided teachers with training, support, time, and resources to create meaning and efficacy for teachers to become life-long learners.

As the district moves from implementation to institutionalization, they have moved from coordination, shared control, pressure and support, ongoing technical assistance, and early rewards for teachers to embedding, linking to instruction, widespread use, removal of competing priorities, and continuing assistance (Fullan, 1991). The job embedded staff development practice of Norwalk Community School District has incorporated teachers sharing and interacting and demonstrated new norms of collegiality through the use of study teams and peer coaching.

## Notes

1. This article appeared in similar form in the *Journal of Staff Development*. Copied with permission. 1995. Vol. 16 No. 3.

## References

Costa, A., & Garmston, R. (Presenters). (1988). *Another set of eyes: Conference skills.* [videotape]. Alexandria, VA: Association of Supervision and Curriculum Development.

Fullan, M. (1990). Staff development, innovation, and institutional development. *Changing school culture through staff development.* 1990 ASCD Yearbook.

Fullan, M. (1991). *The new meaning of educational change.* Columbia University: Teachers College Press.

Fullan, M., Bennett, B. & Rolheiser-Bennett, C. (1990). Linking classroom and school improvement. *Educational Leadership, 47*(8), 13–19.

Hall, G., George, A., & Rutherford, W. (1986). Measuring stages of concern about the innovation: A manual for use of soc questionnaire. Austin, TX: Southwest Educational Development Laboratory (SEDL).

Hord, S., Rutherford, W., Huling-Austin, L., and Hall, G. (1987). *Taking charge of change.* Austin, Texas: Southwest Educational Development Laboratory.

Johnson, D. & Johnson, R. (1989). *Leading the cooperative school.* Edina, MN: Interaction Book Co.

Johnson, D., Johnson, R., & Holubec, E. J. (1988). *Advanced cooperative learning.* Edina, MN: Interaction Book Co.

Joyce, B. and Showers, B. (1988). *Student achievement through staff development.* New York: Longman.

Maeroff, Gene. (1993). *Team building for school change equipping teachers for new roles.* New York: Teachers College.

Marzano, R., Pickering, D., Arrendondo, D., Blackburn, G., Brandt, R., and Moffett, C. (1992). *Dimensions of learning.* Aurora, CO: McREL Institute.

Munger, L. (1991). Support structures for cooperative learning. *Journal of Staff Development,* 12(2), 28–32.

Munger, L. (1990). *Analysis of the effect of a professional development paradigm on the implementation of cooperative learning.* Ph.D. dissertation, Iowa State University.

Sparks, Dennis. (1994). A paradigm shift in staff development. *Journal of Staff Development,* 15(4), 26–29.

# Part IV

## Return to the Vision of Community

ૐ

# 15

## COOPERATIVE LEARNING COMMUNITIES: EXPANDING FROM CLASSROOM COCOON TO GLOBAL CONNECTIONS

*LIANA FOREST*

### Back to the Future

Imagine a community where each baby born has multiple caretakers, some young, some old, some in between. Each of these people cares deeply about that child as a member of their growing family, village, or localized group with a lengthy history. Caretakers share a common value system: children are valuable and enjoyable resources to be cultivated, enjoyed, and included in community endeavors. All persons, of whatever age, involved with that child consider themselves his or her teacher.

When children in such a community become toddlers, they may wander into any home and be fed and played with by everyone there. Everywhere they go, children watch carefully everything older members of the community are doing. They soon form a desire to contribute, to be part of the action. Within a year or two they are allowed to help care for children younger than themselves. Soon young children become members of the workforce within the community: cooking, cleaning, child rearing, planting, harvesting, building, fishing, and celebrating.

Children in this community are never told "you must cooperate, you must be generous." These imperatives are imbedded in the daily tasks and seasonal events participated in by everyone within the community. Not to be a part of this would cause a tremendous sense of loss of identity. Individuals do not see themselves as separate from the group, but as individual resources for and parts of the whole. Without thinking much about it, these children grow up working easily and smoothly with others, caring for those needing care, and developing a sense of pride and competence for what they contribute to family and village efforts.

When I was engaged in studies of naturally cooperative communities such as these (see Graves, 1971; Graves & Graves, 1978a, 1978b, 1983), what puzzled me greatly was why children from them were forced to learn in schools whose values and daily structure contradicted the basic principles of the cooperative community of learners within which they were born and raised. Competitive and individualistic classroom and school cultures imported from modern, urban, and western societies were in direct conflict with these children's accustomed learning style. My concern with cooperation in education began with this dilemma for children who were raised to learn cooperatively but who were compelled to learn to work alone and compete instead (Graves & Graves 1983; 1985).

When I left these settings to return to work in New Zealand and the United States, I began considering a different problem. If children from traditional societies, who took in cooperation with their first foods, were separated from this mode of learning when they entered a school, what about the children in most modern and urban societies who grow up in a totally different context? Their parents may not teach young children how to contribute to the family or the general welfare of their wider community. Their neighborhoods may not be safe places where learning is fostered by caring older children and adults. School could be the only place where they would have a chance to learn what it is like to be a part of a cooperative team, a collaborative community that learns together. Without learning the habits and abilities to build community and collaborate, these young people would have great difficulty in holding down jobs that require these skills. In fact, statistics show that in our culture more people lose their jobs for these reasons than from lack of the academic or technical skills required. What would these young people have to contribute as the citizens and community members of the future? Even if children happen to have a teacher who knows how to build cooperative relations within the classroom, what happens when those children leave his or her class? If the institutions and neighborhoods in which children grow up do not demonstrate that adults can effectively work together toward common goals, these children also will learn something through observation. They will observe that "community" is just a synonym for a place where people live and work, but this does not necessarily include caring about, or even interacting with others. School is a place where you wait out the time until you have to go to work, and how well you do depends on you alone; nor do you care whether your schoolmates succeed. These children could learn to expect others to be untrustworthy, to anticipate the worst, and to dislike those who are different. The alternative to building meaningful community often includes gang membership, violence, and chaos. Building caring community may take more effort now than in traditionally cooperative societies, but can we afford to allow the current trends toward alienation, isolation, and aggression to shape the future?

Moving Toward Educational Community

The movement toward building learning communities (Costa 1992) within school settings has been growing steadily alongside efforts to help students learn cooperatively. *Making the School Everybody's House* (Schmuck & Schmuck 1974) documented early efforts to build community through school reorganization, and other teachers and developers in the 1970s (e.g.: Gibbs 1978 [revised 1987 & 1994]; Stanford 1977) began to consider how to create a caring classroom community. Educators in the field of cooperative learning began early to realize the effects of the lack of a community context in schools adopting cooperative instructional methods. Programs specifically focused on fostering a "climate of cooperation" or "building classroom community," began to emerge, such as Moorman and Dishon's (1983) *Our Classroom* approach, which arose out of a need for better classroom management. The Tribes Program (Gibbs, 1978; 1987) was originally aimed at drug abuse prevention, and Kohlberg's "just community" (1988) was concerned with empowering teenagers to make moral decisions in their own educational setting. The Child Development Project in California began a longitudinal study for promoting prosocial behavior (see Kohn, 1990; Watson, 1990, and chapter 7) which included the establishment of a "caring school community of learners."

There are a number of good educational reasons for promoting classroom and school community in conjunction with cooperative instruction. One is that teachers and principals themselves realize the necessity for a supportive context if cooperative learning is to be completely effective. In 1985 the International Association for the Study of Cooperation in Education conducted a poll to discover what special interest topics attracted members. The poll showed that IASCE members were more concerned with "how to create a cooperative classroom climate" than any other topic, including specific curriculum content areas. This interest has remained high, and recent school restructuring efforts have incorporated collaboration throughout the educational community, including parents and others, as a goal (see Cooper and Boyd, 1995).

Secondly, there has also been a growing interest among educators in more holistic learning that includes the context of the learners, the background experiences they bring to the classroom, and relevant social situations that inhibit or facilitate learning. For many educators, small group learning without considering these factors began to appear as inappropriate as learning to read without considering wider literacy experiences, studying mathematics without real-life problem solving, or most recently, evaluating learning without authentic assessment techniques.

A third consideration is that whole-school cooperative communities have tremendous long-term advantages even though they require additional efforts in the short term. Cooperative learning methods are significantly more effective if all educators in the school are using them to promote pro-social and academic development. Teachers are better able to assess the effectiveness of their interventions by seeing the cumulative effects upon students, and this may take longer than a single year. Colleagues teaching at higher grade levels can give feedback on how one's former students are improving over time. The school as a whole can then develop a unified concept of each student as a growing, developing individual within a supportive, caring community.

In terms of professional development, a cooperative learning community means a more comfortable and inspiring work environment for teachers as well as students. Teachers can expect peers to support and assist them in implementing new instructional strategies, and they can collaborate to develop both methods and curricula. They are empowered to run faculty meetings more actively and efficiently. Staff development becomes community development rather than an externally imposed series of in-service workshops. For example, at Fox School in Belmont, California, a fragmented and isolated faculty was unified with cooperative methods first in faculty meetings, before many teachers began using cooperative learning methods for students. Then teachers helped to plan and implement the use of cooperative learning, integrated with other innovations they felt important, at a pace they found comfortable. The principal helped find ways to release teachers and provide substitutes so that the faculty had time to work together to develop curriculum, to observe and coach one another (Schoneman, 1992).

We can also consider what happens when we do not make the effort to build a community context for cooperative learning within a school. In recent years I visited many schools where extensive staff development in cooperative learning yielded no increase in the use of cooperative methods by most of the staff. Teachers practicing cooperative methods in these schools explained to me why cooperative learning did not "catch on" with the rest of the staff: feelings of being coerced from above or, conversely, lack of administrative support; methods taught with little tailoring to specific school populations or situations; competing demands; no release time for planning and collaborating with colleagues; and colleagues preferring to focus on content and ignore the learning process.

These reasons are related to lack of community in several ways. Teachers in these schools generally do not feel they belong to a common community within which they have a sense of ownership, efficacy, and power leading to real commitment and feelings of responsibility for the school and community as a whole. The quality of teacher action depends on these factors, and without them, most efforts at reform and innovation will ultimately fail. No matter how good a job a teacher does at creating cooperative community within his or her classroom, much of this work can be undone when students move to classes with competitive or alienating environments. In upper-level classes where students have many teachers in a school day, the cooperative classroom may become an oasis for some students, generating jealousy and suspicion from other teachers. Implementers of cooperative methods face negativity from colleagues in some schools and indifference and lack of support in others. For many teachers, a school community where they feel included and empowered is the necessary first step to adopting cooperative learning methods in the classroom.

If we are to remedy this state of affairs, and place cooperative learning in an environment that promotes growth, we need to assure that we understand the components of collaborative community and what steps we must take to develop these components. As Art Costa reminds us, "Recent efforts to bring intellectual, cooperative, and empowered focus to our schools will prove futile unless we create a school environment that signals the staff, students and [wider] community that the development of the intellect, cooperative decision making and the enhancement of individual diversity are of basic importance as the school's core values" (Costa, 1992, p.93). There are no real short cuts to building community thoroughly from the ground up and maintaining it vigilantly over time. Basic to this understanding is a realization that community grows from within. It can be fostered from without—indeed it must be to survive—but it cannot be imposed.

When we do make the commitment and support it with an effort to ensure individuals and sub-groups continue to feel "in community" with others, we see changes (see *Cooperative Learning* magazine's thematic issues on "Creating a Cooperative Learning Community", 1990; and Staff Development: "Building Communities of Learners", 1991/92). Members of a learning community find time to make changes the group decides are necessary, and they energize one another to follow through. Without this initial effort we could lose the tremendous benefits cooperative education can give to teachers and students.

## A Definition of Community

Community can be defined as an inherently cooperative, cohesive, and self-reflective group entity where everyone feels they belong, and whose members work on a regular, face-to-face basis toward common goals while respecting a variety of perspectives, values, and life styles.

*Community Is Where Everyone Feels They Belong . . . Respecting a Variety of Perspectives, Values, and Life Styles.* A comprehensive book on organizing and managing classroom learning communities (Putnam and Burke 1992) gives a similar definition: "a group of people who are associated by common status, pursuits, or relationships." I have added an emphasis on the respecting of variety, or honoring of heterogeneity. Otherwise these groupings could result in the creation of homogeneous clubs or voluntary associations united by a single issue. Putnam and Burke note that "A community is not so much a collection of like-minded believers as a commitment to shared differences. . . . A learning community gathers up differences and celebrates them, because differences are rich resources which improve the quality of group interaction" (1992:40). Increasingly, educators are examining what elements are necessary to a truly cooperative, democratic and inclusive community (Sapon-Shevin, 1991a, 1991b and chapter 10 this volume).

In a cooperative community, everyone is equally eligible for inclusion. No one is ever excluded because of race, religion, personality quirks, differences of perspective, or unconventional attitudes or interests. In such a community, I know I have a place in the group that only I can fill; that I contribute something that is necessary to the group and which is valued by other members. I also know other members well enough to value and respect their unique contributions. Together we define who we are as a group. This definition may change, evolve, and grow, but we construct its meaning together out of what we all have to give. This means we must find out what resources each of us brings and communicate this positively to the group as a whole, not only at the beginning when we are building the group, but before (and often during) every group project: the group must always know what resources it has to do the task at hand. If this process is thorough, members of a community are seen as colleagues, rather than as competitors. In cooperative learning, the identification of such individual contributions, or "multiple abilities," has been most thoroughly developed in Complex Instruction (see Cohen, 1994 and chapter six of this volume). The same care must be taken to identify the unique contributions of faculty colleagues, administrators, parents, and other members of the collaborative learning community.

M. Scott Peck (1987) calls this aspect of community "integrative." He suggests that true community does not try to obliterate diversity, but rather works toward an integrity of the whole. It seeks to balance and reconcile the tension between conflicting interests, needs, and demands, rather than isolating and compartmentalizing them, or reducing them to an average. Community is more like a salad than a sauce. He concludes, "all forms of thinking should be allowed; some forms of behavior should not be" (p. 245). We can no longer afford to have some members of our school and municipal communities feel they do not belong as valued resources of the whole.

*Community Is Where Members Work on a Regular, Face-to-Face Basis Toward Common Goals.* Building community requires sustained interaction developed around common goals, joint tasks, important sharings, and meeting one's and other's needs on a regular basis. More intermittent contacts can comprise a network or a fellowship, but only when people regularly meet, work, and play together does deeper community arise. This kind of regularity, when combined with inclusion, fosters a sense of trust in others' dependability and a feeling of responsibility in oneself to the group. It develops the kind of respect we need in order to risk being vulnerable with others. It fosters the skills to coordinate efforts with balance, compromise, and gain-gain solutions.

Unfortunately, fledgling communities struggle with many competing activities as well as a lack of commitment to regular cooperative meetings and unifying events. The 50–minute classroom hour is especially hampering, both to student cooperation on longer projects, and teacher collaboration in developing and implementing curriculum. School restructuring that considers longer class periods and teacher teams that seek to integrate concepts or methods across subject matter areas can help to build true community for students and teachers. Teacher teams that instruct the same set of students over several years also develop strong community ties. These changes, while initially difficult adjustments, can strengthen classroom, school, and faculty sense of community.

Peer support for teachers often founders because its members are "busy, busy, busy" and "into a thousand different things." In contrast, integration of several aims can help teachers collaborate to reduce instead of increase workloads. For example, a school district in Connecticut found that teacher teams combining cooperative learning methods with an integrated curriculum design and authentic assessment improved all these school initiatives (Hibbard, 1991/1992; Hibbard, 1992). Moreover, providing release time for cooperative support groups can provide teachers with the community backing they need to master difficult innovations in the classroom.

*Community Is a Cohesive Yet Self-Reflective Group.* Schools attempting community need to seek a balance between a sense of solidarity and unity and the ability to self-examine and reflect on the functioning of the group. This may seem to be something of a paradox, since the more we see ourselves as interdependent, standing up for one another, and expressing solidarity, the less willing we generally are to consider improvements in our functioning.

The fear of discovering or exposing disunity (or a lack of information about how to give suggestions or feedback with caring) may be one reason that the "reflection," "processing," or "de-briefing" segment of collaborative meetings often is missing or superficial. It may also help explain why our faculties exhibit a great deal of "pseudo-community" that has little substance when put to the test of making major reforms. However, unless faculty and administrators learn to reflect on the functioning of the group, they will also be unable to convey the necessity for learning this skill to student groups. Putnam and Burke (1992) suggest that "a classroom learning community is characterized by public reflection on what has happened . . . Group reflection on events influences students powerfully to view events as external circumstances to be examined for understanding, and not as internal character flaws to be evaluated and blamed." They note that under these conditions students soon enjoy talking over "great goofs we have made" ( p. 43). The same sort of practice needs to obtain for all segments of a collaborative learning community if it is not to get stuck in the early phases of development.

## Developing Community

Including the three elements defined above is essential but not sufficient for developing collaborative community. Building community is a slow, often difficult, process which develops in stages. These are: forming the community, experiencing community and resolving conflicts, and functioning effectively.

Forming the Community:  Who Are We?

In the early stages of building a community—whether whole school, faculty group, administrative team, or a classroom—members are concerned with finding a place for themselves within the group. This involves becoming acquainted with other group members on a friendly basis, and presenting oneself to the group and being accepted as a valuable member.

Classrooms, schools, or educator support groups are not natural communities; there is usually no built-in reason such as kinship or village ties to bring people together. To encourage strong standards of equality and honoring of diversity, so that each member will come to find her/his place physically, emotionally, and mentally within the growing community, some special efforts need to be taken. Offering opportunities for enjoyable get-acquainted activities, while simultaneously encouraging information exchange and problem solving, is most effective (see Child Development Project, 1995; Graves and Graves 1988, 1990; Kagan, Robertson & Kagan, 1995; and Shaw 1992 for examples). This might include such things as:

- Whole group mixers, ice-breakers, and get-acquainted activities (used when first building community or when new members enter) that introduce members to one another in a light-hearted context. These need to be relevant and authentic experiences, not just silly games. People should learn information they would really like to know about one another or about a topic, such as names, interests, skills, and experiences. These activities also can function to identify particular contributions individuals can make to the group work.
- Whole group challenges that help community members feel they are capable of accomplishing something together as a unit. Faculties may wish to also include social or fund-raising events that parents and wider community members can attend. Learning communities need to include all stakeholders in some way from the beginning, although not at all events.
- Using charts or graphs for discovering and plotting the resources or experiences of faculty task forces, and school site or district level teams along a wide variety of dimensions. The same is done for students in the classroom or school.

Another way of creating an inclusive community is through planning and assessment activities that help the community further learn the resources and needs of its members. For the classroom, Putnam and

Burke suggest students list things they like, things they'd like to change, and things they would like others to support them in doing (1992). A similar exercise would be useful for faculty groups at the beginning of a school year or semester.

A second phase of forming community, once members are acquainted with each other's resources and needs, is finding commonalities and establishing symbols of group identity. The community must continuously reaffirm whole group identity throughout the year.

Whole group identity is balanced by recognizing and incorporating sub-groupings within the larger group. Small learning groups or task forces will need to be formed to get specific work accomplished. At the same time, care should be taken not to allow these small groups to become more important than the class or school community as a whole. Rivalries and factionalism can develop, making it difficult to switch teams and work with someone else. Often in schools, departments or grade-level groupings can siphon off loyalty and leave little energy or time for the entire school community. While practicality and face-to-face interaction needs dictate that we more frequently collaborate in small groups, the composition of these can change, and we can meet with different task forces for different purposes. In addition, structural reorganization in a school which encourages cross-disciplinary and cross-grade level collaboration—for developing integrated curricula or authentic assessment techniques, for example—can help build community. Tutoring programs, set up for older students to help younger ones, can lead to coordination between teachers and their classrooms, strengthening commitment to the school as a whole and helping create more responsible learners.

Developing a sense of joint history also makes for a more cohesive community. J. J. Schwab (1976, p. 246) suggests that celebrations help a community develop a historical memory. One school I know celebrates different classrooms on a rotating basis for their unique contributions to the community, but does not hold contests between them where several classes "fail" while one "wins." Something similar could encourage learning community task forces and enhance intergroup communication.

When teachers make these school-wide efforts to collaborate, they are prepared to deal with cliques developing in their classrooms. When administrators develop ties with teachers, parents, and community representatives, they avoid establishing exclusive educational establishments. Setting norms such as "We can work with anyone," "Everyone knows something, nobody knows everything," or "We each have a piece of the puzzle," is important not just for students but for everyone within the learning community. Short activities such as the Bavelas

5–Squares or "Broken Circles" (Graves & Graves 1990) introduce community members to these norms empirically: consequences of non-cooperation are crystal clear and can be discussed afterwards.

During this formative period, using random group formations for short activities (and changing groups often) helps community members realize the possibility of these norms. In the classroom, giving students a home or family group, with whom they sit to begin and end each day to share personal experiences or write in their journals, can alleviate the group fatigue of moving between different groupings throughout the week. Similarly, teachers may have certain support groups they want to meet with frequently, to balance the variety of groups they are in throughout the community. If there are larger events that incorporate the whole community, the balance between small group and overall community identity will be maintained.

Exploring Community: What Can We Do Together?

At this stage of community development, the work that members collaborate on together becomes very important to them. They ask such questions as "What do we want to accomplish together?" and "What are our group goals?" At times it will be necessary to remind members that group goals are both person-oriented and task-oriented. In addition to learning how to complete a task and achieve a desired outcome for the school and its students, group members are now ready to form deeper connections, to learn to communicate in ways that convey empathy for one and other's feelings, and respect for each other's opinions. Members can learn to own their particular point of view, and after doing that, to step out of their own shoes and into someone else's. During this time communities can benefit by: (1) using team-building activities to build rapport and practice communication skills; (2) adding empathy-building and perspective-taking activities, role plays and role reversals; and (3) including explicit teaching and practice of group formation procedures and cooperative skills necessary for collaborative tasks.

Recent books on general cooperative learning methods often speak directly to faculty groups, and include sections on "climate building" and "team-building" (e.g.: Bennett, Rolheiser-Bennett & Stevahn, 1991; Kagan, 1994). Other excellent resources focusing primarily on classrooms (e.g.: Bellanca 1991; Graves and Graves 1988, 1990; Johnson et. al. 1988; Mc Cabe and Rhoades 1992; Moorman and Dishon 1983) can be adapted for faculty use as well. Susan Ellis' chapter 13 in this volume gives an illustration of the way in which cooperative structures developed for the classroom are equally effective for faculty meetings. Time spent on these preliminary activities pays off in more efficient and smooth team work later on, whether those involved are students, faculty, or a combination of stakeholders in the learning community.

A second component of exploring community at this stage concerns the tasks that group members set out to do together. Members ask such questions as "Who will be responsible for what?," "How much time do we need?," "How will we know when we are finished?," "What will be the expected outcome?" Facilitators, whether classroom teachers, administrators, or faculty leaders, should remember to give groups time to explore these questions, rather than simply deciding this beforehand. If groups are floundering, facilitators can add their suggestions to the list of solutions and remind participants that each group member needs a job, role, or piece of the task. In the interest of promoting effective work, the group needs to explore possible goals, standards, procedures, and expected outcomes.

Examples of how to go about this process cooperatively in the classroom are now widely described. For instance, in Sue Smith's second grade in Rancho Romero School, San Ramon, California, students start with ideas for what kind of classroom they want to belong to. This forms the basis for brainstorming and categorizing guidelines for classroom behavior, and understanding the reasons behind school rules. Thinking and communication skills are thus taught while community expectations are being developed (see this example from a classroom run by a Child Development Project teacher in *Cooperative Learning Magazine*, 1990). Proponents of school change (Fullan, 1994; Glatthorn, 1992) encourage similar standard-setting among all members of the learning community.

In the beginning of working together, the community can learn how to coordinate efforts by tackling tasks where the content is not academic, such as: scheduling daily routines (e.g.: block scheduling); planning future events for the whole community; art projects, room and school environment beautification; and routine school facility tasks.

When tasks are being well-managed collaboratively at this level, then group members may be ready to move on to more intellectually challenging matters, such as integrating curriculum across disciplines, where concerns about the appropriate teaching of subject matter content may arise. Faculties that begin work at this difficult level, however, may have trouble coming to agreement.

This is also the stage when the community develops more self-awareness through practicing reflection. Community members ask and answer such questions as: Are we following the goals we set earlier? Do group members remember what the community expects of them? How well did we organize and carry out our community work, our events, and routines? What are the consequences when this does not happen? What do we want to celebrate?

Although the content of the work goals will differ among the different units of the community (faculty, classrooms, the PTA), the collaborative concerns and process remain basically the same. Faculty meetings, as well as other cooperative small groups functioning as task groups, should be conducted collaboratively with time being set aside for reflection on these issues of group process. While some questions need to be answered by a developing consensus within the whole community, the actual questioning and planning can be done in small groups and reported back to the larger whole, whether the participants are students or faculty. Integrating individual and small group opinions to form decisions for the larger community of the classroom, faculty, or whole school is not only an excellent use of cooperative approaches but develops better thinking skills as well.

Teachers who practice reflection with each other will find time in the classroom for students to address such questions, because they will already have discovered for themselves the value of doing this. In one classroom I visited, children individually consider questions that must be settled in "community meeting," talk them over with parents as homework, then discuss the ideas with their classroom "family group" of four. Finally they add the ideas from their small group to a whole class list, which is discussed with one partner or several (using a concentric circle technique) and eventually voted upon. Where faculty or administrative groups use such procedures, the process will be well understood when transferred to the classroom level.

Functioning Productively and Resolving Conflicts:
How Can We Do Our Best?

Once the group tackles more symbolic, abstract, or complex academic or professional tasks, the community may encounter many internal resistances and obstacles. In the context of dealing with complex and challenging content—on topics where there may be strong differences between members, or when it becomes clear that the outcome of group work seriously and significantly affects each individual—applying cooperative skills becomes much more difficult. Positive interdependence may seem less of a privilege than a pain.

Groups at this stage often lapse into unconstructive fighting and struggle, combined with misguided attempts of members to convert others to the speaker's point of view. Other reactions to this difficult stage may be flight (avoiding troublesome issues through artificial niceness, scapegoating, or ignoring other's feelings), dependency (expecting some authority figure, such as the principal, to solve the problems instead of taking on the challenge of shared leadership), or alliances between some members which exclude others (Peck, 1987). The community may yearn to go back to earlier stages where everything seemed more fun, friendly, and less hard work.

The best way out of this dilemma is to learn conflict resolution, listen to each other's point of view, and take responsibility for finding an adequate balance between the individual and the group. In doing this, groups can also use a number of cooperative structures they have been learning in the context of practical tasks:

- More regular use of roles within the small group and whole group;
- Task structures such as "Round Robin" or "Think-Pair-Share" which build in cooperative skills (Kagan, 1994; Lyman, 1992);
- Interpersonal procedures that ensure equal participation and rapport such as a limited number of counters for each person's contributions to a discussion, or "give two positive comments for every negative feedback" (Graves & Graves 1990);
- "Creative Controversy" techniques which structure disagreement and discussion of conflicting viewpoints (Johnson & Johnson, 1992);
- Conflict management and resolution strategies (Bodine, Crawford & Schrumpf, 1994; Johnson & Johnson, 1991; Kreidler 1984, 1990).

Adult groups are as prone as student groups to fall into chaos and recrimination. They have a harder job, however, since all need to be leaders to suggest approaches, initiate reflection, or volunteer reminders of successes at the darkest times, while students can rely on the teacher to do these things. Professional development at this stage can focus on frameworks for dialogue and skillful discussion (Senge et al., 1994), structured controversy methods (Johnson & Johnson, 1992), or conflict resolution techniques. If adult members of the community can successfully resolve their conflicts, teachers will be less daunted in guiding students through resolving their disputes.

In the classroom, teachers who incorporate cooperative skills into the goals of the lesson, and build in enough time for reflection at the end to assess how well students were able to use them, will avoid many disruptive conflicts. Care must be taken that the members do not become overly dependent on the teacher's structures and unable to operate without them. The ultimate goal is interpersonal sensitivity and the ability to coordinate efforts without losing individual contributions. Including some content-related material which also helps students reflect on issues of fairness, equity, and social problem-solving (Schniedewind, 1992) will make students more aware of their own process in group work.

One caveat: using cooperative approaches does not mean squelching differing opinions or the constructive expression of negative feelings in ways that ultimately help the group and lead to a deepening of relationships. If there is no room for dissent, we have totalitarianism and not democratic community. It must be safe, for example, for faculty to express a difference of opinion with administrators. Although it is difficult, faculty too must examine their procedures for goodness of fit with issues of social justice and equity (Sapon-Shevin & Schniedewind, 1990).

As the community deals with the many structural and personal roadblocks to working together, some may claim that this is diverting them from the school's major intellectual goals. Other members will need to point out to them that the investment in relationships and collaborative structures and skills will pay off in commitment and action. Community members may benefit from remembering the wider applications of cooperation in society, business corporations, and government (Kohn, 1986, 1991). Finally, the complex logistics of scheduling group meetings, classroom demonstrations, or study groups for curriculum change, may seem daunting. Then it is helpful to turn to examples from other schools and districts going through such restructuring efforts (Costa, Bellanca, and Fogarty, 1992; Hibbard, 1991/1992 and Munger, chapter 14 of this volume).

The community will need frequent reminders of their unity and their good times as a broader perspective on their current struggles. The whole group can be used to help small groups brainstorm gain-gain solutions to difficulties in cooperating, taking care not to scapegoat individuals. Cooperative games can lighten the atmosphere. During reflection times, groups can share successes they are having as well as difficulties. A running record of improvements for the community as a whole reduces negative comparisons. Recognition and celebration of tasks completed and conflicts resolved is essential. Every cooperative community will need to recycle the stages of community building, reviving cohesion by once again applying the principles of honoring diversity and taking responsibility.

If conflict is handled creatively, groups will learn to address challenging and relevant content and produce interesting and useful results. Adapting Stanford's (1977) stages of group development, Putnam and Burke (1992:90) place the stage of "supporting and expanding production" after a stage of identifying and resolving conflicts. In practice, we often find productivity and conflict intertwining. Communities can be productive at different levels and with respect to different types of content. Conflicts will differ depending on the degree to which the community has jelled, and also on the complexity of the material with which the group is working. Although conflict changes in character, it can never be considered a stage the community will forever leave behind. The key is to view conflict as a harbinger of further growth, requiring the group to develop a higher synthesis that takes account of differing needs and views. Every roadblock overcome creates stronger community bonds.

Providing Outreach:  How Can We Help Others?

One of the ways a community can choose to celebrate its increasing success in cooperating is to provide services to other groups or communities. This is a normal stage of community development, comparable to publishing written work, displaying visual art, or producing performances, and should be encouraged when the time is appropriate. It also functions as an intrinsic reward for the accomplishment of good group work.

The well-functioning community is now capable of providing a cooperative model to others. Teachers may be willing to have their classrooms serve as demonstration sites for teachers new to cooperative learning. Teacher support groups may find it possible to share resources within their wider school or district communities. Students may wish to present one of their cooperative ventures—such as a cooperative game, radio show, or participatory art project—to the class next door, or at neighborhood homes for the elderly. Classes or whole schools may become involved with projects in their neighborhood or town, and present their findings to civic groups (Kletzien, 1996). Interdisciplinary projects with a social issue emphasis can tie the school to the wider society in which it is embedded and provide positive, authentic outcomes in the form of neighborhood improvement. For example, students in a Santa Cruz, California, high school developed a garden project that regularly sold organic vegetables to the local natural foods groceries. With the advent of relevant, thematic interdisciplinary instructional methods, emphasis on problem solving and thinking skills, and the use of portfolio and authentic assessment methods, this outreach phase is not only an outgrowth of a variety of educational concerns, but promotes advanced collaboration among faculty members, administration, students, and citizens.

All members of the learning community, but especially administrators and teachers, can benefit from extending their boundaries to include networks of educators who are experimenting with cooperative and collaborative structures. These links may begin with local or district interest groups for practitioners using cooperative learning. Later a regional network or association may be established, which eventually may connect educators across national boundaries. Meetings, publications, and exchanges of various sorts may result. Benefits to the learning community include a fresh view, differing perspectives, and complementary models for collaboration, as well as the opportunity to "publish" one's own efforts before a wider audience. Teachers may discover a flair for facilitating others' development in cooperative and collaborative approaches—at first in their own schools, later in these expanding venues.

During the outreach stage we need to ensure that the internal work of the community continues. Too much focus outside the group, especially at an early stage, can deplete community spirit and scatter energy. Outreach can be likened to the biblical saying, "My cup runneth over." Serving others must come from an abundance, creating an exuberant need to share. It is a mistake to push students or teachers to share skills or resources not yet fully under their command. Teachers sent by their district to cooperative learning conferences to "learn all you can so you can come home and teach it to the rest of the faculty," often feel resentful and inadequate. Collaboration for community development is not a set of procedures, but an ongoing experience that deepens with practice. Beginners in building a collaborative learning community need support and freedom from competing demands, not pressure to perform for others.

When Community Must End: How Do We Say Good-bye?

Some educational communities, such as entire schools and certain teacher support groups, may go on developing for years, halving off into new units when they grow too large. Other groups will continue with a constantly changing membership. In these cases, the ongoing maintenance of community identity and incorporation of new members are the major concerns.

But for many groups—such as a specific faculty task force, or a site committee with rotating membership, or a cooperative classroom—there is a definite life expectancy, and we need to plan ahead for this. The greater the group's success, the harder it will be to part. It will be easier to move on if group members know they will be in other collaborative groups and cooperative classroom communities throughout the total learning community of the school.

One method for ensuring continuity throughout a student's tenure in the school is to create vertical groupings across grade levels.

These groupings are termed "houses" in Britain, and "whanau" (the Maori term for extended families) in New Zealand, and "families" in many American schools. All students belong to a vertical group throughout the grades. This also helps students from migrant families who are in and out of school with the seasons. They will at least always come back into their vertical group, where they will be assisted to re-adjust by older "sisters" and "brothers" and in turn, will assist younger "family members." Faculty members can sustain an ongoing identity with these "families," as well.

When a community group of any sort is ending, it is a good time to acknowledge the grief of leave taking, to remember special shared moments, to celebrate successes, and to make a formal ritual of farewell. Members can write letters to one another thanking each person for specific characteristics or acts that were appreciated by the writer. A final party at leave-taking, or a reunion of the group planned for some time ahead may soften the blow. Finally, group members need activities to help them recall all they have gained from taking the risks they took to form community, and to realize that now they have the skills to do it again, and again.

## References

Bellanca, J. (1991). *Building a caring, cooperative classroom: A social skills primer.* Palatine, Illinois: IRI/Skylight Publishing.

Bennett, B., Rolheiser-Bennett, C. & Stevahn, L. (1991). *Cooperative learning: Where heart meets mind.* Edina, MN: Interaction Book Co.

Bodine, R. J., Crawford, D. K. & Schrumpf, F. (1994). *Creating the peaceable school: A comprehensive program for teaching conflict resolution.* Campaign, IL: Research Press.

Child Development Project. (1995). *At home in our schools: A guide to schoolwide activities that Build Community.* Oakland, California: Developmental Studies Center.

Cooper, C. and Boyd, J. (1995). Re-creating the school as a collaborative learning community. In *Cooperative Learning* magazine (1995) 15(1). Montreal, Quebec, Canada: International Association for the Study of Cooperation in Education, CSCP–LB581, Concordia University.

*Cooperative Learning* magazine (1990) 10(3). Theme: Positive social development: Non-academic benefits of cooperative learning. Montreal, Quebec, Canada: International Association for the Study of Cooperation in Education, CSCP–LB581, Concordia University.

*Cooperative Learning* magazine (1990). 11(2). Theme: Creating a cooperative learning community. Montreal, Quebec, Canada: International Association for the Study of Cooperation in Education, CSCP–LB581, Concordia University.

*Cooperative Learning* magazine (1991/92) 12(2). Theme: Staff development: Building communities of learners. Montreal, Quebec, Canada: International Association for the Study of Cooperation in Education, CSCP–LB581, Concordia University.

Costa, A. (1992). The learning community, In A. Costa, J. Bellanca, and R. Fogarty, *If minds matter: A foreword to the future, Vol. I and II.* Palatine, Illinois: IRI/Skylight Publishing.

Fullan, M. (1994). *Change forces.* Bristol, PA: Falmer Press.

Glatthorn, A. (1992). *Teachers as agents of change: A new look at school improvement.* Washington, D.C.: NEA Professional Library.

Gibbs, J. (1994 Third Edition, 1978 & 1987). *Tribes, A new way of learning together.* Santa Rosa, CA: Center Source Publications

Graves, N. B. (a.k.a. L. Forest) (1971). *City, country, and child rearing: A tricultural study of mother-child relationships in varying environments.* PhD dissertation, Boulder: University of Colorado.

Graves, N. B. (a.k.a. L. Forest) & T. Graves (1978a ). Growing up Polynesian: Implications for western education. In B. Shore, C. Macpherson & R. W. Franco, (eds.), *New neighbors: Islanders in adaptation,* Santa Cruz, CA: Center for South Pacific Studies, University of California at Santa Cruz, pp. 161–177.

Graves, N. B. (a.k.a. L. Forest) & T. Graves (1978b). The impact of modernization on the personality of a polynesian people: Or, how to make an up-tight, rivalrous westerner out of an easy-going, generous Pacific islander. *Human Organization* 37:115–135.

Graves, N. B. (a.k.a. L. Forest) & T. Graves (1983). The cultural context of prosocial development: An ecological model. In D. Bridgeman (ed.) *The nature of prosocial development.* New York: Academic Press, pages 243–264.

Graves, N. B. (a.k.a. L. Forest) & T. Graves (1988). *Getting there together: A source book and desk-top guide for creating a cooperative classroom.* Santa Cruz, CA: Cooperative College of California.

Graves, N. B. (a.k.a. L. Forest) & Graves, T. (1990). *A part to play: Tips, techniques and tools for learning co-operatively.* Victoria, Australia: Latitude Media & Marketing; San Juan Capistrano, CA: Kagan Cooperative Learning.

Hibbard, K. M. (1991/1992 Winter). Beyond the first kiss. *Cooperative Learning* magazine 11 (2):29–31.

Hibbard, K. M. (1992). Interdisciplinary instruction: Shining star or black hole? *Cooperative Learning* magazine 12(3):28–31.

Johnson, D. W., Johnson, R., Bartlett, J., & Johnson, L. (1988). *Our cooperative classroom.* Edina, MN: Interaction Book Company.

Johnson, D. W. , Johnson, R. (1991). *Teaching children to be peacemakers.* Edina, MN: Interaction Book Company.

Johnson, D. W. , Johnson, R. (1992). *Creative controversy: Intellectual challenges in the classroom.* Edina, MN: Interaction Book Company.

Kagan, M., Robertson, L. & Kagan, S. (1995). *Classbuilding.* San Juan Capistrano, CA: Kagan Cooperative Learning.

Kagan, S. (1994) *Cooperative learning.* San Juan Capistrano, CA: Kagan Cooperative Learning.

Kletzien, S. B. (1996). Kids around town: Valuing multiple perspectives. In *Creative group expression: An anthology of original essays and practices.* Santa Cruz: The International Association for the Study of Cooperation in Education, pages 45–47.

Kohlberg, L.(1988). *Moral education: Justice and community.* New York: Columbia University Press.

Kohn, A. (1990). The ABCs of caring: A case study of the child development project. *Cooperative Learning* magazine 10(3):6–9

Kreidler, W. J. (1984). *Creative conflict resolution: More than 200 activities for keeping peace in the classroom.* Glenview, IL: Goodyear Books, Scott, Foresman & Co.

Kreidler, W. J. (1990). *Elementary perspectives I: Teaching concepts of peace and conflict.* Cambridge, MA: Educators for Social Responsibility.

F. T. Lyman Jr. (1992). Think-Pair-Share, Thinktrix, Thinklinks and Weird Facts: An interactive system for cooperative thinking. In Neil Davidson & Toni Worsham, (eds.) *Enhancing thinking through cooperative learning.* New York: Teachers College Press, Columbia U.

Mc Cabe, M. & Rhoades, J. (1992). *The cooperative classroom: Social and academic activities.* Bloomington, Indiana: National Education Service.

Moorman, C. & Dishon, D. (1983). *Our classroom: We can learn together.* Bay City, MI: Personal Power Press.

Peck, M. S. (1987). *The different drum: Community making and peace.* New York: Simon & Schuster.

Putnam, J. & Burke, J. B. (1992). *Organizing and managing classroom learning communities.* New York: Mc Graw Hill.

Sapon-Shevin, M. (1991a). Celebrating diversity, creating community: Curriculum that honors and builds on differences. In Stainback, S. & Stainback, W. (eds.), *Adapting the regular curriculum: Enhancing student success in inclusive classrooms.* Baltimore: Paul H. Brookes.

———. (1991b, October). Cooperative learning in inclusive classrooms: Learning to become a community. *Cooperative Learning* magazine, 12(1):4–7.

Sapon-Shevin, M. & Schniedewind, N. (1990). Selling cooperative learning without selling it short. *Educational Leadership* 46(4): 63–65.

Schmuck, R. & Schmuck, P. (1974). *A humanistic psychology of education: Making the school everybody's house.* Palo Alto, CA: Mayfield Publishing Co.

Schniedewind, N. (1992: Spring/Summer). Appreciating diversity, promoting equality: The promise of integrating cooperative learning and the social studies. *Cooperative Learning* magazine 12(3): 4–8.

Schoneman, T. (1992). *Practical ways a principal can build a collaborative school.* Presentation at the Third National Symposium for Cooperative Learning Across the Curriculum, Feb. 6–8. San Francisco, CA

Schwab, J. J. (1976). Education and the state: Learning community. In *The great ideas today.* Encyclopedia Britannica.

Senge, P., Kleiner, A., Roberts, C., Ross, R. B. & Smith, B. J. (1994). *The fifth discipline fieldbook: Strategies and tools for building a learning organization.* New York: Doubleday/Currency.

Shaw, V. (1992). *Community building in the classroom.* San Juan Capistrano, CA: Kagan Cooperative Learning.

Stanford, G. (1977). *Developing effective classroom groups: A practical guide for teachers.* New York: A. & W. Visual Library.

Watson, M. (1990). A talk with Marilyn Watson, child development project program director. *Cooperative Learning* magazine 10(3):15.

# 16

## AFTERWORD: PROMISING PRACTICES AND RESPONSIBLE DIRECTIONS

### CELESTE BRODY AND NEIL DAVIDSON

In this chapter we reflect on the two purposes of this book: helping educators make informed decisions about selecting, teaching, and implementing cooperative and collaborative learning, and considering the goals of teachers' professional development in the context of organizational reforms that create learning communities. We review several themes that are reiterated throughout this book in relation to the questions: What constitutes best practice for the long-term reforms of classroom practices as they relate to cooperative groupwork? What issues were not addressed by the contributors that need further discussion?

### Promising Trends in Professional Development Advocated by Those who Work in Cooperative Learning

As noted in the introduction, the contributors in this volume represent the current shifts in thinking about how to disseminate cooperative learning through professional development practices. There are several promising trends—not without issues, however—that emerge from the discussions in this volume. They are summarized in three areas: (1) the need to adopt multiple approaches and plan long-term, sustained efforts, (2) the need to consider ways to engage and treat the whole organization as a context for learning, and (3) the trend toward understanding constructivist theories as they relate to teacher learning.

#### Multiple Approaches and Long-Term Efforts

Staff developers, teachers, consultants and curriculum specialists who work with teachers should understand or at least be more than familiar with, several approaches to cooperative/collaborative learning and other related programs that foster wholistic approaches to the values of care and cooperation. This understanding includes implicit values and epistemologies, the research base regarding student learning and achievement in cooperative learning, approaches to curriculum, and so on. This standard places a heavy requirement on these educators; nevertheless there is a growing recognition of the need to address the particular requirements and differences in learning environments and contexts. The authors in this volume respond to this issue to some extent.

There are also differences between approaches in terms of how they handle certain practical considerations for teachers, for example, grading (see Kagan & Kagan, chapter 5, as one example of an explicit position on never issuing a group grade), and the importance of developing curriculum for students' pro-social development (see Watson, et.al, chapter 7). These differences need to be recognized and understood by principals, staff developers, and ultimately, teachers.

Differences certainly can be a stimulus for discussion about how best to adapt and situate training and development. One program will not necessarily be best for every school or teacher. This lesson may be the most relevant to educators who work with broad audiences such as university level teachers, or district level personnel. On the other hand, the contributors who have developed research-based approaches recommend the importance of staying with an approach for a long period of time—at least three years. Long-term commitments to particular programs are a fundamental requirement for the staff of most schools to sustain improvements in instruction and ultimately, student achievement and learning. While these two lessons may appear contradictory they point out the complex nature of good professional development.

Considering the Whole School as a Context for Learning

There is a growing recognition that the whole school must be "treated" if there is going to be improvement in student learning. The language—professional development, instead of staff development—communicates this shift in thinking. Part I and III focus on the value of creating learning communities and the different ways to do this. For example, Schmuck (chapter 12) deals with the relationship between organization development and cooperative learning while Ellis (chapter 13) considers how to restructure the staff meetings in which teachers come to talk and solve problems. There are other programs and restructuring efforts that set out to achieve this goal as well. Nevertheless, this is the kind of systemic view that needs to take place at the school or district level. Educators must address these questions continually: How do programs interface with one another? What are the implicit values of such programs? Are they in accord or do they contradict one another? What is the time line needed to create even a modicum of change in student learning? What is the kind of organization we want to create through this professional development effort?

Recent reviews of research about school reform present a pessimistic and quite complex view about an idea that many educators hold: changes in the stucture of the school (e.g., scheduling and teaming) produce changes in teaching practice, that in turn produce changes in student learning (Elmore, 1995). Again, the implication of these findings for cooperative learning is that educators might focus first on changing norms, knowledge, and skills at the individual and organizational level about good teaching as it relates to student learning, before they focus on changing structure.

Constructivist Approaches to Teacher Learning
and Teacher Knowledge

Another promising trend is the shift in the understanding of how constructivist theories of learning apply to teacher learning as well as student learning. One question that generated this volume is a good example of this shift: How do teachers learn and adapt this innovation in light of their own histories and context demands? We have learned that we are still a long way from understanding these. Indeed, producing this volume has left us with more issues than we had when we started, and we are aware how little data there are on the following: What enables some teachers to make dramatic gains in the use of cooperative learning from short-term programs while others require sustained, long-term approaches? For a given teacher, how much and what type of professional development and support is needed to make fundamental, long-term changes? What sorts of professional development plans will make it highly likely that all teachers will successfully implement the innovation, in this case, cooperative learning? How can large-scale, long-term professional development plans in a given school or district take into account the individual needs and concerns of particular teachers? These are very important questions from the outside-in perspective. There is another perspective, however, and that is the teacher's perspective on learning and knowledge.

Clandinin and Connelly (1996) remind us that it is important to understand what teachers know and how they construct knowledge, but in order to do this we must attend to the professional knowledge context in which teachers live and work. This context shapes teachers' personal practical knowledge; it is a landscape of dilemmas inhabited by teachers and it is best understood narratively. When we ask such questions as the ones above, we should remind ourselves that teachers do know what they know; and that much of what they do know about good teaching and learning is conditional; "it depends." When we begin with the need to understand teachers' personal practical knowledge about cooperative/collaborative learning we may ask new questions that could produce different approaches to professional development.

Finally, the goal of all good professional development is student learning and achievement. We assume that readers have access to the research of the last 40 years regarding the value of cooperative learning to promote student achievement; if not, the citations in this volume should help (see chapter 3, Rolheiser and Stevahn in particular, for examples of using the research base). Recent evaluations of other long-term efforts at reform such as the middle school restructuring efforts (Lipsitz, Mizell, Jackson & Austin, 1997) remind us, however, that much professional development still does not provide ample opportunities for study of and reflection on the research base of the innovation as it relates to student learning and achievement. This must be the content at the heart of any effective professional development program.

## Issues and Questions Not Addressed

There are a number of issues that have not been addressed thoroughly in this volume. When we began we wanted to know how educators address situational concerns and contextual considerations, such as issues regarding diversity—ethnic, gender, special needs—in their training for cooperative learning. Do they address these concerns? If so, how? If not, why? And, we asked whether there were differences in how consultants and staff developers approached training and development along grade levels or organizational levels (primary, middle, and secondary). We have learned that both of these—concerns for diversity, and grade level and subject area—are still open questions needing further research and discussion. We will discuss just one, grade and subject level, as an example of where we still need to focus our attention.

### Grade Level and Cooperative Learning Implementation

There is a marked absence of discussing grade-level questions of implementation of cooperative learning and differences among teachers. Certain programs were actually designed with certain levels in mind. For example, the Child Development Project focuses specifically on the elementary level (chapter 7). Most of the programs for cooperative learning have focused on elementary schools. We do know that many approaches to cooperative learning have moved in the direction of specificity to context. Several approaches which were not presented in this volume are good examples of this (see Aronson, et. al., 1978; Clarke, et.al., 1990; Gibbs,1987; and McCabe & Rhoades, 1990 cited in the introduction). Farivar and Webb (chapter 8) and Davidson (1990) are an exception and they consider the demands of mathematics and the grade levels (see also Lotan, Cohen & Morphew, chapter 6 for attention to the middle level).

What is the role of secondary subject subcultures? How do they inhibit educational reform, and how can professional development efforts address these? Anyone who has worked in professional development settings with teachers from elementary, middle, and secondary levels knows that there are many differences among them.

One of the most unappreciated and underrated effects on teachers' willingness to adapt cooperative learning and other school reform efforts at the secondary level, is that high school teachers belong to distinctive subject subcultures. These subcultures are characterized by differing beliefs, norms, and practices about the nature of knowledge, how it is organized and taught. These complicate efforts to restructure high schools and redesign curriculum. Grossman and Stodolsky's (1995) report from surveys and interviews with high school teachers illustrate that school subjects differ with regard to their scope and coherence, and teachers seem to regard conceptions of school subjects as one of the commonplaces of their daily lives. For example Yaakobi and Sharan (cited in Grossman and Stodolsky, 1995) found that humanities teachers differed significantly from language teachers in their attitudes toward academic knowledge, with humanities teachers adopting a more "progressive" perspective on knowledge and teaching. Math teachers along with colleagues in foreign language have stronger beliefs about the extent to which they are free to decide the content of their classes and importance of sequentiality for teaching. Curricular coordination and control, instructional practices and policies relate to disciplinary ways of thinking.

Our own experiences suggest that secondary teachers new to cooperative learning training tend to view this strategy as simply one of several competing views of good teaching; it is another technique to be mastered primarily to extend one's tools for managing groups. Even after long-term staff development, most secondary teachers still rely on cooperative learning primarily for mastery learning and review. Elementary teachers tend to have less interest than middle and secondary teachers in using cooperative learning to achieve improved test scores— except when they are evaluated by their students' performance on nationally normed or statewide tests—although the fact that they can demonstrate improved academic results or explain their approach to others based upon the research on academic achievement, is a secondary reason. Elementary teachers are typically more attracted to cooperative learning to improve classroom relations and class climate than are secondary teachers, but while they recognize that social learning and social values should be made explicit in terms of student learning objectives, many teachers do not do that.

Professional development efforts need to be sensitive to how different orientations toward subject matter and the culture of different grade level organizations may affect teachers' responses to new instructional or curricular practices (Grossman & Stodolsky, 1995, p. 10). Generic approaches to cooperative learning at the secondary level, for example, may ignore the subject-specific concerns teachers raise and how they want to understand this innovation in light of the discourse structure of their subject area. Educators might consider the efforts to reform secondary level teaching from the theoretical perspective of collaborative learning (see the Introduction for a discussion of the differences between cooperative and collaborative learning). It could speak more saliently to the developmental requirements of young adults. Bruffee (1993) suggests that inviting students into the knowledge community requires a different stance toward students and learning. Other trainers who work frequently with secondary teachers get strong results with the structural approach (see Kagan & Kagan, chapter 5 of this volume), especially if they allow time for teachers to discuss applications to different subject areas. But this is a consideration which needs further research and discussion.

## Research About Teachers' Learning and Adaptation of Cooperative Learning

As we mentioned above educators need more discussion regarding research about how teachers learn to adapt and implement cooperative learning. We believe that this is a ripe area for study by those who do formal research, as well as by classroom teachers conducting research on their own teaching. Indeed, the field of cooperative learning may be served by encouraging more teachers to conduct their own classroom research. Those who work with teachers need to discuss the traditional we/they distinction in research, the effect this has on practice, and the promising alternatives of the teacher/researcher and action research for recruiting teachers to direct their own inquiry and professional development (Richardson, 1994; see also the Concerns

Based Adoption Model by Hord, Rutherford, Huling-Austing, & Hall, 1987).

Expert Knowledge and Formal Research Versus Teacher Research

Although there is not much research about how teachers learn to adapt and implement cooperative learning, this situation may be the result of the distinction that exists between those who study teaching and learning, and those who teach and administer from a practical knowledge base. Experts in cooperative learning who have grown from the ranks of school practitioners may not have the same relationship to and investment in doing formal, more traditional research in cooperative learning, as educators whose home bases are teacher education programs at a college or university—nor are we implying that they should. Nevertheless, the deleterious and unfortunate we/they distinction between researcher and practitioner brings us to the question about how we will consider our practice and our inquiry.

Most of the studies on cooperative groupwork and learning were conducted during the 1940s through the 1980s by academics who were simultaneously refining the models and the practices while conducting research on student achievement and pro-social behavior. Many of the practices for teaching teachers about cooperative group methods followed the path from the university teacher education or graduate classroom and research center through school districts' staff development and curriculum programs. Researchers who were also the early disseminators of cooperative learning emphasized correct methods for conducting cooperative groupwork, but local school structures and individual teachers have not adhered so carefully to those models. There are many reasons for this, one of which may be that most of the research on cooperative groupwork has ignored teachers' practical and situated knowledge as discussed above (Clandinin & Connelly, 1992, 1996), and how these affect teacher implementation (Richardson, et.al., 1991). Another reason may be that we have not yet integrated effectively the emerging knowledge about promoting sustained teacher change with professional development practices for cooperative learning. In other words, research on teachers and how they implement such complex practices as cooperative groupwork has not kept pace with local staff development demands. And third, paternalism still emanates from universities to K–12 schools, so that much of the research returns first to the universities before it is laundered and put out for practitioners' consumption. We need to ask: Who "owns" the knowledge in teaching practice, and who benefits from the research?

Educators are standing at a cross-roads, looking down two paths: one well-trodden and familiar to many, based on the currently accepted ideas and forms of inquiry and research about cooperative learning; and the other, rougher, and less familiar path that questions what we know and how we know about the actual implementation of cooperative learning and professional development. This question, and this stance toward inquiry, are fundamental to the purposes of this volume. What data about teacher change, school change, student achievement, and curricula are important for teachers and schools in order to implement cooperative learning effectively? Conversely, how do teachers construct their practical knowledge, and how can professional development programs support teacher inquiry into these questions?

Educators can expect only modest improvements in teachers' development in creating effective contexts for student learning if we simply keep to providing general answers and rule-based responses to the questions raised in this chapter. Approaches to professional development for cooperative learning must leave a great deal of room for teachers to ask and answer their own questions. The future of school reform depends on asking new questions that point us in a different direction. Collaborative approaches to professional development may, indeed, hold one key to school reform. The lessons from cooperative learning are now turning to the education of teachers.

## References

Bruffee, K. (1993). *Collaborative learning: Higher education, interdependence and the authority of knowledge.* Baltimore, MD: Johns Hopkins University Press.

Clandinin, D. J. & Connelly, F. M. (1992). Narrative and story in practice and research. In D. Schon (Ed.), *The reflective turn: Case studies in and on educational practice* (pp. 258–281). New York: Teachers College Press.

Clandinin, D. J. and Connelly, F. M. (1996). Teachers' professional knowledge landscapes: Teachers stories—stories of teachers—school stories—stories of schools. *Educational Researcher* 24(3), 24–30.

Elmore, R. (1995). Structural reform and educational practice. *Educational Researcher.* 24(9). 23–26.

Grossman, P. L. & Stodolsky, S. S. (1995). Content as context: The role of school subjects in secondary teaching. *Educational Researcher,* 24(8), 5–11.

Hord, S, Rutherford, W. L., Huling-Austing, L. & Hall, G. (1987). *Taking charge of change.* Austin: University of Texas Research and Development Center.

Lipsitz, J., Mizell, H. M., Jackson, A. W., Austin, L. M. (1997). Speaking with one voice. A Manifesto for middle-grades reform. Special issue: Research on Middle Grades. *Phi Delta Kappan.* 533–556.

Richardson, V., (1994). Conducting research on practice. *Educational Researcher* 23(5), 5–10.

Richardson, V., Anders, D., Tidwell, D. & Loud, C. (1991). The relationship between teachers' beliefs and practices in reading comprehension instruction. *American Educational Research Journal* 28(3), 559–586.

# CONTRIBUTORS

*James Bellanca* is the President of IRI/SkyLight Training and Publishing Company in Arlington Heights, Illinois.

*Julie Boyd* is Director of Global Learning Communities and the Founder and Director of the Foundation for Global Learning and Co-operation based in Tasmania, Australia.

*Celeste Brody* is Associate Professor of Education at Lewis and Clark College in Portland, Oregon, where she coordinates the pre-service intern program for middle level teachers and field-based inservice masters program for educators.

*Elizabeth Cohen* is Professor of Education and Sociology and Director of the Program for Complex Instruction at Stanford University.

*Carole Cooper* is Director of Global Learning Communities and Director of the Foundation for Global Learning and Cooperation based in Tasmania, Australia.

*Stefan Dasho* is the Senior Staff Developer of the Child Development Project of the Developmental Studies Center in Oakland, California.

*Neil Davidson* is Professor of Curriculum and Instruction at the University of Maryland, and is the immediate past president of the International Association for the Study of Cooperation in Education.

*Susan Ellis* is Program Coordinator for Staff Development and Planning for the Greenwich Public Schools in Connecticut, and a past president of the National Staff Development Council.

*Sydney Farivar* is Associate Professor of Elementary Education at the California State University in Northridge.

*Robin Fogarty* is the Vice President of Publishing for the IRI/SkyLight Training and Publishing Company in Arlington Heights, Illinois.

*Liana Forest* is a psychological anthropologist, writer, and former Executive Editor of Cooperative Learning Publications for the International Association for the Study of Cooperation in Education.

*David Johnson* is Professor of Educational Psychology with an emphasis in social psychology at the University of Minnesota and Co-Director of the Cooperative Learning Center at that university.

*Roger Johnson* is Professor of Curriculum and Instruction with an emphasis in science education at the University of Minnesota and Co-Director of the Cooperative Learning Center at that university.

*Miguel Kagan* is Marketing Director for the Kagan Cooperative Learning Company in San Clemente, California.

*Spencer Kagan* is the President and Director of Kagan Cooperative Learning in San Clemente, California, and a former Professor of Psychology at the University of California, Riverside.

*Sylvia Kendzior* was Staff Development Director of the Child Development Project of the Developmental Studies Center in Oakland, California.

*Rachel Lotan* is the Associate Director of the Program for Complex Instruction at Stanford University.

*Christopher Morphew* is an Associate of the Program for Complex Instruction at Stanford University.

*Linda Munger* is an independent consultant for many school districts, based in Des Moines, Iowa.

*Carol Rolheiser* is an Associate Professor at the Ontario Institute for Studies in Education of the University of Toronto and is Associate Chair of the Curriculum, Teaching, and Learning Department.

*Patricia Roy* is director of the Center for School Change at Delaware State University in Dover, and is a past president of the National Staff Development Council.

*Stanley Rutherford* is a writer and materials developer for the Child Development Project of the Developmental Studies Center in Oakland, California.

*Mara Sapon-Shevin* is Professor of Education at Syracuse University in New York and Co-President of the International Association for the Study of Cooperation in Education.

*Richard Schmuck* is Professor of Education with an emphasis in organization development at the University of Oregon.

*Nancy Schniedewind* is Professor of Educational Studies at the State University of New York in New Paltz.

*Daniel Solomon* was the Director of Research at the Developmental Studies Center in Oakland, California until his recent retirement.

*Laurie Stevahn* is Director of Professional Development Associates in Minneapolis, Minnesota, and an Associate of the Cooperative Learning Center, University of Minnesota.

*Marilyn Watson* is the Program Director of the Child Development Project of the Developmental Studies Center in Oakland, California.

*Noreen Webb* is Professor of Educational Psychology in the Graduate School of Education at the University of California, Los Angeles.

# INDEX

References to *figures* and *tables* are identified by *f* and *t* respectively.